What Drives Third World City Growth?

What Drives Third World City Growth?

A Dynamic General Equilibrium Approach

ALLEN C. KELLEY

and JEFFREY G. WILLIAMSON

PRINCETON UNIVERSITY PRESS

Copyright © 1984 by Princeton University Press
Published by Princeton University Press, 41 William Street,
Princeton, New Jersey 08540
In the United Kingdom: Princeton University Press, Guildford, Surrey

Library of Congress Cataloging in Publication Data will be found on the
last printed page of this book

ISBN 0-691-04240-3 (cloth)
0-691-10164-7 (paper)
This book has been composed in Lasercomp Times Roman
Clothbound editions of Princeton University Press books are printed
on acid-free paper, and binding materials are chosen for strength and
durability. Paperbacks, although satisfactory for personal collections, are
not usually suitable for library rebinding

Printed in the United States of America by Princeton University Press
Princeton, New Jersey

Contents

Contents vii

Figures

Tables

Preface

This book has been more than a dozen years in the making. It had its beginning around 1970 when we were both teaching and doing research in economic development and economic history at the University of Wisconsin. While these two fields had at that time just emerged from an exciting decade of intellectual growth, they still lagged behind in the application of modern analytical tools to a key problem—the sources of economic growth and structural change.

Development economics had become increasingly quantitative. Developing economies in the Third World were analyzed by the extensive application of partial-equilibrium analysis, and econometric studies abounded (including descriptions of long-run growth). However, most models of national development were too aggregative and relative prices were commonly ignored. In addition, production and consumption functions were excessively rigid, often exhibiting fixed coefficients or simple input-output relationships. While short-run macro stabilization models were common, long-run general equilibrium models were virtually absent from the literature—an odd state of affairs given that all development economists seemed to agree that the "structure" of an economy influenced its growth potential. The partial-equilibrium orientation of the development economist persisted in spite of his qualification that "of course, general equilibrium effects may matter," in spite of a qualitative economic history literature that has always been dominated by a general equilibrium tradition (the "seamless web of history" and "everything depends on everything else"), and in spite of the pioneering empirical studies of long-run growth by Abramovitz, Kuznets, and others. While less formal, this literature highlighted general equilibrium interactions and portrayed growth and structural change in nonlinear terms.

In a sense, "new" economic historians were drifting in a similar direction. Coming from a tradition that described development as highly complex and richly interdependent, "cliometrics" in the late 1960s nonetheless focused on partial-equilibrium topics (e.g., industry studies), or applied partial-equilibrium techniques as a first pass at analyzing general equilibrium problems. There were still no cliometric examples of formal general equilibrium modeling.

By 1970, it seemed to us that the time was ripe to incorporate more historical content and more explicit general equilibrium modeling into development economics. Similarly, the time seemed ripe to apply formal general equilibrium models to the traditional problems of economic history, refreshed by new insights coming from development economics.

To this end we entered into a collaboration that resulted in two books. The first, with Russell J. Cheetham (*Dualistic Economic Development: Theory and History*), set out a simple general equilibrium model of dualistic development. The model was analyzed using the standard tools of growth theory as well as computer simulation techniques. The latter was essential if the empirical properties of the dualistic model were to be understood. The goal was to move well beyond growth theory's emphasis on long-run asymptotic properties, and to investigate empirically relevant paths of structural change as the economy underwent its "industrial revolution." *Dualistic Economic Development* was followed by *Lessons from Japanese Development: An Analytical Economic History*, where we embraced the cliometrician's counterfactual in order to make sense out of some important economic issues of Japanese history from the beginning of the Meiji Restoration to the Great Depression. Among the topics examined were the origins of the "Japanese Miracle," the impact of Japanese militarism on subsequent development, the role of demographic change on economic growth, and the impact of "surplus labor" on industrialization. Counterfactual experiments relevant to each of these topics were made possible by the application of a computable general equilibrium (CGE) model to Japanese history.

Our collaboration ended in 1974, but after a four-year hiatus, it began anew as a result of a conversation in which we speculated on the future directions of CGE modeling. Our thoughts on needed future research directions were amazingly congruent: there was much more to be learned about Third World countries through the application of dynamic CGE models, CGE models should expand dimensions of demographic analysis, and CGE models should incorporate several new specifications that had been underplayed in the previous literature, including our own early work.

CGE modeling seemed particularly relevant for Third World city growth problems, a topic that was attracting much attention and debate. Centering as it does on factor movements between sectors and across space, as well as on the role of wage and price signals to guide this transformation, urban growth not only lends itself to CGE modeling, but CGEs may also represent an indispensable tool for the analysis. This is in spite of the proclivity of urban economists to think almost exclusively in partial-equilibrium, and the overriding commitment of demographers to fixed-coefficient, reduced-form models to project future trends in city growth. We felt the time was appropriate to apply general equilibrium analysis to problems of Third World city growth. This book reports the fruit of that enterprise.

We have accumulated many debts along the way. Financial support was provided by the Ford Foundation, the National Science Foundation, the Esmeé Fairbairn Research Center (Edinburgh, Scotland), the International Institute for Applied Systems Analysis (Laxenburg, Austria), Duke University, the University of Wisconsin, and the World Bank. In addition to financial support we are particularly indebted to IIASA, Kelley's home while on sabbatical in 1978–79 and Williamson's home while a frequent visitor between 1978 and 1980, and the World Bank, where Williamson spent his sabbatical in 1981–82. Our friends Andrei Rogers at IIASA and Douglas Keare at the World Bank vigorously encouraged and supported the project throughout.

Others who contributed at various points in our research include Brian Arthur, Charles Becker, Lars Bergsman, Hollis Chenery, Donaldo Colosio, Vernon Henderson, Bruce Johnston, Urban Karlstrom, Nathan Keyfitz, Gregory Ingram, Jacques Ledent, Desmond McCarthy, Edwin Mills, Lennart Ohlsson, Andras Por, Hisanobu Shishido, Lance Taylor, George Tolley, and Andrzej Wierzbicki.

Three other individuals deserve special mention. Sherman Robinson not only shared his wisdom on computer algorithms, but he supplied bubbling enthusiasm for, and intimate knowledge of CGEs, which helped sustain our own commitment to the project. Warren Sanderson was exceptionally generous in sharing ideas that proved invaluable in formulating our theoretical framework. And most important, Robert Schmidt gave tirelessly of his time and creative energy to the computational aspects of the project. Without his contribution, *What Drives Third World City Growth?* would never have made it.

ACK
JGW
September 1983

What Drives Third World City Growth?

CHAPTER ONE

The Third World City Growth Problem

1. THE CITY GROWTH PROBLEM

The past quarter century has witnessed unprecedented economic progress in the Third World as gauged by the standards of history since the first Industrial Revolution in Britain. Economic success of that magnitude has always created problems of dislocation and structural adjustment, many of which are spatial. City growth is one such problem, and given the unprecedented economic progress in the Third World, their city growth problems, not surprisingly, seem to be unprecedented as well. By the end of this century, the United Nations forecasts urban population growth rates three times those of rural areas. Two billion people, exceeding 40 percent of the Third World population, will live in cities; some cities will have reached extremely large size—Mexico City at 31.6 million, São Paulo at 26 million, and Cairo, Jakarta, Seoul, and Karachi each exceeding 15 million. Current rates of Third World city growth border on the spectacular, averaging between 4 and 5 percent per annum.

Analysts and policymakers are sharply divided on the city growth problem. Pessimists stress the Third World's inability to cope with the social overhead requirements of rapid urban growth and high urban densities, citing environmental decay and planning failure as evidence of impending crisis. They tend to view Third World city growth as another example of the "tragedy of the commons," a classic example of overuse of a collective resource. In contrast, optimists view city growth as a central force raising average living standards. They view urbanization as the natural outcome of economic development, and a necessary requirement for the more rational use of economic resources. To the optimist, the tragedy of the commons is really nothing more than an example of poor economic planning and inappropriate prices. Debate over public policy options remains intense, the optimists favoring an open city approach, the pessimists searching for ways to close them down.

This debate is hardly new, and can be found as early as the 1830s in the British Parliamentary Papers, in treatises by political economists, and in the British press. Nothing ever changes, it seems, and we still don't have good answers to the question "what drives city growth?"

2. SETTING THE STAGE

Cities are capital-intensive, a stylized fact that has led many pessimists to conclude that current rates of Third World city growth cannot be sustained. To make matters worse, cities are excessively capital-intensive, stocked as they are with public capital whose user charges are low or zero. It follows that since the social costs of in-migration exceed private costs, cities are created that are both too large and too many. To make matters "worse," increasing urban land scarcity encourages the substitution of capital for land, further increasing the cities' capital intensity. What happens when the national economy can no longer finance the cities' voracious appetite for saving and accumulation? So it is that pessimists stress the Third World's inability to cope with the social overhead and housing requirements generated by rapid urban growth.

Pessimists also stress that the Third World has "over-urbanized," a situation that will require painful structural adjustment in the near future. This disequilibrium view is based on the premise that migrants are attracted to the cities in the hope that they (or their children) will be selected for training and employment in the favored high-wage sectors. The disequilibrium view also believes that new immigrants accept underemployment in the (allegedly) low-wage traditional service sectors while waiting for more suitable employment. According to the pessimists, the new immigrants will wait only so long before social discontent erupts. Do labor markets in Third World cities really exhibit this kind of disequilibrium, and is the Third World over-urbanized as a consequence?

Pessimists also observe that the sources of past Third World urban "excesses" can be traced to the availability of cheap energy, technological diffusion from the developed world that favored modern urban sectors, heavy capital inflows, world trade liberalization, a drift toward domestic price distortions favoring city output, and unusually rapid population growth. These conditions now show signs of changing, suggesting that Third World countries may have over-urbanized in the recent past, at least based on likely future economic and demographic conditions. Thus, projected high rates of urban growth may not be reached over the next two decades, given further OPEC-induced fuel scarcity (cities being fuel-intensive); technological regression in modern sectors which have borrowed heavily from advanced countries (themselves now undergoing productivity slowdown); diminished capital transfers due to economic austerity in advanced countries; a retreat toward protectionism in industrial-ized countries; and retardation in economywide population growth rates.

In short, the pessimists offer three sources of an incipient urban crisis in the Third World: a savings constraint that will bridle the growth of capital-intensive cities; a labor market disequilibrium that has made over-urbanization a temporary, but serious problem of overshoot; and the disappearance of unusual external conditions that were favorable to urban growth in the recent past. While the pessimists have established a plausible case, no one to our knowl-edge has offered a quantitative assessment of the importance of these forces over the past two decades. Without such an assessment, debate over future Third World trends will be dominated by allega-tion and anecdotal evidence. It is our view that the debate can be better informed by the application of a general equilibrium model of Third World development which includes some of the costs of urbanization so that "natural limits" to urban growth can be eval-uated, and the impact of changing economic-demographic condi-tions assessed.

3. WHAT'S WRONG WITH OUR MODELS OF MIGRATION AND CITY GROWTH?

Rapid city growth implies heavy rural-urban migration. Indeed, demographers have shown us that the more rapid the city growth, the more important is in-migration as a share of the city population increase. For that matter, the urban transition—epochs of first rising then falling city growth rates associated with long-run urbaniza-tion—has always been driven by changes in the rate of in-migration. What, then, do we know about migration itself?

The Rational Migrant in Partial Equilibrium

An enormous empirical literature on migration behavior in the Third World accumulated during the 1960s and 1970s. These studies offered explanations of migration by the application of partial-equi-librium models. The central issue in that stream of early migra-tion research—led by the human-capital approach embodied in Sjaastad's (1962) classic contribution—was a test of economic ratio-nality. Do Third World households respond to economic incentives in selecting employment locations? The answer was a resounding "yes," since earnings differentials consistently appeared as an im-portant determinant of migration (Beals et al., 1967; Sahota, 1968; Yap, 1976b; Beier et al., 1976) in a variety of Asian, African, and

Latin American labor markets. The postulate of rationality has been confirmed most recently by Gary Fields (1982) and T. Paul Schultz (1982), who deal with place-to-place lifetime migration in Latin America.

In 1969, Michael Todaro raised another issue, one that influenced much of the research in the 1970s, including the pessimists' view of city growth. If migrants are rational, why do "wage gaps" between urban and rural areas persist and why does migration to the city continue in the face of the (alleged) urban unemployment or low-productivity underemployment? To explain these apparent anomalies, Todaro offered a simple thesis: migrants do not respond solely to current earnings differentials but rather to *expected* earnings differentials. Expected earnings are conditioned by migrants' expectations of securing jobs in the favored urban formal sector. Debate ensued over the form of the expectations function as well as its empirical relevance, but the Todaro model quickly became the conventional wisdom underlying discussion of Third World urban labor markets. Obviously, it implies over-urbanization.

A key premise of this new conventional wisdom has been that the in-migrant accepts informal service sector employment (or, indeed, unemployment) at a wage below that prevailing in the rural area so that he may remain in the urban labor queue, hopeful for employment in the formal high-wage sector. Accumulating revisionist research has cast doubt on this premise. For example, Fishlow's (1972) work on Brazil, Bellante's (1979) on the American South, Merrick's (1973) on Belo Horizonte, and Mazumdar's (1976, 1979) on India, all suggest that observed nominal wage gaps are in large part a reflection of skill, age, sex, and occupational differentials, rather than wage gaps per se. Furthermore, Yap (1976a; 1976b; 1977) has shown that recent in-migrants to Brazilian cities do *not* have incomes lower than that which they would have received in the rural areas they vacated; they do *not* appear in informal sector employment with much greater frequency; and furthermore, they improved their relative income position very quickly after arriving in the city. Even more recently, Mohan (1980) has shown that underemployment in Bogota is *not* extensive and in any case not specific to recent in-migrants, that migrants are *not* poorer, and that the so-called informal sector is extremely hard to distinguish from alternative employment in the city. Similar findings can be cited for other countries, like India (Mazumdar, 1976, 1979).

Much of the research on Third World migration suffers from another flaw: rarely do empirical studies take adequate account of cost-of-living differentials. When they do, the cost-of-living indices almost always exclude rents, since they are so difficult to measure, especially in squatter housing. The exclusion is troublesome since rents rise with density and crowding, and thus cities, especially large ones, tend to have high rents. Nominal wage differentials therefore tend to overstate the advantage of city life. When cost-of-living differentials are included, much of the nominal gap disappears (Fishlow, 1972; Thomas, 1978, 1980; in contrast, see Meesook, 1974). Furthermore, it is the non-food component of cost-of-living that explains most of the differentials (Thomas, 1980, p. 89).

In addition, these migration studies seldom give serious empirical attention to urban amenities and disamenities, an issue that has been recently examined both for developed economies (Nordhaus and Tobin, 1972; Rosen, 1979) and for important historical cases like the British Industrial Revolution (Williamson, 1981). But little work has been done along these lines for Third World societies, which is certainly surprising given the general concern with the quality of life among the Third World urban poor (e.g., see Beier et al., 1976 and Linn, 1979, chaps. 3, 4, and 5). Such evidence is likely to be important in modeling the potential limits to urban growth.

Migration in General Equilibrium

If economic factors play a critical role in determining rural-urban migration, then urbanization and city growth are surely determined by those same factors. It follows that urbanization and city growth cannot be analyzed without explicit attention given to the interaction between rural and urban labor markets. Furthermore, those labor markets cannot be fully understood without explicit modeling of labor supply and demand forces in both the sending and receiving regions. In short, *urbanization and city growth can only be understood by embedding the process in a general equilibrium model.* This conclusion has slowly emerged over the past decade or so as economists and demographers have become increasingly sophisticated in their study of the sources of urbanization. Furthermore, we have learned that comparative statics are not sufficient to the task since it is now generally believed that while economywide growth influences the rate of urbanization, urbanization may also influence aggregate growth—an issue ignored in most urban studies except those that appeal to city-scale economies.

Based on the firmly held belief that the current structure of an economy—including urbanization levels—can influence its subsequent growth performance, macro models of Third World societies have stressed sectoral detail from the start. The classic examples are offered by the dual economy models pioneered by Lewis (1954), Fei and Ranis (1964), and Jorgenson (1961), the latter extended by Kelley, Williamson, and Cheetham (1972). Central to these models and their more elaborate extensions are the output gains associated with resource transfers from "traditional" low-productivity sectors to "modern" high-productivity sectors. Such resource transfers—labor migration in particular—have spatial implications, the most notable example being urbanization. In the classic labor surplus version, modernization (or urbanization) augments aggregate output both through short-run efficiency gains and long-run growth effects. In the short run, labor resources with low marginal productivity are shifted to high marginal productivity employment. In the long run, accumulation rates are raised since savings rates are higher in the modern sectors—indeed, in the extreme version only capitalists save, and capital is an argument in the modern, urban-based production functions only: ". . . rural-to-urban migration with its consequent dampening of urban wages, increases profits. Hence it leads to higher savings, investment, and output growth" (Stark, 1980, p. 97). Rising (urban) accumulation rates imply increased rates of modern-sector job vacancies, a rural-urban migration response, and further urbanization. Thus, output growth, trend acceleration, and increasing urbanization are the likely outcomes of the labor surplus model. The neoclassical dual economy makes the same prediction (Kelley, Williamson, and Cheetham, 1972; Dixit, 1973), at least for the long run.

What forces tend to inhibit the rate of ubanization in these dual economy models? Obviously the share in urban areas cannot exceed 100 percent. Thus, in the very long run, urbanization rates will slow down as this limit is approached and city growth rates will decline to the national population growth rate. But what about the medium term, perhaps a few decades hence? In the medium term, increasing labor scarcity is typically the only source of retardation in the rate of urbanization, even when such models are expanded for demoeconomic simulation (e.g., Tempo-II, Bachue, Simon, FAO, and KWC; see Sanderson, 1980). The rise in the real wage serves to choke off the rise in the saving rate, to reduce the rate of urban capital accumulation, to retard the rate of increase in new urban job vacancies, and thus to limit urban growth. The ultimate source of the limits to urban growth in models of this sort is agriculture, either through the disappearance of a rural labor surplus and/or through the rise in the relative price of agricultural products—the key wage good in such models.

Nowhere in this account are competing, and potentially voracious, urban "unproductive" investment demands on the national
saving pool considered. In addition, while inelastic agricultural land
supply insures an eventual constraint on urbanization through
rising food costs and real wage increases, nowhere is the impact of
inelastic *urban* land supply on city rents—another key wage good—
and urban cost-of-living considered. Nor, for that matter, is there
any concern with inelastic urban land supply on density, crowding,
and urban disamenities. It seems to us that such models are poorly
equipped to confront urbanization problems in the Third World.
They say nothing about the costs of urbanization, and are equally
silent on the possible limits to urban growth generated within the
growing urban sector itself. If our understanding of Third World
urbanization is to be enriched by macro modeling, existing multisectoral models must be revised to capture the potential impact of city
costs on urban population growth through migration.

4. LIMITS TO URBAN GROWTH

How might our models of development be revised to better capture the costs of urbanization? If there are endogenous forces that
tend to inhibit the rate of urbanization independent of overt anti-
urban policy or unfavorable exogenous demoeconomic events, what
are they? How potent might these forces be? Could they impose important limits to urbanization?

No doubt rapid rates of population growth explain much of the
spectacular growth of cities in the Third World. Furthermore, one
could appeal to the mechanics of the demographic transition as a
potential limit to urban growth. It is well known that fertility rates
are lower in the cities than in the countryside, thus implying an
eventual retardation in population growth rates as urbanization
proceeds. However, it is doubtful that these long-run demographic
transition forces will play a significant role over the next two
decades.

It seems likely that more insight into the limits of urban growth
might be gained by examining various urban costs that influence
the migration decision, on the one hand, and rising urban investment requirements that compete with "productive" capital accumulation, on the other. First among these influences are inelastic urban
land supplies. Urban land constraints serve to raise (market or
shadow price) rents, augment urban relative to rural living costs,
and inhibit in-migration to the city. To the extent that rising rents

and urban disamenities are both caused by density, crowding, and other manifestations of inelastic urban land supplies, then city rents reflect more than living costs alone, but the quality of urban life as well. The importance of these urban land constraints on city rents can only be evaluated in a general equilibrium model which, at the very minimum, admits housing service activities and confronts issues of equilibrium land use. Furthermore, any urban land use characterization must allow for a variety of urban land requirements—residential squatter settlements, factory sites, land use for public social overhead, and luxury housing sites.

Second, the housing-cum-social overhead investment requirements of city growth must be confronted. "Unproductive" urban investments of this type, which do not create capacity for future urban employment, may well take priority over those forms of accumulation that do create capacity for future urban employment (first analyzed by Coale and Hoover, 1958). In any case, "unproductive" urban investment requirements compete directly with "productive" capital accumulation. Any model of urban growth must deal with these competing requirements since new urban housing-cum-social overhead requirements may very well serve to check urban growth. Of course, if the housing-cum-social overhead investment is forgone, then housing costs will rise and the quality of urban services fall, further discouraging in-migration to the city. In short, the rise in the relative cost of living in the city may impose a limit to urban growth and/or the rise of urban unproductive investment requirements may diminish the rate of productive urban capital accumulation and new urban job vacancies, thus limiting urban growth.

There are other possible constraints on urbanization worth considering. Modern sectors tend to be relatively intensive in both skills and intermediate inputs, particularly imported inputs. The most visible manifestation of the latter influence is the cost of energy. As far as skill bottlenecks go, there is considerable debate. If capital and skills are complements, and labor of different skills poor substitutes for each other, then rapid rates of urban capital accumulation imply increasing demands for skilled labor. Any model of the limits of urban growth must take these potential skill bottlenecks into account for they may place important constraints on capacity expansion in the modern urban sectors, retard the rate of growth in urban employment demand in general, and thus place further limits on urban growth. Any effort to relax this constraint by skill accumulation is likely to compete with productive urban capital accumulation and thus offer an alternative limit to urban growth.

We have no way of appreciating how important these and other limits to urban growth may be without their explicit evaluation in a general equilibrium model of Third World development.

5. OVERVIEW OF THE BOOK

This book offers a quantitative assessment of the sources of Third World city growth past, present, and future. Not only will it offer a framework capable of replicating the so-called "urban transition," but it will also make it possible to assess the impact of various economic and demographic events on the pace and character of that urban transition.

Chapter 2 develops an eight-sector general equilibrium model of a developing economy (where rural-urban features are highlighted). The model is dynamic, and thus is capable of making predictions about the patterns of growth and structural change over time. It makes predictions about growth, accumulation, and inequality; about industrialization; about changes in employment distribution and the structure of wages; about relative prices and the structure of trade; and about the rise in government. But most important, the model makes predictions about in-migration, city growth, and urbanization. The model makes predictions about other aspects of urban development, too—trends in density, crowding, and land scarcity; urban land values and squatter settlement sprawl; excess housing demands and residential construction activity; and relative costs of city life. But the key force driving these urban events is the rate of city in-migration, and it is the endogenous explanation of rural-urban migration that motivates construction of the model.

Chapter 3 turns to the empirical record of the Third World since 1960 and asks "fact or fiction?" Is the model capable of replicating Third World experience in the recent past? It appears so, at least based on pre-OPEC Third World history.

Having established the model's empirical credibility, the remainder of the book focuses on analysis. Chapter 4 explores the workings of the model by detailed examination of short-run impact multipliers. Here we begin to seek to determine which exogenous variables and which policy parameters have had the greatest impact on city growth by exploring the impact of five key macro events: unbalanced productivity advance, world market conditions and domestic price policy, capital accumulation, demographic change, and land scarcity. Each of these is computed with reference to Third World conditions around 1970, but the chapter goes on to ask whether things were any different in 1960, or in 1980, or, for that matter, if they would be different in the year 2000. The chapter concludes with an examination of the impact of two policy variables that have received much attention in the literature over the past decade, urban wage policy and government attitudes toward urban squatter settlements.

Guided by the new knowledge as to which factors most influence city growth, Chapter 5 moves on to counterfactual analysis. What explains rapid Third World city growth over the past two decades? What accounts for the modest slowdown more recently? Were exogenous conditions unusually favorable for rapid city growth in the 1960s? Did these conditions dramatically reverse in the 1970s? Or can the city growth slowdown be explained by forces endogenous to Third World economies themselves? The analysis applies the historians' counterfactual by asking how Third World cities would have grown under alternative conditions. The exercise turns out to be extremely relevant in guiding our expectations about the future.

What will the year 2000 be like? Demographers have certainly supplied answers to such questions, but since all of them take migration as exogenous, none of them offer truly endogenous explanations of future city growth. Chapter 6 offers our "predictions" or "projections" and compares them with those of the demographers. The differences are striking, and we are able to tell the reader exactly what the source of the differences is. In any case, the chapter shows how the model replicates the urban transition, a stylized fact of long-run urban development. Using alternative scenarios and policy regimes, the chapter also assesses those factors that are likely to be most critical to Third World city growth over the next two decades.

An agenda is now established. What, then, drives Third World city growth?

CHAPTER TWO

Modeling Third World Urbanization
and Economic Growth

1. AN OVERVIEW OF THE MODEL

Our purpose in this chapter is to construct a dynamic model of Third World urbanization and city growth in which city in-migration is fully endogenous. It is a long-run model of what the demographers call the "urban transition," but one that contains sufficient economic and demographic detail such that later in the book we can explore the impact of various macro events on the pace and character of Third World city growth.

To begin with, the multisector general equilibrium model developed in the pages that follow possesses a high degree of what the specialist calls "closure." Most input and output prices are determined endogenously. Neoclassical production functions are assumed and price-responsive aggregate demand functions are implied by the household demand system postulated. A period-by-period equilibrium is imposed on the economy whereby factors move between and within sectors, minimizing rate of return and earnings differentials, subject to various institutional constraints and imperfect information about the future. Optimization at the microeconomic level is imposed on firms and households that independently maximize returns and utilities subject to budget constraints.

Given this introduction, it should already be apparent that our model of Third World city growth descends from a robust family tree: small-scale general equilibrium models of dualistic development, large-scale computable general equilibrium models, multi-sector interindustry models in the Leontief tradition, and even macroeconomic-demographic models which highlight population policy options.[1] This is an impressive ancestry indeed. While none

---

[1] Early dualistic models include those of W. A. Lewis (1954), J. C. Fei and G. Ranis (1961, 1964), and D. W. Jorgenson (1961, 1967). A review and extension of these and other models can be found in A. C. Kelley, J. G. Williamson, and R. J. Cheetham (1972) and C. Lluch (1974). The earliest equilibrium multisectoral framework revealing interindustry linkages is by L. Johansen (1959). Recent applications include I. Adelman and S. Robinson (1978), L. Bergsman (1978), and K. Dervis, J. de Melo, and

of these models have, to our knowledge, been applied to Third World city growth problems, nevertheless it might still prove useful to stress the novelties of our own framework from the start.

We distinguish between *tradeables* and *nontradeables*, the latter including various location-specific services. This is hardly the first multisectoral model to recognize nontradeables but it is the first spatial dualistic model that stresses the importance of nontradeables as an influence on migration behavior. The presence of nontradeables implies urban-rural cost-of-living differentials. Since migrants are assumed to move in response to improvements in expected earnings adjusted for cost-of-living differentials, the latter may exert an important impact on the rate of urban growth. For example, rapid city growth will increase density and congestion, and housing (and public support service) scarcity—all related to the short-run rise in structure rents and deteriorating city services, and to the long-run rise in urban disamenities and land rents. As a result, the city will be somewhat less appealing to potential rural out-migrants. Furthermore, new house building (and social overhead) serves to diminish the rate of productive capital accumulation in the city and thus diminishes the rate of growth of job vacancies in the modern urban sector, further reducing the attraction of the city. Matters may be made even worse as capital is substituted for scarce urban land, the city's capital-intensity rises, and labor absorption rates decline. Urban growth, therefore, has embedded in it countervailing forces that may produce an eventual retardation, a characterization consistent with the stylized facts of history.

Development economists have long emphasized the importance of *human capital accumulation* (T. W. Schultz, 1961, 1972), but it has appeared in formal models only infrequently. The emphasis almost always has been on conventional physical capital. In contrast to the Coale and Hoover (1958) tradition, a broader view of accumulation is taken in the present model where demographically-induced expenditures on education are not considered unproductive consumption financed at the expense of productive investment. Modern urban sectors utilize skilled labor and these skills are assumed to be complementary to physical capital. Imperfect capital markets exclude individual investment in human capital, but firms invest in skills

S. Robinson (1982). Macroeconomic-demographic models of limited closure originated with the work of A. Coale and E. Hoover (1958). Later contributions include R. Barlow (1967), R. Barlow and G. W. Davis (1974), F. Denton and B. Spencer (1976), S. Enke (1971), G. Rodgers, M. Hopkins, and R. Wéry (1978), and J. L. Simon (1976).

accumulation through training programs. This investment decision is made by comparing the discounted flow of augmented profits to the current training cost, namely the average return on investment in physical plant and equipment. The accumulation of human capital is thus determined by its return to the using firms as well as by the demographic trends influencing the stock of "potential trainables."

While growth and development theory has made significant strides in confronting issues of labor heterogeneity, a symmetric treatment of capital is less common. Of course capital has multisector uses, and frequently capital is treated as "putty-clay" so that once in place there are in effect many types of physical capital stocks. But rarely do multisectoral general equilibrium models focus on various forms of accumulation requiring many capital goods producing sectors. In contrast, our model explicitly confronts *a portfolio of heterogeneous capital stocks* consisting of "productive" conventional capital (plant and equipment), "unproductive" capital in residential structures (housing), and human capital (training and skills accumulation), each produced by a different capital goods sector. All are financed by a common savings pool, and new investment is allocated according to its greatest marginal return *subject to the constraints of capital market fragmentation*. While the allocation of saving between productive and unproductive uses obeys traditional neoclassical rules, institutional and political realities of the undeveloped Third World capital market constrain that allocation. These constraints include:

—the absence of a mortgage market so that all housing must be self-financed;
—the absence of a household loan market so that individual investment in human capital is suppressed;
—demographic restrictions on the stock of "potential trainables," thus inhibiting firms' investment in human capital and making it possible for the rate of return to human capital to remain at high levels;
—the immobility of physical capital once in place, making it possible for rate-of-return differentials across sectors to persist over long periods of time.

These capital market imperfections provide abundant options for government policy to eliminate (or exacerbate!) inefficient resource allocation and market failure induced by the disequilibrating impact of successful growth.

Typically, development models incorporate very simple specifications for land use, restricting it to agricultural production alone. This treatment may be appropriate for some purposes, but it is unacceptable in a model where the focus is city growth and urban problems. In our model *optimal urban land use* is explicitly confronted, although we do not employ the urban economist's land-gradient function. Our urban land use specification has potentially important implications. Urban growth will bid up the price of urban land largely due to the requirements for residential structures and social overhead. Because land is immobile, it shares the same characteristics as nontradeables. Thus, endogenously determined land use and rents can produce spatial cost-of-living differences with a resulting impact on rural-urban migration and city growth. Furthermore, the model is equipped to deal with two additional urban problems: first, rising urban population densities and the disamenities associated with such crowding; and second, the dramatic rise in urban land values widely observed in the Third World.

Government activities are typically specified as exogenous in formal models of development. However, given the accumulating evidence that government spending exhibits systematic patterns related to growth and structural change, it seems appropriate to move toward a specification of *endogenous government fiscal behavior* (Heller, 1975). In our model, government spending is constrained by the availability of public income, stemming from endogenous tax revenues and exogenously determined international capital flows. The latter is specified in a manner that places us in the "revisionist" foreign-aid camp since foreign capital does not augment the domestic savings pool dollar for dollar. Furthermore, the government allocates its capital budget to maximize returns while the current account is determined in response to social preferences. In addition, spending has an urban bias. The government's domestic revenue sources are numerous, thus providing an opportunity to assess the effects of alternative government taxation policies on city growth, structural change, the commodity price structure, growth, and distribution.

While these are the most novel features of our model, it should be emphasized that our framework also attempts a synthesis from a growing literature on general equilibrium systems.[2] Many of

---

[2] Studies using this approach include: A. C. Kelley, J. G. Williamson, and R. J. Cheetham (1972); L. Yap (1972, 1976a); J. G. Williamson (1974); A. C. Kelley and J. G. Williamson (1974); F. Ahmed (1974); L. de Bever (1976); B. Edmonston, W. C.

the functional specifications here can be found elsewhere. To our knowledge, however, these specifications have yet to be combined in a single model capable of confronting many of the key macro-development issues of the 1980s. For example, *nested constant elasticity of substitution production functions* have been employed by Bergman (1978) and Edmonston, Sanderson, and Sapoznikow (1976), but the former incorporates only a limited role for demand, while the latter is not designed to confront urbanization issues. *Labor market fragmentation* has been highlighted by Yap (1972, 1976a), but endogenous demand forces are suppressed in her model. Similar observations may be made for the treatment of *imported energy requirements*, or the use of the *extended linear expenditure system.*

All of these remarks are directed toward the economic model discussed below. We have said nothing about the demography with which such a model might interact. The demographic model could involve urban and rural age-sex-specific schedules of mortality, fertility, and migration. The demographic model could determine new urban and rural labor force entrants; the economic framework could determine labor force needs as well as the equilibrating mechanism for matching demands with supplies from period to period. Demography could enter directly by its influence on the level of demand and its composition (especially through housing requirements), by determining labor force growth through age-sex-location labor force participation rates, by its impact on regional settlement patterns and land use, and by modifying the distribution and availability of new investment or capital formation through the urban-rural remittance mechanism. Population growth rates could be determined exogenously given the constancy of the various demographic schedules, although aggregate population growth could change due to inter-

---

Sanderson, and J. Sapoznikow (1976); J. G. Williamson and L. de Bever (1977); R. Mohan (1977); F. J. Lysy and L. Taylor (1977); I. Adelman and S. Robinson (1978); J. de Melo (1978); J. de Melo and S. Robinson (1978); K. Dervis and S. Robinson (1978); J. de Melo and S. Robinson (1980); J. G. Williamson and P. H. Lindert (1980); and K. Dervis, J. de Melo, and S. Robinson (1982). The most recent review and presentation of a variety of general equilibrium models can be found in A. C. Kelley, W. C. Sanderson, and J. G. Williamson (1983). It should be pointed out that this stream of literature stresses the importance of multisectoral modeling. We obviously agree, and thus reject the view (Taylor, 1979) that the economic content of multisectoral computable general equilibrium models can be reduced to simple one- and two-sector paradigms and still maintain their effectiveness for empirical analysis and policy motivation.

sectoral migration. While this book does not offer such demographic detail, the model could be readily extended to do so.[3]

A final distinguishing feature of our model relates to the forces motivating its development and choice of specifications. Our model is not designed to explain the behavior of a specific low-income country. A case study approach is more appropriate to this task.[4] Rather, our goal has been to capture the key features of a group of Third World, growing countries which are price-takers in international markets. Ours is a model of "representative" Third World countries, an approach discussed at length in Chapter 3 and documented empirically in Appendix B. In developing our theoretical specifications, we have benefited from results of extensive empirical analysis undertaken on a sample of such countries. For this purpose data from the World Bank, the United Nations, the International Labour Office, country studies, and the general economics literature have all been systematically exploited. It is our view that theorizing is most likely to succeed where there is sensitivity to empirical reality. Moreover, a model of theoretical elegance that cannot be empirically implemented is of little use. In many instances our theoretical specifications have been conditioned by this constraint. While the present chapter focuses on *modeling* urbanization and economic growth, it is to be emphasized that the model has already drawn upon an extensive data base.

2. COMPARATIVE STATICS

Sectoral Activities

Our economy consists of eight sectors, each of which produces a single homogenous commodity or service. These sectors have a specific spatial location, urban or rural, and produce tradeables and nontradeables. As we shall see, the distinction between tradeables and nontradeables is central to cost-of-living differentials between regions, and thus potentially important to both the migration process and to urbanization. The tradeable and nontradeable distinction is also relevant to the international exchange and specialization choices open to the economy. While the inclusion of nontradeable service activities has become familiar in the literature on computable

---

[3] A demographic model capable of interaction with the economic model developed in this chapter has already been developed by R. M. Schmidt (1981, 1983), although we did not have the time and resources to introduce it into this book.

[4] One such example is an ongoing project on Indian urbanization involving one of the present authors (Becker, Mills, and Williamson, ongoing), for the World Bank.

general equilibrium models, we feel they are especially important in understanding the urbanization process and have yet to receive the emphasis they deserve.

There are two commodity-producing sectors in the model: manufactures and primary products, both of which are tradeable internationally and interregionally. Their empirical counterparts are the following: the manufactures sector M includes both mining and manufacturing, since these sectors have comparable technological characteristics. The primary product sector A includes agriculture, forestry, and fishing. The M-sector is an urban activity while the A-sector is rural.

Service-sector activities are highlighted in the model, especially those that are not tradeable between locations. There are six service-sector activities. The modern or "formal" capital-cum-skill intensive service sector KS has, as its empirical counterpart, the combination of electricity, gas, water, transportation, communications, defense, education, other government services, and construction of what we call urban high-cost housing stocks. While the output of the KS sector cannot be traded internationally, it *can* be traded interregionally within the economy. It is urban location-specific and is the central activity supplying the final demand needs generated by the government sector. Given the demand conditions discussed below, the KS sector can be expected to be one of the "leading" growth sectors in our developing economy, a feature commonly ignored in development models.

Recent qualitative models of migration (Todaro, 1969; Corden and Findlay, 1975; Yap, 1972, 1976a) have focused at length on the urban traditional or "informal" service sector as a source of low-productivity urban employment, and we have already seen in Chapter 1 how it has figured importantly in current conventional wisdom regarding the determinants of rural-urban migration and the rate of urbanization in the Third World. The literature has made no effort, however, to introduce similar activities for the rural sector, ignoring Hymer and Resnick's (1969) useful emphasis on rural "Z goods" activities. We have chosen to follow Hymer and Resnick by introducing symmetry into the model. The rural labor-intensive service sector RS and the urban labor-intensive service sector US both produce services with empirical counterparts including domestics, personal services, and the construction of lower-quality housing stocks for relatively low-income wage earners. These two traditional labor-intensive service sectors do not produce outputs tradeable between regions, and here lies one potential source of cost-of-living differences between urban and rural areas.

The model is completed by the addition of three remaining service sectors, all of which produce housing (and support) services from location-specific housing stocks. The rural sector has only one such housing activity, *H, RS*, since housing stocks there appear to be predominately low-cost, labor-intensive structures. The model will be developed to permit house rents to be lower in rural areas, thereby providing the farm sector with a cost-of-living advantage. Relatively cheap rural labor might yield that result by itself, but high site rents attached to scarce urban land is likely to be the main cause of the rental differential. There are two housing activities in the urban sector: a higher-cost housing sector, *H, KS*, constructed by relatively capital-intensive methods and consumed by higher income groups; and a lower-cost housing sector, *H, US*, constructed by traditional labor-intensive methods, generating lower-quality housing for urban poor at low rents. Accessibility of this low-cost housing, the government's attitude toward squatter settlements, and thus the level of urban rents will figure importantly in migration decisions in our model.

In reality, there is a continuum of housing units by quality. The dichotomy embedded in our model reflects an important aspect of that continuum—the differing nature of construction technology as well as the different costs implied. Since housing represents the most important asset in the household's portfolio, and accounts for most of the household's investment activity, we felt it important to elaborate on its nature, especially in the urban area where issues of migration and asset accumulation, related to housing, may be particularly important to the process of development and structural change.

Technological Conditions and Factor Inputs

Like all models of economic dualism, ours stresses production dualism. (A complete mathematical statement of the model can be found in Appendix A. Equation numbers in the text are consistent with those in the Appendix.) Thus, the eight sectoral activities exhibit quite different rates of technical progress, factor-intensity, distributional attributes, and substitution elasticities. Furthermore, technological dualism is not simply an attribute of the well-known rural-urban dichotomy, but an urban attribute too.

It is assumed that the production process in all sectors (except rural housing) can be described by a continuous, twice-differentiable, single-valued function. Conventional physical capital, *K*, is used in agriculture, manufacturing, and the modern service sector, although it is specific to a given sector once in place. Unskilled labor, L, is used in all sectors except housing, and is mobile between them, subject to migration rules to be discussed later. Skilled labor, S, is utilized in the M and KS sectors only, while land, R, is used as an input in both agriculture and urban housing. Each of these five factors of production is homogeneous. Production is subject to constant returns to scale and diminishing marginal rates of substitution are assumed to prevail. Joint products are excluded and external economies (and diseconomies) do not exist. It is assumed that factor-augmenting technical change applies to capital, skills, and labor but not to land. Thus each sector is analogous to a large firm or industry having a production function and exhibiting optimal behavior. Such behavior implies cost minimization with respect to inputs and revenue maximization with respect to outputs.

The production processes in the two modern urban sectors are viewed to be more capital-cum-skill intensive than in agriculture. The importance of factor-intensity differentials has been appreciated since Eckaus (1955) brought it to our attention. He argued that in underdeveloped economies agriculture was far less capital-intensive, which, together with differences in elasticities of factor substitution, gave rise to the phenomenon of "technological dualism." We shall impose alternate restrictions consistent with his view: namely, the current elasticity of substitution in urban modern sectors is less than one, while it is equal to one in agriculture (i.e., Cobb–Douglas). There is abundant empirical evidence supporting this view (Chenery and Raduchel, 1971; Fallon and Layard, 1975; Yotopolous and Nugent, 1976).

The modern or formal urban-sector production functions must capture these overall attributes, but the presence of three factors of production makes the conventional constant elasticity of substitution (CES) production function inappropriate. Since it is not possible to confront the issue of earnings distribution without paying explicit attention to labor heterogeneity, we have insisted that the working population be distinguished, at the very minimum, as skilled and unskilled labor. Furthermore, we are convinced by several empirical studies that the elasticity of substitution between each of the three pairs of inputs in these modern sectors is not the same. Rather, we are persuaded that conventional capital and skills are relative complements (Grilliches, 1969; Fallon and Layard, 1975; Kesselman, Williamson, and Berndt, 1977; Hamermesh and Grant, 1979) and that this fact goes a long way in accounting for the phenomena of rising skilled-wage premia, "wage stretching" (Morley and Williamson, 1977; Beier et al. 1976, pp. 381–82), and increased earnings inequality in much of the Third World where capital accumulation is so rapid.

Given the need to specify modern-sector production functions that allow for relative complementarity between skilled labor and capital, the usual CES production function cannot be employed. The most useful specification for our purposes is the two-level or nested CES first proposed by Sato (1967) and since applied to developing economies in a number of case studies (Bowles, 1970; Fallon and Layard, 1975; Edmonston, Sanderson, and Sapoznikow, 1976; Lysy and Taylor, 1977; Adelman and Robinson, 1978). This function separates factors into groups and generates an index for one group using the CES function in its usual form. This index is then combined in another CES function to generate value-added output. In our case, ϕ_i is a composite index of conventional and human capital (skills) inputs, ξ_i' and ξ_i are distribution parameters, and σ_i' and σ_i are elasticities of substitution. Following Eckaus and the "structuralists" (Chenery and Raduchel, 1971), we anticipate that these substitution elasticities will generally fall below unity.

Furthermore, we anticipate that the elasticity of substitution between capital and skilled labor will be significantly less than that between unskilled labor and composite capital, thus conforming to the capital-skill complementarity hypothesis. The implication of this hypothesis is that rapid physical capital accumulation in the modern sector tends to raise the demand for skilled relative to unskilled labor. Accumulation tends to breed earnings inequality in our model as a result.

Moving from a value-added to a gross-output production function where intermediate inputs are specified explicitly, we shall consider separately those inputs supplied domestically and those obtained from abroad. Imported intermediate inputs Z_i, including fuel, have been incorporated in both modern sectors. Intermediate input demands are almost always captured by fixed coefficients in development and planning models. Such Leontief-like specifications might be appropriate in short-run applications, but they are unacceptable in a model covering as much as four decades, especially given the OPEC shocks of the 1970s (Hoffmann and Jorgenson, 1977; Berndt and Wood, 1975). Since it is mandatory to admit the possibility of economizing on imported raw material inputs if the longer-run implications of OPEC pricing policies are to be sensibly investigated, substitution between imported inputs, domestically supplied intermediate inputs, and the conventional primary inputs must be allowed.

Imported non-competitive inputs are combined with other domestic and primary factor inputs following a Cobb–Douglas specification. While this specification introduces greater flexibility into our economy's structure, aspects of import dependency associated with modern-sector expansion can still be investigated. In particular, our specification permits analysis of unbalanced sectoral growth on aggregate imported intermediate inputs, especially fuels, given different import intensities by sector. Chenery and Raduchel (1971) have demonstrated that the latter can be a relatively important aspect of import dependency in a typical developing country. This specification also makes it possible to explore the impact of changes in the price of such imports on industrialization and urbanization. Since Z_i is imported at exogenous world market prices, the impact of changes in such prices, attributable, for example, to OPEC policy, can be readily explored.

The model also allows for domestic intermediate inputs, although we take a somewhat restricted view of their importance. The output of both traditional service sectors is treated as satisfying final demand only, a reasonable assumption since they are dominated by domestics, personal services, and highly labor-intensive low-cost housing construction. Neither of these two sectors enters into the intersectoral production flows. The same is true of housing services, or the rental stream generated by housing stocks. The motivation for the addition of the remaining intersectoral production flows is to recognize the direct and indirect output mix changes induced by demand or supply changes in a given sector. One of our interests is to account for trends in the distribution of income and earnings. By focusing on direct factor requirements only, and given factor-intensity differences across sectors, we would surely exaggerate induced changes in factor demand were we to ignore these indirect factor requirements induced by the input-output relationships.

The two modern-sector production functions take the following form:[5]

$$Q = A_i Q_i^{\alpha_{i,F}} z_i^{\alpha_{i,Z}} \prod_{j=A,M,KS} Q_{i,j}^{\alpha_{i,j}}, \qquad i = M, KS \neq j$$

$$Q_{i,F} = \{\xi_i \phi_i^{(\sigma_i-1)/\sigma_i} + (1-\xi_i)[zL_i]^{(\sigma_i-1)/\sigma_i}\}^{\sigma_i/(\sigma_i-1)},$$
$$i = M, KS$$

$$\phi_i = \{\xi_i'[xK_i]^{(\sigma_i'-1)/\sigma_i')} + (1-\xi_i')[yS_i]^{(\sigma_i'-1)/\sigma_i'}\}^{\sigma_i'/(\sigma_i'-1)},$$
$$i = M, KS$$

$$\sum \alpha_{i,j} = 1, \qquad i = M, KS \neq j = F, Z, A, M, KS$$

(1),(2)

where Q_i is gross output in sector i, Z_i is imported raw materials,

[5] Equation numbers correspond with the mathematical statement in Appendix A.

$Q_{i,j}$ are intersectoral inputs (excluding intrasectoral inputs), $\alpha_{i,j}$ are the cost shares of each factor in gross sales, ϕ_i is a composite input index of conventional and human capital (skills), ξ_i and ξ'_i are distribution parameters, and σ_i and σ'_i are substitution elasticities. Factor-augmenting technical progress determines the level of $x(t)$, $y(t)$, and $z(t)$; xK_i, yS_i, and zL_i will be referred to as "efficiency capital," "efficiency skilled labor," and "efficiency labor" in what follows.

Agriculture's production function is specified as Cobb–Douglas:

$$Q_A = A_A[xK_A]^{\alpha_{A,K}}[zL_A]^{\alpha_{A,L}}R_A^{\alpha_{A,R}}Z_A^{\alpha_{A,Z}} \prod_{j=M,KS} Q_{A,j}^{\alpha_{A,j}} \qquad (3)$$

$$\sum \alpha_{A,j} = 1, \qquad j = K, L, R, M, KS, Z$$

where Q_A denotes gross agricultural output, and R_A the endogenously determined stock of land, unaugmented by technical progress.

Following the now standard conventions in the formal literature (Mazumdar, 1975), the traditional service sectors utilize unskilled labor inputs only. In the absence of sector-specific technological change, the average physical product of efficiency labor diminishes with the continued application of labor, and the law of diminishing returns is held to prevail ($\alpha_i < 1$). Thus,

$$Q_i = A_i[zL_i]^{\alpha_i}, \qquad 0 < \alpha_i < 1, \qquad i = US, RS \qquad (4), (5)$$

Below we shall assume that labor in the traditional service sectors is paid its average product, thus satisfying product exhaustion. Since much of the traditional service labor is self-employed (e.g., barbers, vendors; see Mazumdar, 1976), the difference between average and marginal product may be considered as a reward for entrepreneurship.

Housing services are produced by the combined inputs of existing residential structures and land. Housing is obviously quite different from the other five commodity and service activities since it utilizes neither labor nor productive capital. Housing is, therefore, discussed below in conjunction with land-market and optimal land-use issues.

Commodity Price and Tax Policy

Prices of manufactured and agricultural goods are determined exogenously by the combined influences of world market conditions and the country's commercial policy, although the latter is not treated separately. That is, the country is assumed to be a price-taker in world markets. This characterization describes the bulk of developing countries but excludes, most notably, those that are endowed with exceptional deposits of exportable raw materials, where these exports loom large not only in the country's exports, but in world trade as well. Thus, for manufactures,

$$\bar{P}'_M = \bar{P}_M - \bar{P}_Z \frac{Z_M}{Q_M} - \bar{P}_A \frac{Q_{M,A}}{Q_M} - P_{KS} \frac{Q_{M,KS}}{Q_M} \equiv \alpha_{M,F} \bar{P}_M \qquad (9)$$

where $\bar{P}'_M$ denotes the value-added price and $\bar{P}_M$ the (tariff-distorted) domestic selling price.[6] Domestic agricultural prices are also taken as exogenous and distorted by policy in the following way:

$$\bar{P}'_A = \bar{P}_A - \bar{P}_Z \frac{Z_A}{Q_A} - \bar{P}_M(1 + \tau_{A,M}) \frac{Q_{A,M}}{Q_A} - P_{KS} \frac{Q_{A,KS}}{Q_A}$$

$$\equiv (\alpha_{A,K} + \alpha_{A,L} + \alpha_{A,R}) \bar{P}_A \qquad (10)$$

where $\bar{P}_A$ refers to the domestic selling price, $\bar{P}'_A$ refers to the value-added price (received by farmers), and $\tau_{A,M}$ refers to the domestic tax or subsidy on purchased inputs in the agricultural sector. The relative magnitudes of $\tau_{A,M}$ and $\bar{P}_A$ reflect the extent to which agriculture is squeezed by policy. Note that export taxes are also embodied in $\bar{P}_A$, and these may serve to squeeze the farm producer as well (Johnston and Kilby, 1975; T. W. Schultz, 1978), driving a wedge between world market prices, $\bar{P}^W_A$, and domestic selling prices, as in Figure 2.1. An increase in the export tax serves to diminish domestic output, to increase domestic demand at the lower domestic price (a source of subsidy to the urban work force at the farmers' expense), and to diminish exports. The export tax may, however, have little impact on government tax revenues (shown as the shaded area in Figure 2.1), depending on domestic demand and supply elasticities. We shall assume as much since tax revenue effects will be ignored in all experiments involving $\bar{P}_A$ in the chapters that follow.

---

[6] It should also be noted that per unit value-added should exhaust total factor payments per unit of output. Thus,

$$\bar{P}'_M = w_{M,S} a_{M,S} + w_{M,L} a_{M,L} + r_M a_{M,K} \equiv a_{M,F} \bar{P}_M$$

where $w_{M,j}$ are wage rates, r_M is the return to capital, and $a_{M,j}$ is the endogenous input-output ratio of factor j to value added. Similar conditions hold for all other sectors.

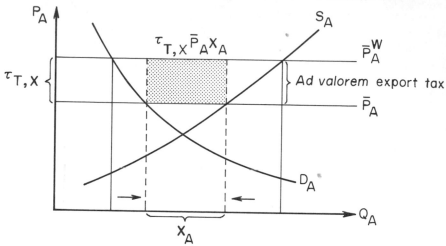

Figure 2.1 Partial Equilibrium Analysis of the Export Tax

The remaining prices in our model (rural services, P_{RS}; urban traditional services, P_{US}; urban modern services, P_{KS}) are all determined endogenously where, in addition,

$$P'_{KS} = P_{KS} - \bar{P}_Z \frac{Z_{KS}}{Q_{KS}} - \bar{P}_M \frac{Q_{KS,M}}{Q_{KS}} - \bar{P}_A \frac{Q_{KS,A}}{Q_{KS}} \qquad (11)$$

following the same notation as above. (Rents are discussed below.) There are other commodity taxes present in the model, but since they appear as expenditure or sales taxes, we need not discuss them until we confront the government sector and the private sector demand system later in this chapter.

Labor Demand, Labor Supply, and Wage Determination

Economywide supplies of skilled and unskilled labor are exogenously given at any point in time in the static model. This is not true over time, of course, since skills are augmented endogenously and unskilled labor grows in response to long-run demographic forces. Although total labor supplies are given by previous history in the static model, the distribution of the labor force over space and across sectors is not. The next section will analyze the migration behavior embedded in the model that determines labor allocation. The present section will focus on labor demand and wage determination in the absence of migration forces.

There are five sectors that employ unskilled labor:

$$L_U = L_M + L_{KS} + L_{US} \tag{47}$$

$$L_R = L_A + L_{RS} \tag{48}$$

$$L = L_U + L_R \tag{49}$$

where L_R is the total rural unskilled labor force and L_U is the total urban unskilled labor force. Overt unemployment is not an attribute of our model since very few unskilled laborers in the Third World can afford the luxury, having few or no assets to finance significant periods of overt unemployment. Apparently this characteristic holds true even for rural immigrants to some Third World cities, since the evidence suggests that they secure employment relatively soon after arrival (Yotopoulos, 1977, chap. 6; Yap, 1976a, 1977). Low-productivity underemployment in the traditional service sectors appears to offer a better measure of the extent of labor surplus (Mazumdar, 1975).

With the exception of the two labor-intensive service sectors, efficiency factors are assumed to be paid their marginal value products, provided that, at each point in time, the marginal value product of efficiency labor in each sector is sufficient to allow every member of the unskilled labor force to consume at levels that satisfy subsistence. We interpret "subsistence" to be the level of per capita consumption considered by households to be essential for their welfare. This minimum level of consumption will be defined explicitly when we turn to the household demand system, but for the moment we shall assume that it is above the caloric level at which starvation occurs, and that it also exceeds levels at which marginal increases in consumption significantly influence productivity, efficiency, and thus earnings. (See Fei and Chiang, 1966; Mirrlees, 1975.)

Defining $\tilde{w}_{i,L}$ to be the wage per efficiency unskilled laborer in the ith sector, annual earnings can be denoted by $w_{i,L} = z\tilde{w}_{i,L}$ where, we will recall, z is a factor of augmentation through technical change (or utilization). Thus, wage equations for these five sectors can be written as

$$\tilde{w}_{i,L} = P_i' \frac{Q_i}{Q_{i,F}} (1 - \xi_i) \left[\frac{Q_{i,F}}{zL_i} \right]^{1/\sigma_i} = \frac{w_{i,L}}{z}, \tag{17}, \tag{18}$$

$$i = M, KS, \text{ and where } P_M' = \bar{P}_M'$$

$$\tilde{w}_{A,L} = \bar{P}_A \alpha_{A,L} \left[\frac{Q_A}{zL_A} \right] = \frac{w_{A,L}}{z} \tag{19}$$

$$\tilde{w}_{i,L} = \frac{P_i Q_i}{z L_i} = \frac{w_{i,L}}{z}, \qquad i = US, RS \qquad (20), (21)$$

Note that marginal product pricing does not hold in the informal service sectors, but rather average value product determines wages there. It may be appealing to view wage determination in traditional services as the result of income sharing. Alternatively, the output produced above the laborer's marginal product may be considered a premium of entrepreneurship distributed back to the laborers—a view consistent with the fact that self-employment and family enterprise dominate this sector.

It might be helpful to emphasize two issues at this point: the distinction between wage rates and annual earnings, on the one hand, and the structure of earnings by occupation-sector, on the other. Both of these issues are important to income distribution patterns generated by the model. First, we have shown elsewhere that wage rates and earnings can behave quite differently over time in the developing economy, depending on the character of technical progress and labor utilization rates. (See Kelley, Williamson, and Cheetham, 1972, chaps. 4, 5, and 8.) As we shall see below, labor-saving technological change implies rapid increases in z, an influence that serves to suppress the rise in the real wage rate, confirming the historical evidence of wage stability (for unskilled labor). Yet that influence also seems to drive a wedge between wage rates and annual earnings, the latter rising even in the face of wage-rate stability. Thus, stability in the wage-rate of efficiency unskilled labor does not necessarily imply stability in wage earnings or, for that matter, stability in the unskilled labor's share. Second, our choice of migration rules will be crucial in determining the structure of earnings among the unskilled in our model. If we were to assume complete factor mobility between sectors, and thus wage equalization, there would be no room for anything other than a fully egalitarian distribution of unskilled earnings: all earnings inequality would take the form of wage differentials between skilled and unskilled labor. Migration specifications become important, therefore, to the distribution patterns generated in any model of Third World economies.

Equations (17)–(21) can be readily converted into sectoral (un-skilled) labor requirements, demand conditions that are central to issues of employment, labor migration, income distribution, and urbanization. Sectoral unskilled labor demands are, therefore, writ-ten as the combined influence of technology, output levels, and, of course, real wages themselves:

$$L_i = \left[\frac{w_{i,L}}{P'_i}\right]^{-\sigma_i} [Q_i(1 - \xi_i)Z^{(\sigma_i - 1)/\sigma_i}Q_{i,F}^{(1 - \sigma_i)/\sigma_i}]^{\sigma_i} \qquad i = M, KS$$

$$L_A = \left[\frac{w_{A,L}}{\bar{P}_A}\right]^{-1} \alpha_{A,L}Q_A$$

$$L_i = \left[\frac{w_{i,L}}{P_i}\right]^{-1} Q_i, \qquad i = US, RS$$

It should be clear from these labor demand functions that wage elasticities vary across sectors, being higher in agriculture (unity) than in the modern sectors where σ_i is usually less than unity.

Consider next the skilled labor market. Skilled labor supplies, S, are given at some exogenous level in the static model, depending on previous experience with skill accumulation. Since skilled labor is utilized only in the two modern urban sectors, it follows that

$$S = S_M + S_{KS} \qquad (50)$$

Defining $\tilde{w}_{i,s}$ to be the wage per efficiency skilled laborer in the ith sector, his annual earnings can be denoted by $w_{i,s} = y\tilde{w}_{i,s}$ where y is a factor of augmentation comparable to that for unskilled labor. Once again marginal productivity conditions are invoked so that

$$\tilde{w}_{i,s} = P'_i \frac{Q_i}{Q_{i,F}} \xi_i(1 - \xi_i) \left[\frac{Q_{i,F}}{\phi_i}\right]^{1/\sigma_i} \left[\frac{\phi_i}{yS_i}\right]^{1/\sigma_i} = \frac{w_{i,s}}{y}, \quad (22), (23)$$

$$i = M, KS \text{ and where } P'_M = \bar{P}'_M$$

As with unskilled labor, these two wage equations can be converted into skilled-labor demand functions:

$$S_i = \left[\frac{w_{i,s}}{P'_i}\right]^{-\sigma'_i} [Q_i\xi_i(1 - \xi_i)Q_{i,F}^{(1 - \sigma_i)/\sigma_i}\phi_i^{(1 - \sigma'_i)/\sigma'_i}y^{(\sigma'_i - 1)/\sigma'_i}]^{\sigma'_i} \quad i$$

$$= M, KS$$

Labor Migration and Wage Gaps

Research on the determinants of labor migration in developing economies has proceeded along two lines. The first has its source in formal dualistic labor transfer models where the treatment of migration has typically been quite simplistic. The Lewis (1954), Fei–Ranis (1961), Jorgenson (1961, 1967), and Kelley–Williamson–Cheetham (1972) models all exploit the hypothesis that current wage differentials induce labor migration between sectors. Since the significance of wage differentials as a determinant of migration is well documented (Beals et al., 1967; Sahota, 1968; Yap, 1976b), the hypothesis would hardly seem contestable. Yet, this evidence hardly justifies the extreme but common assumption in the general equilibrium literature that wages are in fact equalized by the process of migration. In fact, nominal wage equalization is not observed in the Third World (L. G. Reynolds, 1965; Johnston and Nielsen, 1966; Johnson and Whitelaw, 1974), although the lion's share of the observed nominal wage gaps appears to be due to skill and cost-of-living differences. (On the alleged Brazilian "low-wage" Northeast, see Fishlow, 1972; on the alleged American low-wage South, see Bellante, 1979; similar findings are found in Merrick, 1973 and Mazumdar, 1976, 1979.) Since it is widely recognized that wage differentials are not the sole determinant of migration, and that all determinants are not necessarily economic, we cannot adopt wholesale the simple wage equalization assumptions of the simpler general equilibrium models in a more policy-oriented framework, especially one like ours that focuses on the urbanization process.

A second line of thought extends the classical treatment of the migration decision. Either it includes an urban unemployment (or underemployment) variable, and thus focuses on expected annual earnings differentials (Todaro, 1969; Harris and Todaro, 1970; Zarembka, 1972; Corden and Findlay, 1975), or it utilizes a capital theoretic framework that explicitly introduces present value calculations, migration costs, job search, and distributed lags (Sjaastad, 1962; Kelley, Williamson, and Cheetham, 1972; Williamson and de Bever, 1977). In particular, the Todaro framework has enjoyed considerable popularity over the past decade and there have been many attempts to introduce this hypothesis into static and dynamic intersectoral development models.

The Todaro hypothesis is simple and elegant. While similar statements can be found elsewhere (Harris and Todaro, 1970; Stiglitz, 1974), the most effective illustration can be found in Corden and Findlay (1975), reproduced in Figure 2.2 (which assumes perfect capital mobility). There are only two sectors analyzed, but they are sufficient to illustrate the point. Under the extreme assumption of wage equalization through migration, and in the absence of wage rigidities, equilibrium is achieved at E (the point of intersection of the two labor demand curves, AA' and MM'). Here $w_A^* = w_M^*$ and the urbanization rate is $O_M L_M^*/L$, where M denotes the manufacturing sector and A denotes agriculture. In addition, the Corden–

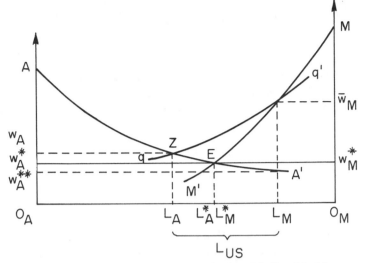

Figure 2.2 The Harris–Todaro–Corden–Findlay Model

Findlay model incorporates the widely-held belief that the wage rate of Third World manufacturing sectors is pegged at artificially high levels, say at $\bar{w}_M$. If overt unemployment is assumed away, then all who fail to secure the favored jobs in the M sector would accept lower-paying jobs in the A-sector at w_A^{**}.

Clearly, the level of employment in the urban sector has been choked off by the high wage in the manufacturing sector and both migration and urbanization have been forestalled. As Todaro initially pointed out, however, urbanization rates have been dramatic in the Third World and furthermore there has been an expansion in traditional urban service underemployment (see also Sabot, 1975; Mazumdar, 1975; Rogers, 1977; Merrick, 1978). Todaro explains this apparent conflict (e.g., migration in the face of urban underemployment) by developing an expectations hypothesis which, in its simplest form, states that the favored jobs are allocated by "lottery," that the potential migrant calculates the expected value of that lottery ticket, and compares it with the certain employment in the rural sector. Migration then takes place until the urban expected wage is equated to the rural wage. Given the pegged $\bar{w}_M$, at what rural wage would the migrant be indifferent whether he had underemployment in the traditional urban service sector or employment in the agricultural sector? If his probability of getting the favored job is simply the ratio of L_M to the total urban labor pool, L_U, then the expression

$$w_A = \frac{L_M}{L_U}\, \bar{w}_M$$

indicates the agricultural wage at which he is indifferent about employment locations. This is in fact the qq' curve in Figure 2.2. The equilibrium agricultural wage, w_A, and urban underemployment (e.g., the size of the traditional, unorganized sector) is thus given at Z.[7]

While this conventional wisdom is elegant, it has not been sustained in many empirical tests (Mazumdar, 1976, 1979; Yap, 1976a, 1976b, 1977; Linn, 1979; Mohan, 1980). We adopt it here only with qualifications. These qualifications are motivated by the following observations. First, we are not convinced that $\bar{w}_M$ can be viewed as pegged in the Third World and independent of market forces. (See Mazumdar, 1975, 1976; House and Rempel, 1978; Henley and House, 1978.) Put differently, the apparent wage rigidity attributed to institutional factors (unions, government regulations) may in fact be explained by market forces, with institutions merely responding to those forces (Taylor, 1979, chap. 5; Stark, 1980, p. 98). In any case, we have no way of projecting such a fixed wage into the future, and without that information dynamic analysis is limited to ad hoc guesses.

Second, we agree with Willis (1979) that the lottery view of who gets favored jobs is naive and ignores property rights. It seems to us that the allocation of new job vacancies in the favored sectors is hardly random, but rather very much a function of bribes, nepotism, employment search costs, union dues, and the like. That is, these favored jobs have property rights earning rents that command an implicit or explicit price. Third, the Todaro formulation ignores the obvious fact that the majority of the favored jobs are more skill-intensive than either farm labor or traditional urban service activity. Thus, unskilled in the favored sectors tend to be prime-aged males with higher educational attainment. Finally, and we think most important, the formulation ignores spatial cost-of-living differentials.

Our own approach is a hybrid which attempts to meet at least some of these criticisms. On the one hand, we assume perfect mobility of unskilled labor *within* the rural sector since free entry and

---

[7] The Harris-Todaro curve, qq', is a rectangular hyperbola with unitary elasticity. The elasticity of the labor demand curve in the urban modern sectors is assumed to be less than unity in Figure 2.2 according to our expectations revealed in the previous section on labor demand.

costless mobility seem to be reasonable approximations there (Beier et al., 1976, p. 381). We make the same assumption for both skilled and unskilled labor between the two modern urban sectors, certainly an acceptable premise to the Todaro adherents given their willingness to aggregate all modern-sector activities. Thus,

$$w_{A,L} = w_{RS,L} \tag{24}$$

$$w_{M,S} = w_{KS,S} \tag{25}$$

$$w_{M,L} = w_{KS,L}$$

On the other hand, we model the unskilled wage gap between traditional urban services and the modern sectors by inserting an exogenous differential κ that reflects both the costs of the property right as discussed above as well as the fact that informal service employment is dominated by "workers outside the prime age group, females, and with lower levels of education" (Mazumdar, 1976, p. 675)—that is, labor of lower quality. Thus,

$$w_{M,L} = w_{KS,L} = \kappa w_{US,L}, \qquad \kappa > 1 \tag{26}$$

Finally, the rural-urban migration process must be specified. Here we adopt a position which is closer in spirit to the Todaro hypothesis but, we feel, with more to defend it. The potential urban-rural migrant is assumed to behave as if he calculates an expected urban nominal wage, w_U. This wage is simply the weighted average of potential urban unskilled earnings and skilled earnings (net of taxes), where the weights are marginal probabilities, rather than average probabilities as in the simple Corden–Findlay version. Thus

$$w_U = \left[(1 - \tau_Y) w_{M,S} \right] \left[\frac{\dot{S}(-1)}{L_U(-1)} \right] + \left[1 - \frac{\dot{S}(-1)}{L_U(-1)} \right]$$
$$\left[w_{M,L} \frac{L_M(-1)}{L_U(-1)} + w_{KS,L} \frac{L_{KS}(-1)}{L_U(-1)} + w_{US,L} \frac{L_{US}(-1)}{L_U(-1)} \right] \tag{28}$$

where τ_Y is the income tax rate on high-wage skilled labor. The migrant has accessible current information on city wages, but not on his employment probabilities. Thus employment weights are lagged one year in the migrant's calculation of expected urban income.[8] In

---

[8] In our specification of skill augmentation and training, eq. (82), we introduce a longer lag for migrants in obtaining skilled employment. For simplicity, this feature has been suppressed in the migration equation, since it would introduce unnecessary complexity of little empirical consequence.

summary, the migrant is induced into the cities with the anticipation of having the chance of gaining one or two favored modern-sector jobs: either unskilled employment at a higher wage rate, or training and perhaps subsequent skilled employment at an even higher wage. (Training and skills creation will be discussed below when we confront the dynamic specifications in the model.)

We assume that the migrant is motivated by real (expected) income differentials, rather than by nominal wage gaps. Thus,

$$\frac{w_{A,L}}{COL_R} = \frac{w_U - c_M}{COL_{US}} \qquad (27)$$

where the location-specific cost-of-living indices, COL_i, are influenced by price differentials for nontradeables as well as budget weights. This specification will be discussed at greater length when we confront the household demand system. In addition, c_M is an exogenous parameter reflecting the nominal costs of migration—both direct transportation costs and indirect opportunity costs associated with job search.

In summary, our model is capable of generating an endogenous earnings structure in four dimensions: rural unskilled earnings, urban traditional-sector unskilled earnings, modern-sector unskilled earnings, and skilled earnings. The wage spread over these employment categories will be determined by the endogenous forces of market demand, supply, and the migration process itself. The speed of urbanization will be determined by the same set of forces. While expectations of favored sector employment may well generate the Todaro result of "over-urbanization," it is also possible that cost-of-living influences may choke off that tendency without the overt introduction of government policy. The issue is an empirical one.

"Productive" Capital Markets

Our assumption that efficiency factors are paid their marginal value products applies not only to labor, but to physical capital as well. Thus, the sectoral rates of return r_i are written as

$$\tilde{r}_i = P_i' \frac{Q_i}{Q_{i,F}} \xi_i' \xi_i \left[\frac{Q_{i,F}}{\phi_i} \right]^{1/\sigma_i} \left[\frac{\phi_i}{xK_i} \right]^{1/\sigma_i} = \frac{r_i}{x}, \qquad (29), (30)$$

$$i = M, KS, \text{ and where } P_M' = \bar{P}_M'$$

$$\tilde{r}_A = \bar{P}_A \alpha_{A,K} \left[\frac{Q_A}{xK_A} \right] = \frac{r_A}{x} \qquad (31)$$

We assume capital immobility, so after-tax rates of return need not be equalized between sectors. That is, once investment is allocated to a given sector and used to augment the capital stock there, the new stock of capital becomes specific to that production activity. Thus, any economic event that serves to raise the rate of return in one sector relative to another, will tend to generate rate of return differentials, a disequilibrium attribute typical of most developing economies, and often labeled as "market failure."

On the other hand, we assume that the current pool of productive investment goods can be allocated freely between sectors. Indeed, both private investors and government authorities are assumed to allocate current saving (excluding, of course, that earmarked for housing investment) so as to minimize rate of return differentials. The rate-of-return differentials minimized, however, are not simply the net returns on existing capital, since these are determined primarily by the sectoral capital stocks that are fixed in the current time period. Rather, private and public agents form expectations of projected rates of return based on investment plans that will serve to augment sectoral capital stocks in the next time period. Thus, the differentials minimized by current investment allocation decisions might be called *ex ante* net (after tax) rates of return or quasi rents. Formally, where the $\tau_{\Pi,i}$ are "corporate" tax rates ($\tau_{\Pi,M} > \tau_{\Pi,KS}$), we wish to

$$
\underset{I_{i,M}}{\text{MINIMIZE}}
\begin{bmatrix}
\text{RETURN DIFFERENTIALS} \\
= \left| [\tilde{r}_A^* - \tilde{r}_M^*(1 - \tau_{\Pi,M})] \right| \\
+ \left| [\tilde{r}_A^* - \tilde{r}_{KS}^*(1 - \tau_{\Pi,KS})] \right| \\
+ \left| [\tilde{r}_M^*(1 - \tau_{\Pi,M}) - \tilde{r}_{KS}^*(1 - \tau_{\Pi,KS})] \right|
\end{bmatrix}
\tag{32}
$$

such that

$$
I_M = \sum_i I_{i,M}, \qquad i = A, M, KS
$$

where

$$
\tilde{r}_i^* = \left\{ \tilde{r}_i + \frac{\partial r_i}{\partial K_i}(-1) \bigg|_{K_i} [I_{i,M} - \delta_i K_i] \right\} - \delta_i \bar{P}_M, \qquad i = A, M, KS
$$

It is quite possible, indeed likely, that the current net investment pool is insufficient to equalize quasi rents, and differentials between *ex post* rates of return may persist or increase over periods of time. Even so, some readers might wish to see more evidence of capital market fragmentation and ineffective financial intermediation introduced into the model.

Indeed, there is a growing empirical literature that emphasizes capital market fragmentation (Gurley and Shaw, 1955, 1956, 1967; Patrick, 1966; E. Shaw, 1973; Tybout, 1981), although development economists have found it difficult to model the process (McKinnon, 1973; de Melo, 1976, 1977). We certainly agree with this emphasis. As a result, critical elements of capital market imperfection and fragmentation are introduced explicitly into the model when we consider investment in human skills (individuals cannot borrow to finance skill acquisition), as well as investment in housing (households are restricted to self-finance and mortgage markets are nonexistent).

Given these elements of capital market fragmentation, we consider it relatively unproductive to add more capital market realism to our model at this point. In an earlier work (Kelley, Williamson, and Cheetham, 1972, chap. 7), we did make an effort to formulate a disequilibrium dualistic model which incorporated capital market imperfections in the allocation of conventional physical capital. That exercise pointed out the heavy empirical requirements that this move toward realism implies. It also underscored the ad hoc devices used in the literature to circumvent the explicit estimation of key parameters. The most popular device has its origin with Rosa Luxemburg, who assumed that all rental income was reinvested in the sector of origin. Many have followed in her footsteps. A recent example offered by Yap (1972), who assumed that 80 percent of a given sector's savings was reinvested while the remaining 20 percent was allocated in response to rates of return.

We do not find these ad hoc approaches to capital market fragmentation appealing, and believe that the assumptions embedded in our basic model supply the best starting place for an analysis of Third World urbanization. For example, capital market imperfections in the skill acquisition process are already in our model; the absence of a mortgage market is also there; and the immobility of current stocks of physical (productive) capital adds another market-clearing constraint. All of these capital-market attributes are likely to produce the relevant stylized facts of Third World development: persistent rate of return differentials, sectors starved for funds, heavy reliance on self-generated funds, high reinvestment rates, thin intersectoral savings flows, and an urban investment bias. The latter is assumed since increasing government expenditure can be satisfied in our model only by the expansion of the KS sector (e.g., education, health, defense, communications), and increases in the KS sector's output implies a rise in investment requirements there (e.g., the construction of school buildings, medical facilities, harbors, airports, roads). By definition, such investment is urban based. There are also other forces in our model that are likely to make the rural sector appear starved for funds.

Finally, in the remainder of this exposition we shall find it useful to make reference to an "economywide discount rate." In what follows, this percentage rate will be defined as the average net (after taxes, excluding depreciation requirements) rate of return to productive physical capital. Equation (33) supplies the calculation where sectoral capital stocks are used as weights in computing the average:

$$i = \left[\sum_i (1 - \tau_{\Pi,i}) x K_i \tilde{r}_i^*\right]\left[\bar{P}_M \sum_i K_i\right]^{-1}, \qquad i = A, M, KS \quad (33)$$

This economywide discount rate will appear as an opportunity cost facing competing investment alternatives in skills accumulation and housing.

Education, Training, and Skills Formation

The availability of skilled labor can have a potent impact on growth and distribution. Slow rates of growth in the stock of skills can constrain expansion in the two modern sectors where skilled labor is utilized in production. Demand shifts favoring these skill-intensive sectors will serve to raise the skill premium, and produce "wage stretching" and earnings inequality (Chiswick, 1974; Beier et al., 1976; Phelps–Brown, 1977; Morley and Williamson, 1977; Williamson and Lindert, 1980). The importance of a possible skills bottleneck depends critically on the degree to which unskilled labor and capital can be used as substitutes for skills.

Debate on this issue has been extensive and until recently divided into two camps: the manpower "structuralists" who see little opportunity for substitution between labor of different skills, and their opponents who argue that, on the contrary, substitution elasticities are very high between labor of different skills (Bowles, 1970). The issue has apparently been resolved by recent empirical research (Grilliches, 1969; Fallon and Layard, 1975; Kesselman, Williamson, and Berndt, 1977) which finds elasticities with intermediate values. (These results are discussed at greater length in Appendix B; they have been incorporated in the production function specifications discussed earlier in this chapter.)

The importance of a skilled labor bottleneck also depends on the response of skill accumulation to demand conditions. Skill formation rates are a function of three forces in the specification which follows: the stock of "trainable" urban labor, the relative scarcity of skills (measured most commonly by the skill premium) which offers incentives to engage in training, and the level of government expenditures on formal education which influences the ease with which trainables can, in fact, be converted to skilled labor. We are aware that many Third World economies appear to exhibit a glut of formal school graduates. The specification which follows is designed to account for a variety of Third World experience, since the model may generate abundance or scarcity of those formally schooled. In any case, the stock of trainables will be limited to urban workers only. This seems reasonable: rural workers, regardless of educational training, must first migrate to urban areas before being considered for training. This in itself supplies an incentive to migrate. Furthermore, to the extent that such education (or health facilities) is more accessible in the city, a household head may well migrate to insure the education (or health) of his children (an urban amenity motive perhaps mislabeled as "bright lights").

How, then, is the skills-acquisition process modeled in our economy? We shall assume the training to be financed by the industries that utilize skilled labor. Either due to insufficient funds implied by capital-market imperfections, or due to the absence of an effective private schooling industry, or both, we shall assume that individuals cannot gain access to training unless selected for such training by firms who find it profitable to make such investments. The full cost of the training is, therefore, borne by the industries rather than the individual. (Trainees do bear the time cost of training, but only in forgone leisure.) Furthermore, we shall treat the two industries as if in collusion on their training investments, and that neither industry tries to obtain a free-ride simply by hiring newly skilled workers after the other industry has made the necessary investments. Both industries invest in training, if profitable, and they jointly share the fruits of that investment.

The procedure involves first, determining the returns to investment in training (and thus the demand function for skills), second, determining the costs of training (and thus the supply function for skills), and third, determining the supply of workers actually trained. Given the latter, the training activity can be priced and thus the total investment requirements computed. These investment requirements become one component of the current saving pool. The economy therefore accumulates three types of long-lived assets—physical capital, housing, and skills.

We are conscious of the fact that the KS sector relies heavily on skilled workers drawn directly from the formal education sector (clerks, bureaucrats, teachers, and doctors), while the M sector normally relies on blue-collar workers who acquire skill by on-the-job training. Yet, our simplification does not appear to be inappropriate. Public education is determined in part by government investment decisions, and thus the formal-education-using KS sector can also be viewed in the same light as the M sector. Moreover, considerable training may even be required in government activity to convert the formally educated student into a worker of more immediate use.

After taxes, total profits in industry j ($j = M, KS$) are simply $r_j(1 - \tau_{\Pi,j})K_j$. Total profits are augmented by the marginal addition of one more trained skilled worker as follows:

$$\frac{\partial(r_j[1 - \tau_{\Pi,j}]K_j)}{\partial S_j} = K_j \frac{\partial r_j[1 - \tau_{\Pi,j}]}{\partial S_j} + r_j[1 - \tau_{\Pi,j}]\frac{\partial K_j}{\partial S_j}$$

With physical capital stocks fixed in the short run,

$$\frac{\partial(r_j[1 - \tau_{\Pi,j}]K_j)}{\partial S_j} = K_j[1 - \tau_{\Pi,j}]\frac{\partial r_j}{\partial S_j}\bigg|_{s_j + \dot{s}_j} = \phi_{s,j} \qquad j = M, KS$$

$$(78), (79)$$

where $\phi_{s,j}$ is the marginal after-tax revenue from the addition of one skilled worker.

For the purposes of simplification, assume for the moment that the per unit cost of training a worker is constant at c, a parameter over which the government has some control. These are marginal (and average) costs common to both industries. While these training costs are all incurred in the current time period, the revenue stream will continue throughout the working life of the skilled worker. We shall assume that firms find it profitable to train only young workers with a long working life ahead of them. For computational simplicity, we shall also assume that firms compute the present value of these anticipated returns supposing 1) naive expectations that $\phi_{s,j}$ shall prevail indefinitely and 2) that the young skilled laborer can be viewed, at least approximately, as an asset with infinite life. The resulting present value of the benefit stream generated by current investment in training is simply

$$\hat{r}_{s,j} = \frac{\phi_{s,j}}{i}, \qquad j = M, KS \qquad (80), (81)$$

where i is the economywide discount rate, taken here as the weighted average of returns to physical capital in the various sectors, following equation (33) above. Thus, we have explicitly introduced the notion that training must compete with alternative investments in economywide physical accumulation. Presumably, the firm is indifferent between investment in training and alternative modes of accumulation such that current costs and capitalized benefits are equated:

$$\hat{r}_{s,j} = c, \qquad j = M, KS \qquad (83), (84)$$

What determines the stock of potential trainables? Generally, this includes all of last year's unskilled workers (excluding deaths and retirements) plus all new entrants who are children of urban households, but excludes any of this year's rural in-migrants. The exclusion of recent in-migrants is based on a two-staged view of in-migration: only those of the unskilled who have already had some exposure to urban work are considered trainable by modern-sector firms. The urban unskilled are also distinguished by their level of formal education (Ed), the latter dictated by previous government educational policy and the demographic structure of the urban population. Thus, the stock of urban trainables by formal educational achievement is, in the current period, determined exogenously. Furthermore, we shall assume that the trainability of the urban unskilled worker is a function of formal education: those with high formal-educational attainment tend to be relatively cheap to train, e.g., exhibit lower c's in the training production function, but the same opportunity costs, $w_{M,L}(-1)$, in unskilled formal sectoral occupations. A step cost function of the following kind is postulated:

$$c = \begin{cases} c_0 w_{M,L}(-1), & 0 \le \dot{S} \le L_{U,0}, & k = 0, Ed > n \text{ years} \\ c_1 w_{M,L}(-1), & L_{U,0} < \dot{S} \le L_{U,1}, & k = 1, n-1 < Ed \le n \\ \vdots & & \vdots \\ c_n w_{M,L}(-1), & L_{U,n-1} < \dot{S} \le L_{U,n} & k = n, & Ed = 0 \end{cases} \qquad (82)$$

where k represents the formal-education class ($k = 0$ denoting highest attainment), and the total trainables constraint is

$$\dot{S} = \sum_j \dot{S}_j \le L_U, \qquad j = M, KS \qquad (85)$$

where $\dot{S}$ are total workers trained.

Figure 2.3 portrays the training market (where for simplicity $w_{M,L}(-1) = 1$). Anticipated returns and the discount rate dictate the aggregate demand function for training. High anticipated returns generate buoyant demands in the two industries combined; such high anticipated returns may manifest themselves by skill bottlenecks with sizeable skill premia. Low rates of return to physical capital investment in A, KS, and M would yield the same result; investment in training would appear relatively profitable. Figure 2.3

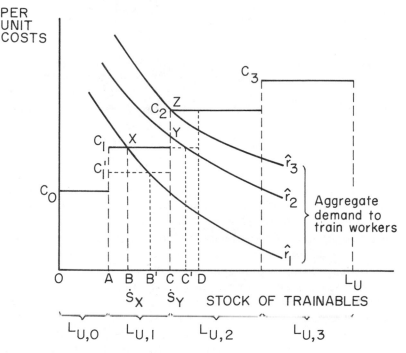

Figure 2.3 The Skills Investment Market

illustrates two possibilities. At point X, demand ($\hat{r}_i$) is slack and a substantial share of those in the $k = 1$ educational class would find themselves glutting the market and thus employed at unskilled tasks. (In the $k = 1$ class $\overline{AB}$ workers will be trained and $\overline{BC}$ workers will remain untrained.) In contrast, at point Y, a much larger share of those with formal education are trained as skilled workers, leaving perhaps only elementary school graduates ($k = 2$) and dropouts, plus illiterates ($k = 3$), in unskilled jobs. Note, too, that an expansion in demand for skilled workers may in some circumstances be met with a rise in skilled wages and no additional training (Y to Z), while in other circumstances the training rate may rise (X to Y). The stock of trainables by k class as well as the height of the step in the cost function both matter to this result.

Total training costs, or total investment in training, can be written in either of two ways:

$$\text{TRAINING COSTS} = w_{M,L}(-1)\left\{\sum_k c_k L_{U,k} + c_l\left[\dot{S} - \sum_k L_{U,k}\right]\right\}, \quad (86)$$

$$k = 0, \ldots, l - 1$$

and

$$\text{TRAINING COSTS} = P_{KS} I_{S,KS} \qquad (87)$$

where l is the optimal class trained satisfying (83) and (84). These training costs may lay claim on some real resources in the economy; that is, some capital goods sector must allocate resources to that investment activity and the investing firms's training cost must accrue as income to some sector. As is apparent in equation (87), it seems sensible to us to assign this capital goods activity to the KS sector since K_S includes formal education. We are aware that this specification may have important implications for wage inequality dynamics: high skill premia and earnings inequality imply profitability of investment in skills acquisition. The training investment response places demands on the KS sector. These added demands for KS output imply the augmentation of demand of skills (since they are used especially intensively there), and thus the wage premium may remain high in spite of rapid skills accumulation.

Finally, it should be noted that the training activity has another cost to the firm since the unskilled urban labor force is diminished by the training activity. Unskilled labor scarcity may cause a short-run rise in costs as a result. To the extent that rural labor supplies are elastic, urban unskilled labor scarcity is unlikely to persist for the longer run.

The model of skills accumulation presented to this point is one of firms investing in vocationally-oriented training according to their profit-maximizing calculus, given an exogenously determined cost-of-training function. While our model does not explain the cost function, changes in it can influence the rate of skills accumulation. These changes will have their source primarily in government education policies which, while implicit in our exposition, can now be elaborated. Two such policies are illustrated in Figure 2.3.

For simplicity, consider the case where the share of education in the government's budget is constant, and two alternative policies are evaluated. The first policy represents a reorientation of the curriculum for the $k = 1$ education class toward more vocational training. This will reduce the training costs facing the firm from c_1 to c_1' and, for a given demand (say $\hat{r}_1$), result in an expansion in skills investment by $\overline{BB'}$. The second policy represents a reallocation of the education budget toward producing $k = 1$ students at the expense of $k = 2$ students. This will expand the numbers in the $k = 1$ education class to $\overline{AD}$. If the firms' aggregate demand for skills were represented by $\hat{r}_2$, the new education policy would increase the number of unskilled laborers by $\overline{CC'}$. These two examples illustrate the analytical as well as the policy-related features of our skills-generation framework.

It should be apparent that we do not view education solely as a consumer durable. Rather, educational outputs can play a productive role in the economy; human capital accumulation is important in explaining the process of growth and development. The specific way education enters is complex, and in our model determined by the interplay of production possibilities, demographic forces, and government education policies.

Housing, Land Markets, and Land Use

There are two competing uses to which land stocks can be put in our model—farming and urban residential land sites. We shall assume that urban residential sites implicitly include, in fixed proportion, factory site requirements as well as public land (parks, roads, schools). The fixed proportion assumption will simplify the analysis considerably, since we can focus exclusively on the residential-site demand component of urban land use. Furthermore, we shall assume that "wasteland" exists in the rural area. This wasteland has no competing use, has no inherent site value, but it can be used for rural housing construction. In the real world, of course, wasteland can be and is exploited for both urban and farmland expansion through drainage, clearing, and filling. These activities involve investment, and to confront land accumulation endogenously would require the explicit introduction of urban and rural land-supply functions, presumably inelastic to capture investment costs, and competitive with other investments in housing, training, and physical accumulation. We ignore such complications and take the expansion of productive land as exogenously given, although not necessarily constant. To do otherwise would take us far afield and empirical implementation would be much too demanding.

We begin with a model of partially segmented land markets; that is, rural and urban land uses are completely non-competitive, but all intraurban land uses are competitive. The stock of agricultural land is given by R_A while the urban land stock is

$$R_U = R_{U,US} + R_{U,KS} \tag{51}$$

where urban land sites are utilized for two types of housing—low-cost "squatter settlements" ($R_{U,US}$) and high-cost "luxury housing" ($R_{U,KS}$).

The urban housing market is central to migration behavior and thus to our analysis of the urbanization process. One of the limits on urban growth rates in the Third World is the availability (and cost) of urban housing facing new urban households, whether the housing is of the informal, labor-intensive, owner-occupier type in squatter settlements—typical of rapidly expanding Third World cities—or more substantial dwelling units constructed by capital-intensive techniques and rented in a formal housing market. Any serious model of urbanization must admit this possible source of limits to urban growth. The limits may take various forms, but we shall stress two.

First, urban rents may rise in the long run due to the inflation of urban site rents as in classical urban location theory (Mills, 1972; Henderson, 1977). In addition, urban rents may also rise in the short run if investment in new structures lags behind demands generated by rapid urban population growth (Song and Struyk, 1976; Mills and Song, 1977). Second, to the extent that investment in housing responds to those demands generated by the in-migration, aggregate saving available for productive accumulation or training will contract and thus the rate of output expansion will suffer economy wide (Coale and Hoover, 1958). Since physical capital and skills are used most intensively in the modern sectors (M and KS), the rate of urban labor absorption is diminished. In-migration to the cities and urbanization rates may slack off as a result. Our model incorporates these forces so that over-urbanization (Hoselitz, 1955, 1957; Sovani, 1962; Kamerschen, 1969; Preston, 1979; Ledent and Rogers, 1979) in our economy may be forestalled.

As pointed out above, there are two housing types in our model: low-cost squatter settlements and high-cost luxury housing. In this we follow the United Nations' Habitat (1976, p. 70) where they state:

> In many less developed countries building is characterized by the existence of two sectors: a) a multitude of very small enterprises ... which operate in the rural and peri-urban areas, belonging almost entirely to the informal sector of the economy; b) a small number of large firms using modern techniques and organization,

and their Global Review of Human Settlements (UN, 1976, p. 11) where squatter settlements

> ... generally refer to areas where groups of housing units have been constructed on land to which the occupants have no legal claim. In many instances housing units located in squatter settlements are shelters or structures built of waste materials without a predetermined plan. Squatter settlements are usually found ... at the peripheries of the principal cities.

According to the same source, these squatter settlements are by no means a small share of total urban dwellings, but account for the bulk of the growth in cities throughout the Third World (see also Mohan, 1979, chap. 1 and Linn, 1979, table II-7). It seems to us important to distinguish between two types of urban dwellings, to indicate the different sectors that produce them as well as the different socioeconomic classes that consume the rental services that flow from these residential structures. Thus, the quality of housing is denoted by a jth subscript in the production functions which follow.

Urban housing services are produced under constant returns to scale with housing structures, H_j, and land, $R_{U,j}$, as inputs. While estimates of the elasticity of substitution between land and structures in residential-housing production functions vary considerably (Muth, 1969, 1971; Arnott and Lewis, 1977; Ingram, 1977; Henderson, 1977), estimates are almost always quite high, implying that rising urban land scarcity fosters capital substitution, making cities even more capital-intensive. Since the most recent review of the econometric evidence suggests support for the Cobb–Douglas specification (McDonald, 1981), we adopt

$$Q_{H,j} = A_{H,j} H_j^{\alpha_{H,j}} R_{U,j}^{\alpha_{R,j}}, \qquad j = US, KS \qquad (6), (7)$$

where $\alpha_{H,j} + \alpha_{R,j} = 1$, US denotes squatter settlements, and KS luxury housing. In contrast, rural housing services do not require the input of land of significant site value, so that a fixed coefficient production function is assumed to apply:

$$Q_{H,RS} = \frac{H_{RS}}{a_{H,RS}} \qquad (8)$$

This asymmetric treatment can be defended by appealing to qualitative evidence, but the quantitative evidence would appear to support it too. For example, poor rural households spend a far lower share of income on rent than do poor urban households (by a ratio of 5 to 1 in the case of Peru; Thomas, 1978, tables 33, 37–39). An even more relevant example would be the rapid rise in urban relative to rural property values, as in Korea (Mills and Song, 1977).

This rural-urban asymmetric treatment of housing insures that rising land prices and increased site rents will have a disproportionate effect on the cost-of-living in urban areas as urbanization proceeds. Perhaps this can be seen more clearly when the total rental price of urban housing is rewritten as

$$P_{H,j} = \frac{r_{H,j}^{\alpha_{H,j}} d_U^{\alpha_{R,j}}}{A_{H,j} \alpha_{H,j}^{\alpha_{H,j}} \alpha_{R,j}^{\alpha_{R,j}}}, \qquad j = US, KS$$

where d_U is the site rent and $r_{H,j}$ is the structure rent. Of course, the real estate market never decomposes total rental price into these two component parts, and in our model all dwellings are owner-occupied. (In Korea, for example, 94 percent of rural and 83 percent of urban households were owner-occupiers in 1975 [Suh, 1979, table 11, p. 47].) Nevertheless, it will still prove analytically useful to decompose total rental prices in this fashion. In percentage rates of change (denoted by an $*$), these rental prices are related by

$$\overset{*}{P}_{H,j} = \alpha_{R,j}\overset{*}{d}_U + \alpha_{H,j}\overset{*}{r}_{H,j}, \qquad j = US, KS$$

Land's share, $\alpha_{R,j}$, has been estimated to be about 0.10 (Muth, 1969, 1971; Henderson, 1977; and Ingram, 1977). It follows that modest increases in urban rental prices may be consistent with dramatic increases in urban site rents (called the "magnification effect" in the urban literature). Dramatic increases in urban site rents imply equally dramatic increases in urban land prices and the latter have become a notable feature of twentieth-century development even in the Third World. For example, urban land prices in Korea have been rising in real terms at 16 percent per annum since the early 1960s. (Mills and Song, 1977. For information on the boom of urban land values in the Third World, see Woodruff and Brown, 1971, pp. 16–25, and chaps. 5, 6, and 9. The same phenomenon can be found in postwar Japan. See Mills and Ohta, 1976.)

What, then, determines land rents, land prices, and land use in our model?

The agricultural production function is Cobb–Douglas. Under competitive assumptions, land rents per hectare can be written as

$$d_A = \bar{P}_A \alpha_{A,R} \frac{Q_A}{R_A} \tag{43}$$

Alternatively, expression (43) can be written as a derived demand function for farmland:

$$R_A = \bar{P}_A \alpha_{A,R} Q_A d_A^{-1}$$

where the derived demand function has an elasticity of -1. Cobb–Douglas production functions in urban housing imply similar derived urban land demands for residential purposes (recalling that residential requirements embody commercial, factory, and public site needs). Thus

$$d_{U,j} = P_{H,j}^s \alpha_{R,j} Q_{H,j} R_{U,j}^{-1} \qquad j = US, KS \tag{44, 45}$$

where $P_{H,j}^s$ is the net rent received by the owner (imputed, not cash) after paying an urban property tax. Since it is not our purpose here to determine the distribution of urban populations across urban space—as in classic urban location theory—nor to confront the Third World reality that squatter settlements tend to be located at the fringe of the city while luxury housing tends to be located nearer the central business district (Mohan, 1977; Ingram and Carroll, 1978; Mills and Song, 1977), we shall assume that urban site rents are the same for all urban households. Thus,

$$d_U = P^s_{H,j} \alpha_{R,j} Q_{H,j} R^{-1}_{U,j}, \qquad j = US, KS$$

or

$$R_{U,j} = P^s_{H,j} \alpha_{R,j} Q_{H,j} d^{-1}_U \qquad j = US, KS$$

Like farmland, these derived demand functions for urban land also have an elasticity of -1. The aggregate derived demand function for urban land is simply

$$R_U = d^{-1}_U \{ P^s_{H,US} \alpha_{R,US} Q_{H,US} + P^s_{H,KS} \alpha_{R,KS} Q_{H,KS} \}$$

Our model is in no way a true spatial framework since distance plays no role in either of the two sectors. Thus, farmgate prices do not rise with greater proximity to urban markets and therefore farmland does not exhibit a rental gradient reflecting such heterogeneity. Similarly, proximity to the central business district does not offer any of the advantages typically postulated in conventional urban location theory (savings in transport costs and commuter time). There is, therefore, no urban rental gradient implied.

If land markets were fully integrated, the extramarginal rent on the fringe of the city would matter in determining land use. Figure 2.4 supplies the optimal land-use solution under integrated land market conditions. The equilibrium rent is denoted by $d^* = d_U = d_A$, and the optimal land-use mix is derived accordingly. What seems interesting to us is how many central land-use issues are captured by this simple framework. Three such issues are confronted in what follows:

—Does the model predict rising urban densities over time?
—Can it account for the dramatic rise in urban land values?
—Will it produce an encroachment on farmland over time?

It is a common theorem of growth theory that factors in relative inelastic supply will increase in relative rent (and thus price or value) unless technology tends to be very factor-saving of the inelastically-supplied input (e.g., Nichols, 1970). In our model, capital accumulates, skills are augmented through training, population growth swells the labor force (and thus residential housing stocks),

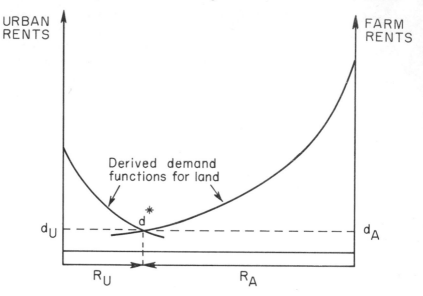

Figure 2.4 The Determinants of Land Rents and Optimal
Land Use under Integrated Land Markets

but the stock of land grows exogenously, and presumably at relatively low rates. The presumption is that relative rents will rise over time unless technological change serves to save on land. If one focuses only on land for agricultural use, technological change surely does tend to save on land, since the agricultural sector declines in relative size with successful economic growth.

On the other hand, our model explicitly introduces an additional land use—urban residential-site needs—and since successful economic growth implies rapid urbanization, the land-saving attributes of the simpler growth model are no longer so relevant. Indeed, while our urban housing production function specifications include the possibility of extensive substitution of structures for land (guaranteeing that urban densities will increase in the face of rising land rents), rapid urbanization implies a relatively voracious demand for land and the encroachment of farmland at the cities' margins. Additionally, there are forces at work in agriculture that will shift outward the derived demand for farmland: e.g., the rising price of foodstuffs and the accumulation of agricultural capital. In short, we expect the model to produce an outward shift in the derived demand for land in both uses, and we also expect that the derived demand for urban land will shift outward at a more rapid rate. The long-run implications of such derived demand growth under integrated land markets would be:

—Urban and rural rents would rise at a rapid (and identical) rate;
—Land use would shift in favor of urban residential use, but the rate of shift would be choked off by two forces—the downward sloping character of the derived demand for farmland and the tendency for urban housing to consume less space as land gets scarcer;
—Urban land density would rise.

All of these attributes are stylized facts of urbanization in the Third World.[9]

While the integrated land market assumption seems to conform to some stylized facts of urban development, it fails to conform to others. The most serious limitation stems from two assumptions: the possibility of farmland conversion at the city's margin at zero cost, and the absence of an urban rental gradient. These assumptions combined insure that urban land supplies will be relatively elastic. We find this characterization unattractive, and it certainly makes it impossible for the model to predict rising relative scarcities of

---

[9] This analysis ignores both property and capital-gains taxes. Very few Third World economies utilize such taxes, but they may well be introduced in the near future. As a result, we thought it useful to introduce such tax parameters into the model to allow exploration of their potential impact. The value of urban property is

$$V_{H,j} = \frac{P_{H,j} - \tau_{H,j} V_{H,j}}{i} = \frac{P_{H,j}}{(i + \tau_{H,j})}, \qquad j = US, KS \qquad (13), (14)$$

or, alternatively,

$$V_{H,j} = \frac{P_{H,j}^S}{i}$$

where $P_{H,j}$ is the (imputed) rent on the jth type of housing—a "demand price," $P_{H,j}^S$ is the (imputed) net rent after property taxes on site and structure—a "supply price," and τ is the urban property tax rate (most likely zero rated on squatter settlements). Therefore,

$$V_{H,j} = \frac{P_{H,j}^S}{i} = \frac{P_{H,j}}{(i + \tau_{H,j})}$$

so

$$P_{H,j}^S = \left[\frac{i}{(i + \tau_{H,j})} \right] P_{H,j}, \qquad j = US, KS \qquad (15), (16)$$

the demand price for housing exceeding the supply price by

$$\frac{i + \tau_{H,j}}{i} \geq 1.$$

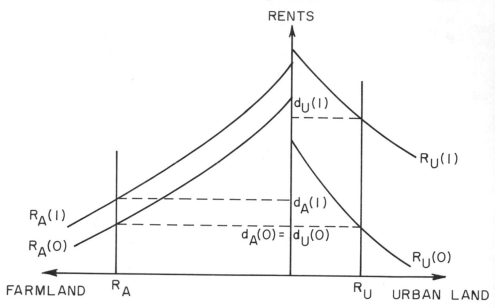

Figure 2.5 Shifts in Land's Derived Demand over Time with
Segmented Land Markets

urban compared with farmland, a stylized fact that may prove important to long-run urbanization and city growth. To provide a more attractive characterization of land use and relative scarcity, we have rejected the integrated land market assumption in favor of *segmented* land markets. This alternative is summarized in Figure 2.5, where both total urban and farm land are given exogenously, and no conversion is allowed at the city's margin. Unbalanced derived demand growth favoring urban land generates a rent gap, $d_U - d_A$ (here simplified by fixed land stocks). If land values are calculated assuming naive expectations regarding the behavior of future rents (i.e., d is expected to prevail at the current rate forever), the urban-rural "land value" gap, $V_U - V_A$, will replicate rent gap trends. More realistic expectations might have land value gaps rising more sharply.

Balance of Payments and Foreign Trade

Since there are no monetary variables in our model, the balance of payments must always be in equilibrium. We assume, therefore, that the foreign-exchange rate is consistent with the balance of payments equilibrium such that the external clearing equation is satisfied by

$$[\bar{P}_M M_M - T_M + \bar{P}_Z(Z_{KS} + Z_M + Z_A)] - [\bar{P}_A X_A + T_X + \bar{F}] = 0 \quad (52)$$

where $\bar{P}_A X_A$ are export earnings, $[\bar{P}_M M_M + \bar{P}_Z(Z_{KS} + Z_M + Z_A)]$ are foreign-exchange requirements for imports, $\bar{F}$ denotes exogenous levels of net foreign aid and private capital imports, T_M are tariff revenues, and T_X are export taxes. Equation (52) hides more than it reveals and what follows is an elaboration of our implicit assumptions regarding trade relationships.

Our model is a conventional "vent for surplus" paradigm. That is, our economy is viewed as a price taker with $\bar{P}_A$, $\bar{P}_M$, and $\bar{P}_Z$ all determined in world markets.[10] Given domestic demand and supply conditions, excess supplies of the primary product can be "vented" on world markets and excess demands for manufactured goods can be satisfied in the same fashion. It should be noted that this approach focuses attention exclusively on the net trade of both commodity types. The model does not confront gross trade relationships, including dynamic changes in the mix of commodity trade within these export and import categories. Thus, while the model is fully capable of explaining the net impact of dynamic comparative advantage, it cannot deal with any tendency toward specialization in the export of labor-intensive consumer goods in exchange for more capital-cum-skill intensive producer durables.

It does seem likely, however, that the observed tendency of comparative advantage to shift specialization from primary products to manufactured goods will be captured by the model. This process of dynamic comparative advantage can be seen in the conventional trade diagram in Figure 2.6, where P_0 represents an initial production mix (i.e., Q_A and Q_M), and C_0 initial domestic consumption mix (i.e., D_A and D_M). Relatively rapid capital and skill accumulation, compared to unskilled labor and land, as well as unbalanced total-factor productivity growth favoring manufacturing, is likely to shift the production possibility frontier in such a fashion that (at C_1 and P_1) *net* dependence on exports of primary products will diminish unless domestic demand conditions are highly biased toward manufactured goods. Indeed, the model may well yield a shift in comparative advantage to a net *export* of manufactured goods, although Figure 2.6 does not elaborate on this case.

Net foreign capital inflows $\bar{F}$ are given exogenously. This treatment of "foreign aid" may, at first sight, appear to be in the tradition

---

[10] We invoke the "law of one price" here. See, however, Isard, 1976; Kravis and Lipsey, 1977; and Dervis and Robinson, 1978.

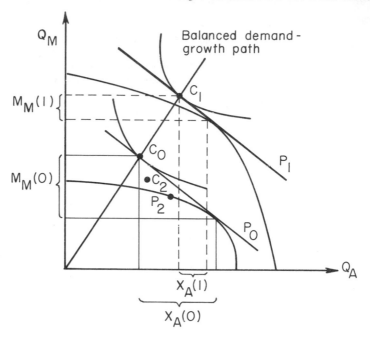

Figure 2.6 Dynamic Comparative Advantage and
"Vent-for-Surplus"

of the "two-gap" literature (Chenery and Strout, 1966), but it actually conforms more readily with the revisionist literature which has developed in recent years (Griffen and Enos, 1970; Weisskopf, 1972; Papanek, 1973; Heller, 1975; Bhagwati and Grinols, 1975; Grinols and Bhagwati, 1976). That literature has pointed out that domestic saving appears to bear a negative correlation with foreign aid levels, implying that the domestic-savings effort is relaxed with the addition of foreign aid. Presumably, the relaxation of the domestic-savings effort lies primarily with the government sector where, it is thought, the tax effort is diminished and current expenditures are expanded at the expense of government saving. As we shall see in the next section, our model does indeed capture such behavioral responses. On the other hand, since the rate of return plays no direct role as an influence on domestic savings in our model, the possibility that $\bar{F}$ may crowd out private savings (McKinnon, 1973) is ignored. Our own view is not that crowding-out forces are irrelevant, but rather that development economists have not yet successfully accounted for their quantitative influence (see, however, Heller, 1975; Ortmeyer, 1979).

The Government Sector

The government has two sources of revenue in our model: endogenously determined taxes and exogenous levels of net foreign aid and private foreign capital, the latter assumed to flow through government channels. These revenues form the total government budget constraint which is allocated between saving and consumption. With the exception of current education expenditures, the empirical counterpart of these two spending categories are the government's capital and current budgets, respectively.

The inclusion of education expenditure in government saving represents a break with the conventional treatment of government in most growth and development models. Typically, the government is modeled so that its consumption does not directly contribute to household income or utility, nor does it contribute to future output expansion. While this is a useful abstraction for some purposes, especially given the difficulty of valuing and allocating public goods to consuming units, it will not suffice in our model. In particular, education expenditures may well yield consumption utility to its recipients, but in our model they have an impact on future income as well. This reality is explicitly incorporated in our model since skills are produced by training investment and these compete with alternative modes of accumulation. It seems appropriate, therefore, to include this category of government expenditure as savings. While other categories of government expenditure might also qualify (e.g., health expenditures), our approach can be considered as, at least, a partial rectification of an anti-growth bias attributed to government in most development models.

All government final demands are produced by the capital-cum-skill intensive KS service sector, and government demand dominates this sector's total output. We make no distinction between governmental and privately owned and operated enterprises, focusing instead on the demand characteristics of government activities.

Taxes come from a wide range of sources. These include:

1) taxes on households' consumption of M sector goods,

$$\tau_M [\bar{P}_M D_M]$$

2) taxes (or subsidies) on agricultural intermediate inputs purchased from manufacturing,

$$\tau_{A,M} [\bar{P}_M Q_{A,M}]$$

3) taxes on urban property (including housing),

$$\tau_{H,US} [V_{H,US} Q_{H,US}] + \tau_{H,KS} [V_{H,KS} Q_{H,KS}]$$

4) taxes on enterprise income (net of depreciation allowances) in the M and KS sectors,

$$\tau_{\Pi,M}[r_M - \delta_M \bar{P}_M]K_M + \tau_{\Pi,KS}[r_{KS} - \delta_{KS}\bar{P}_M]K_{KS}$$

5) taxes on distributed profits,

$$\tau_Y\{\psi_M[(1 - \tau_{\Pi,M})(r_M - \delta_M \bar{P}_M)]K_M + \psi_{KS}[(1 - \tau_{\Pi,KS})$$
$$\times (r_{KS} - \delta_{KS}\bar{P}_M)]K_{KS} + r_A K_A\}$$

6) taxes on rental income in agriculture,

$$\tau_Y[d_A R_A]$$

7) taxes on skilled labor's income,

$$\tau_Y[w_{M,s}S_M + w_{KS,s}S_{KS}]$$

8) taxes on foreign trade (given exogenously),

import duties T_M

export taxes T_X.

For the most part the tax specification is straightforward, but tariffs and export taxes pose some technical difficulties. Treating import tariffs and export subsidies as *ad valorem* rates, foreign trade tax revenues would have been endogenous and equal to $\tau_{T,M}[\bar{P}_M^W M_M] + \tau_{T,s}[\bar{P}_A X_A]$, where $\bar{P}_M^W$ denotes world prices. As we pointed out in the previous section, however, our model examines *net* imports of manufactured goods M_M and *net* exports of primary products X_A, a feature common to this type of model where the composition of imports and exports is suppressed. Since the composition of imports and exports shifts systematically as economic development takes place, and since *net* imports of manufactured goods decline through import substitution (with perhaps the country even becoming a net exporter of manufactures), a tax function based on net trade flows would yield inappropriate estimates of revenues derived from international trade. To avoid this problem, we have chosen instead to take revenues from import duties (T_M) and export taxes (T_X) as exogenous.

The government tax-revenue function can now be summarized in equation (53)

$$\begin{aligned} T = &\tau_M[\bar{P}_M D_M] + \tau_{H,us}V_{H,us}Q_{H,us} + \tau_{H,KS}V_{H,KS}Q_{H,KS} \\ &+ \tau_{A,M}[\bar{P}_M Q_{A,M}] + \tau_Y[\psi_M(1 - \tau_{\Pi,M})(r_M - \delta_M \bar{P}_M)K_M \\ &+ \psi_{KS}(1 - \tau_{\Pi,KS})(r_{KS} - \delta_{KS}\bar{P}_M)K_{KS} + r_A K_A + d_A R_A \\ &+ (w_{M,s}S_M + w_{KS,s}S_{KS})] + \tau_{\Pi,M}(r_M - \delta_M \bar{P}_M)K_M \\ &+ \tau_{\Pi,KS}(r_{KS} - \delta_{KS}\bar{P}_M)K_{KS} + T_M + T_X \end{aligned} \tag{53}$$

This tax function exhibits an urban bias, a feature documented in surveys of fiscal finance in low-income countries. Only labor income of the relatively highly-paid urban skilled worker is taxed. In addition, since urban activities tend to be capital-intensive, and since capitalist income is subject to relatively heavy taxation, urbanization implies an expanding tax base on that score too. The urban bias is also evident in our treatment of commodity taxation of manufactured goods, as well as the tax on urban residential property.

Another characteristic of the tax function is its apparent high elasticity with respect to the Gross National Product (GNP) and the attributes of structural change that accompany economic growth: an increase in the share of manufactured goods in total household expenditures, a rising share of modern-sector output, a shift of the labor force into higher-skilled occupations, and an increasing inequality in the distribution of income in the early to intermediate stage of economic development. A rising share of taxes and government spending in GNP is a likely outcome from our model, and such patterns would conform to empirical studies (Bird, 1976; Bolnick, 1978; Chelliah, 1971; Chelliah, Bass, and Kelley, 1975).

One qualification of the tax function is in order. While the profits of the *KS* sector are taxed, a major portion of this sector produces government goods and services. This is a mixed public-private sector, a reality captured in the model by specifying lower "corporate" tax and payout rates in the *KS* than in the *M* sector, i.e., $\tau_{\Pi,KS} < \tau_{\Pi,M}$ and $\psi_{KS} < \psi_M$.

Unlike most general equilibrium models (but see Heller, 1975), government spending is not exogenously given in our model. Such a hypothesis would not only be at variance with the empirical literature (Gandhi, 1971; Kelley, 1973, 1976a; Thorn, 1967), but is also unappealing for a model that accounts for the sources of growth and structural change in the long run. The present model attempts, albeit in a highly simplified fashion, to capture aspects of government spending over time by appealing to the same forces that determine private consumption and saving behavior. The government is assumed to allocate its budget to saving, G_S, in response to increments in the resources available to it from taxes and foreign sources, and in response to demographic and urban pressures—by assumption, the main source of public investment demands. Thus,

$$G_S = \alpha_G + \beta_G[T + \bar{F}] + \gamma_G[\dot{N}_U(-1)] \tag{54}$$

$$G_{KS} = [T + \bar{F}] - G_S \tag{55}$$

We anticipate that the government's marginal propensity to save, β_G, will exceed that of the private sector, based on the literature accumulated to date on this issue (Mikesell and Zinser, 1973; Yotopoulos and Nugent, 1976; Williamson, 1979). We also expect, consistent with the Coale and Hoover (1958) hypothesis, that public saving will be negatively related to increasing urban population, $\gamma_G < 0$. Some analysts, like Michael Lipton (1976), would view this prediction as an accurate reflection of the realities of the urban bias in world development. The pooled sample of Third World economies covering the 1960s and early 1970s confirms both expectations. Indeed, Appendix B.6 reports estimates of $\hat{\beta}_G$ and $\hat{\gamma}_G$ as 0.34 (11.37) and -0.11 (1.09), respectively (*t*-statistics in parentheses). This result is not conditional on our definition of saving since similar results are forthcoming when expenditures on education are excluded from government saving, although both $\hat{\beta}_G$ and $\hat{\gamma}_G$ are somewhat lower when G_S is defined to exclude educational expenditures.

Finally, since $\hat{\beta}_G < 1$, changes in the levels of foreign aid do not augment the resource pool for accumulation by an equal amount, but by only $\hat{\beta}_G d\bar{F}$. This places us squarely in the "revisionist" foreign aid camp discussed above. To repeat, the revisionist literature has argued that the domestic savings effort is relaxed with the exogenous infusion of foreign aid. In our model, the relaxation of the domestic saving effort lies with the government sector where the additional foreign aid is dissipated by a rise in current public expenditures. While *total* savings do not decline in the face of additional foreign aid, it is still true that domestic investment increases by only a third of it ($\hat{\beta}_G = 0.34$).

Household Demand and Saving

One of the ironies of the development planning literature is the relative inattention to the role of demand in the process of growth and structural change. There are few models that admit prices as an influence on demand, and simultaneously permit demand to influence prices.[11] We agree with Lluch, Powell, and Williams (1977)

---

[11] This is becoming less true with the recent proliferation of computable general equilibrium models, primarily produced by World Bank economists and consultants. See, for example, Lysy and Taylor (1977), Blitzer, Clark, and Taylor (1975), and the recent large-scale model by Adelman and Robinson (1978). It still remains true of economic-demographic models (e.g., the Bachue, Tempo, and Simon models discussed earlier in this chapter) and world models like Meadows et al. (1974) and Leontief et al. (1977).

who note:

> ... the bulk of models of economic development have been based on the assumption that commodity prices are of little or no significance in determining the crucial aspects of economic behavior. The oil crises may or may not constitute a convincing rebuttal of this proposition, but investigation of the role of prices remains high on the list of priorities in economic development modeling. Prices cannot be investigated meaningfully without also examining the structure of demand. (p. xxii).

To explore the issues surrounding the role of demand in economic development, we have selected the Extended Linear Expenditure System (ELES), initially proposed by Lluch (1973) and investigated on Third World data by Lluch, Powell, and Williams (1977). The ELES framework captures most of the stylized demand facts associated with modern economic growth in the Third World. In particular it:

—captures Engel effects;
—incorporates dualistic elements in demand behavior across regions and socioeconomic classes;
—provides an important role for demographic influences;
—offers explicit empirical content to the concept of "subsistence" in the low-income societies.

Equally important, the framework can be derived from reasonable postulates of behavior (Goldberger, 1967; Brown and Deaton, 1972; Howe, 1975) and satisfies the adding up property common to several modern integrated demand systems. Its only serious competitor is the direct addilog system first developed by Frisch (1959) and extended by Houthakker (1960) and Sato (1972). The ELES has the advantage, however, of having been estimated with data for Third World economies underlying our representative-economy model.

In its simplest form, the Extended Linear Expenditure System assumes that the household allocates its disposable income (y^*) between various commodities ($q_1, \ldots, q_n$) and savings where prices ($p_1, \ldots, p_n$) are exogenous to the household, and saving is the difference between total income and the sum of all commodity expenditures ($y^* - c$, where $c = \sum p_i q_i = \sum v_i$). The model further assumes that the household's utility function is such that each commodity potentially possesses a minimum subsistence demand ($\gamma_i \geq 0$) which must be fulfilled before the remaining "supernumerary" income ($y^* - \sum p_i \gamma_i$) is allocated at the margin between the various commodities and saving. This paradigm of household saving and spending is represented by the expenditure equations

$$v_{i,j} = p_{i,j}\gamma_{i,j} + \beta_{i,j}\left\{y_j^* - \sum_k p_{k,j}\gamma_{k,j}\right\},$$

$$k = A, M, T, S, H$$

$$c_j = \sum_i v_{i,j}$$

$$s_j = y_j^* - c_j$$

(56)

A graphical presentation of the ELES for the two-commodity case is provided in Figure 2.7. Based on the utility function $u(q_1, q_2)$, and assuming $q_i > \gamma_i$, the household's expenditure and savings allocation follow directly: for q_1, γ_1 represents subsistence needs, $B - \gamma_1$ is supernumerary expenditure on this commodity, and saving is measured by the value of q_1 not consumed, S/p_1. An analogous accounting holds for q_2. Such a representation highlights the role of prices in saving-expenditure allocation decisions, a feature captured in our general equilibrium model which utilizes the ELES.

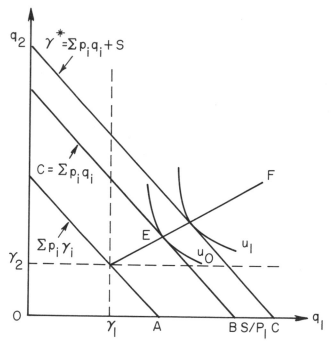

Figure 2.7 The Two-Commodity Case of ELES

By rotating the three parallel lines, alternative prices would prevail; these would elicit quite different allocations between q_i and s.

The ELES is similar to the more familiar Linear Expenditure System (LES), with one notable difference: in the extended system, total consumption out of disposable income is determined endogenously. Thus, the sum of the marginal budget shares and savings exhausts disposable income. In the LES, the sum of the marginal budget shares exhaust total *expenditure*.[12] The ELES thus does not utilize the strong separability assumption between saving and expenditure embedded in the LES, but rather views the household as determining its expenditure allocation simultaneously with its total consumption decision, an appealing premise.

The ELES implies a Keynesian saving specification except that supernumerary disposable income is the determinant of household saving, not disposable income. The qualification is important, since it implies that the ELES predicts a non-linear relation between average household savings rates and income. (See also Bhalla, 1980 for an alternative explanation of this non-linearity on Indian data.) While savings specifications which take account of rates of return and asset portfolio preferences would be desirable (see, for example, Cooper and McLaren's [1981] extension of ELES), they are too complex to incorporate into this version of our basic model and, in any case, debate still continues over the appropriate empirical characterization of interest elasticities in household saving functions. Yet, our savings specification does respond to the appeal by Mikesell and Zinser (1973) who, in their survey of the literature for developing countries, urged the exploration of savings behavior of various types of households. Compositional influences will be captured in our framework to the extent that there may be a shift in the distribution of income to higher-saving households as economic development takes place.

Our savings specification also permits commodity prices to influence saving. Based on ELES estimates of saving and expenditure allocation for seventeen countries, Lluch, Powell, and Williams (1977) found that for low ranges of per capita income, a 1 percent rise in the price of food will elicit a 1.8 percent decline in the saving rate (p. xxv). If this quantitative result has general validity, then

---

[12] The LES is therefore a subset of the ELES, where saving is determined exogenously. To see this, sum the expenditure equations in (56) to obtain $c = (1 - \mu) \times \sum p_i \gamma_i + \mu y^*$, where $\mu = \sum \beta_i$. By obtaining an expression for y^* in terms of c, and substituting into (56), the more familiar LES results, $v_i = p_i \gamma_i + \hat{\beta}_i (c - \sum p_i \gamma_i)$, where $\hat{\beta}_i = \beta_i / \mu$.

omitting prices from the saving decision, as would be implied by household systems based on the strong separability assumption, may provide quite misleading results concerning the role of demand in economic development.

The treatment of subsistence consumption is a particularly interesting feature of the ELES. The concept has many interpretations in the economic development literature, ranging from the biological-requirements-for-survival notion in early dualistic models (Jorgenson, 1967), to the more recent policy discussions relating to "basic needs," a set of socially desired minimum consumption standards (Srinivasan, 1977; Streeten and Burki, 1978; Hopkins and Norbye, 1978). The ELES demand system provides an interpretation of subsistence which lies between these two extremes. In particular, the γ_i's are determined by the household's own preferences and thus represent an aggregation of biological requirements, individual preferences, and social norms. The composition of the γ_i's, as well as their aggregate size, may vary across individuals in society. While our model will treat the γ_i's as parameters constant to a household type, subsistence demand may change over time, due, in part, to shifts in the distribution of income across households. The γ_i's have particular relevance, therefore, to interpreting the consequences of specific types of income-expenditure distribution policies in the low-income country.

Recent empirical investigations of the ELES utilizing microeconomic data from Mexico, Korea, Chile, Yugoslavia, and several Latin American cities (Lluch, Powell, and Williams, 1977) have established differences in household demand behavior related to selected demographic characteristics, location (largely urban and rural), and socioeconomic class, even after controlling for the level of household income. Based on this and similar findings (Kelley and Williamson, 1968; Kelley, 1969, 1976b; Blitzer, Clark, and Taylor, 1975; Betancourt, 1980), we have elected to disaggregate our households into several categories: urban and rural, on the one hand, and skilled labor, unskilled labor, and property income recipients on the other. This will permit the investigation of the role of demand through systematic changes in the composition of households as development takes place, and in particular, the impact of urbanization, changing income distribution, and skill accumulation. The possibility that we will be able to assess the role of household final demand effects, adjusted to indirect derived demands originating through the interindustry structure, represent an interesting feature of the model, although Appendix B will show how the quantitative evidence serves to limit that effort. Subject to these qualifications, we should be able to provide at least one empirically relevant test of the competing hypotheses concerning the relative importance of demand variations, versus supply changes operating through technical change and resource availabilities, on the patterns and rates of economic change. (See Chenery, 1960; Kuznets, 1957, 1966; Clark, 1957; Chenery and Syrquin, 1975.)

A full statement of the household demand system, as well as statements summarizing their aggregation into final demand categories corresponding to our model's production structure, is provided in Appendix A as equations (56)–(59). Each household's demand statement, irrespective of location or socioeconomic class, possesses the form presented above in equation (56). In addition, Appendix A provides a side equation (57) for the cost of living relevant to various types of households. This statistic will be important in assessing the impact of economic policies on various aspects of household welfare, especially those policies relating to income distribution and migration.

Housing Investment and Aggregate Saving

Aggregate saving determines accumulation possibilities in our model, and this savings pool is generated by three sources: retained after-tax corporate and enterprise profits, government saving, and household saving. (Foreign saving serves to augment government resources and thus indirectly appears as a component of government saving.) These three sources can be written as

$$
\begin{aligned}
\text{SAVINGS} = {} & (1 - \psi_M)[(1 - \tau_{\Pi,M})(r_M - \delta_M \bar{P}_M) K_M] + \delta_M \bar{P}_M K_M \\
& + (1 - \psi_{KS})[(1 - \tau_{\Pi,KS})(r_{KS} - \delta_{KS} \bar{P}_M) K_{KS}] \\
& + \delta_{KS} \bar{P}_M K_{KS} + s_{US} L_{US} + s_M L_M + s_{KS} L_{KS} \\
& + s_R L_R + s_C C + s_S S + G_S
\end{aligned}
\tag{88}
$$

where all parameters and variables have been previously defined.

There are three competing demands on this savings pool: investment in physical (productive) capital, investment in human capital (training), and investment in (unproductive) housing. Following the conventional emphasis in the development literature, physical capital accumulation is written as a residual in equation (89)

$$
\bar{P}_M I_M = \text{SAVINGS} - \text{HOUSING} - \text{TRAINING COSTS}
\tag{89}
$$

but it should be emphasized that these three modes of accumulation are determined simultaneously and in competition. Investment allocation rules dictating the intersectoral allocation of $\bar{P}_M I_M$ and the determinants of training investment were both discussed in previous sections. This section will focus on housing investment under imperfect capital markets. It will then conclude with a summary of the mechanism that dictates overall investment allocation in the model.

Following Coale and Hoover (1958), our model distinguishes between productive and unproductive investment. Unproductive investment is captured by housing requirements, a component that is sensitive to demographic and urbanization forces. Furthermore, housing investment (no doubt grossly understated in the squatter settlements) was as high as a fifth of fixed capital formation and a third of construction in twenty-five LDCs in the early 1970s (Linn, 1979, table VI-3). Housing investment will be viewed in much the same way that subsistence consumption requirements are treated in the consumer demand system. That is, private households behave in a fashion such that housing needs receive first priority in their investment portfolios. Only after these investment needs are satisfied do households release their residual savings for productive accumulation purposes through banks, non-bank financial institutions, and informal curb markets. This characterization is motivated by McKinnon's (1973) emphasis on financial market fragmentation.

Since the formal mortgage market is poorly developed or nonexistent in much of the Third World, we have assumed that *none* of the three private housing sectors (rural, urban squatter settlements, urban luxury housing) is able to secure external finance to satisfy investment requirements. Housing investment is, therefore, self-financed by each household sector independent of other surplus-generating sectors. While this specification eliminates the possibility of *inter*sectoral housing financial flows, it does not exclude the possibility of *intra*sectoral housing financial flows. For example, fathers may loan to sons, but middle-class skilled households never loan to poor unskilled households. Certain sectors may therefore be starved for housing finance while others have a surplus which they allocate to the national saving pool for productive accumulation or training investment.

Under conditions of rapid population growth, it is quite possible that household savings will be fully exhausted by housing investment requirements. This potential demographic burden is reinforced in our model by rapid rates of urbanization. This follows from the fact that housing is location-specific; thus, migration of even a stable aggregate population requires new housing construction in the receiving regions, and net investment economywide. Furthermore, given the cost-of-living adjustment embedded in the model's migration function, rapid in-migration and urbanization may well be forestalled by the urban housing requirements that these population movements imply. An urban housing investment shortfall will result in a rise in urban rents, thereby attenuating in-migration. Alternatively, increased urban housing investment serves to inhibit the accumulation of productive capital, and we know that the rate of productive capital accumulation is a central determinant of the relative expansion of employment in the modern urban sectors.

This treatment illustrates the importance of general equilibrium paradigms in accounting for the sources of growth and structural change. Consider the analysis of intersectoral migration. The benefits of migration in reallocating labor to its highest productivity will be partially offset in our model by the costs resulting from the diversion of productive investment funds to unproductive urban housing. The rate of urbanization will tend to diminish as a result. A similar impact results from rising urban housing rental prices. Thus, rapid rates of urbanization will trigger endogenous forces tending to suppress over-urbanization, a result that may provide a very different characterization of intersectoral labor transfers than would be forthcoming from partial equilibrium demographic estimates of urban change. Projections of city populations exceeding 30 million (UN, 1976) are likely to merit serious qualification in the face of economic adjustments like those contained in our model (see also Beier et al., 1976). Only general equilibrium modeling of the sort contained in our housing-cum-migration specification can capture the various countervailing forces associated with urbanization, economic growth, and structural change.

What remains is to convert these qualitative descriptions of investment demand in housing under capital market fragmentation into explicit quantifiable equations. At given prices and incomes, we specify the following type of urban housing investment demand equation:

$$I_{H,j} = \text{Min}\{s_j L_j P_j^{-1}, I_{H,j}^N + \delta_{H,j} H_j\},$$

$$I_{H,j} = \text{Max}\{0, I_{H,j}\},$$

where $s_j L_j P_j^{-1}$ is the saving generated by households consuming the jth type of housing (deflated by P_j and thus converted into housing investment quantities), $I_{H,j}^N$ is net investment in housing, and $I_{H,j}$ is gross investment in housing. The first expression simply states that household saving in sector j may be binding on housing investment in that sector. If not, dwelling investment will not exhaust the sector's household saving and a surplus will be available for accumulation in other forms. Our expectation is that rural households will consistently have a surplus available for accumulation in other forms in spite of a low per capita income. This may also hold for the urban skilled and property income recipient classes, but is less likely for the urban unskilled household sector. The second expression given above simply states that gross investment cannot be negative. This expression is unlikely to be binding under conditions of rapid population growth, even with substantial rural out-migration rates. Depreciation requirements are given by $\delta_{H,j} H_j$.

In discussing the determinants of net investment, $I_{H,j}^N$, it will be helpful to define the following terms, some of which are new while others are added to refresh the reader's memory:

$\hat{r}_{H,j}$ = an index of profitability of housing investment in the jth housing stock, a benefit-cost ratio computed as the ratio of the discounted stream of net rents to current construction costs;

P_j = per unit construction costs of H_j;

$r_{H,j}$ = per unit "structure rent" on H_j (a shadow price since owner-occupied status is assumed, and thus rents are fully flexible with no market stickiness);

i = the discount rate, or average rate of return on physical capital economywide;

$P_{H,j}$ = total rental price, including both the site and structure rental components.

Using these definitions, net investment in housing in the jth sector is written as

$$I_{H,j}^N = \theta_{H,j}[\hat{r}_{H,j}^{\varepsilon H} - 1]$$

where $\hat{r}_{H,j}$ is the index of investment profitability:

$$\hat{r}_{H,j} = [(r_{H,j} - \delta_{H,j} P_j)i^{-1}]P_j^{-1}, \qquad j = US, KS, RS \quad (71)-(73)$$

High values of $\hat{r}_{H,j}$ indicate high profitability with positive gaps between capitalized anticipated net rents and current construction costs.[13] This expression also states that net investment in housing should be zero when the benefit-cost ratio is unity, that is, where the economywide percentage rate of return equals the rate of return on sector j's new housing investment. Higher values of $\hat{r}_{H,j}$ imply more housing investment at the expense of alternative investment elsewhere in the economy.

It should be apparent from Figure 2.8 that net investment in housing can take on negative values as the benefit-cost ratio falls

---

[13] We assume naive expectations and infinite life for simplicity. Furthermore, ε_H is taken to be common to all types of housing investment.

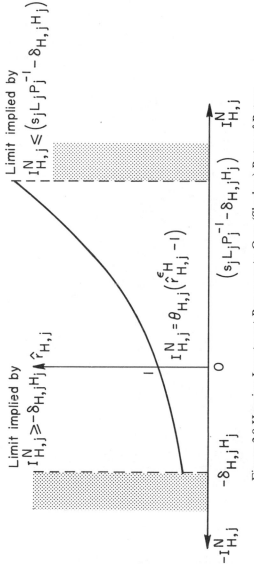

Figure 2.8 Housing Investment Response to Own (Shadow) Rates of Return

below unity, but since gross investment is restricted to non-negative values, a limit on the size of the negative values of net housing investment is implied as

$$I_{H,j}^N = \theta_{H,j}[\hat{r}_{H,j}^{\varepsilon H} - 1] \geq -\delta_{H,j}H_j$$

The previous expression simply postulates that new housing investment is responsive to profitability in a non-linear way as in Figure 2.8.

The housing investment demand equations for all three sectors can now be written formally as

$$\left. \begin{aligned} I_{H,RS} &= \text{Min}\{s_R L_R P_{RS}^{-1}, I_{H,RS}^N + \delta_{H,RS}H_{RS}\} \\ I_{H,RS} &= \text{Max}\{0, I_{H,RS}\} \\ I_{H,RS}^N &= \theta_{H,RS}[\hat{r}_{H,RS}^{\varepsilon H} - 1] \end{aligned} \right\} \qquad (68)$$

and

$$I_{H,US} = \text{Min}\{[s_{US}L_{US} + s_M L_M + s_{KS}L_{KS}]P_{US}^{-1}, I_{H,US}^N + \delta_{H,US}H_{US}\}$$
$$I_{H,US} = \text{Max}\{0, I_{H,US}\} \qquad (74)$$
$$I_{H,US}^N = \theta_{H,US}[\hat{r}_{H,US}^{\varepsilon H} - 1]$$

and

$$I_{H,KS} = \text{Min}\{[s_S S + s_C C]P_{KS}^{-1}, I_{H,KS}^N + \delta_{H,KS}H_{KS}\}$$
$$I_{H,KS} = \text{Max}\{0, I_{H,KS}\} \qquad (70)$$
$$I_{H,KS}^N = \theta_{H,KS}[\hat{r}_{H,KS}^{\varepsilon H} - 1]$$

As equations (71)–(73) reveal, structure rents are central to the determination of $\hat{r}_{H,j}$. Given Cobb–Douglas housing-service production functions, urban structure rents are

$$r_{H,j} = \left\{ \frac{A_{H,j}P_{H,j}^S \alpha_{H,j}^{\alpha H,j}\alpha_{R,j}^{\alpha R,j}}{d_{U,j}^{\alpha R,j}} \right\}^{1/\alpha H,j}, \qquad j = US, KS \quad (74),(75)$$

Recall that $r_{H,j}$ is a shadow price since all housing is owner-occupied in our model. Note, too, the presence of $P_{H,j}^S$ in the expression for $r_{H,j}$. It is the total rental price after urban residential property taxes have been assessed and paid. (See equations (15) and (16) and the discussion above.) Since wasteland has no value in rural areas and since we assume the absence of rural property taxes, rural rents implied by the fixed coefficient production function are

$$r_{H,RS} = P_{H,RS}a_{H,RS}^{-1} \qquad (76)$$

Finally, ε_H is an unknown parameter in (68)–(70), but we shall experiment with alternative values.

There are three sectors involved in housing construction in our model. $I_{H,RS}$ represents rural dwellings produced by the informal *RS* sector, perhaps even constructed by the occupying household itself and with "waste" materials. $I_{H,US}$ represents similar low-cost urban dwellings (shanty housing or squatter settlements) produced by the informal labor-intensive *US* sector, also perhaps even constructed by the occupying household itself. $I_{H,KS}$ denotes high-cost housing, produced by the formal construction sector, which, as part of *KS* activities, is relatively capital- and skill-intensive, and generates intermediate input demands in the primary product and manufacturing sectors. When these housing-investment requirements are valued by current construction costs, P_j, total investment demand for housing is obtained in value terms:

$$\text{HOUSING} = P_{RS}I_{H,RS} + P_{US}I_{H,US} + P_{KS}I_{H,KS} \tag{77}$$

It might be helpful to summarize saving, accumulation, and capital-goods sector activity at this point. In terms of the majority of computable general equilibrium models, ours is unusual in its treatment of accumulation. There is not just one mode of accumulation, but rather there are three (skills, physical capital, and housing). There is not just one capital-goods sector, but rather four (*KS* producing skills; *RS*, *US*, and *KS* constructing dwellings; and *M* producing physical capital goods). Since each of these capital-goods producing sectors is characterized by quite different factor-intensities, changes in the mix of accumulation over time can have important implications for the structure of output, price patterns, and the derived demands for inputs. This distinguishes our model from the tradition that has flowed from Uzawa's classic contributions.

Uzawa (1961, 1963) found that a sufficient condition for uniqueness of static equilibrium was that the consumption-goods sector be more capital-intensive than the capital goods sector. While Gordon (1961) has suggested that this assumption may not be unreasonable for higher-income economies, it appears artificial when applied to less-developed societies. It seems to us more appropriate, in any case, to stress that factor-intensity even in the static model is endogenous and conditional upon the direction that the economywide portfolio mix takes. Shifts in favor of skills investment imply skill-intensive capital goods activity (increasingly *KS*-oriented); shifts favoring conventional physical capital accumulation imply capital-intensive capital goods activity (increasingly *M*-oriented); shifts favoring low-cost housing imply labor-intensive capital goods activity (increasingly *RS*- and *US*-oriented). These forces have potentially important implications for the distribution of income.

Note, too, that the three modes of accumulation are explicitly competitive. Skills accumulation takes place up to the point where rates of return are equated to the economywide rate on physical capital accumulation. Physical capital goods are allocated across the three capital-using sectors so as to minimize rate of return differentials. Dwelling investment will utilize household saving only up to the point where rates of return are equated to the economywide rate on physical capital accumulation. Of course, there are institutional and technological features that seriously restrict the economy's ability to equate rates of return at the margin. Any of the three dwelling markets (rural, urban squatter settlements, and formal urban luxury) may be starved for funds since the absence of an intersectoral mortgage market may leave housing investment requirements in excess demand. The immobility of physical capital stocks between sectors makes it possible that current physical investment allocations are insufficient to equalize rates of return to capital between *A*, *M*, and *KS*. Indeed, the larger are housing requirements, the smaller is the residual pool available for physical capital accumulation and the more likely that current investment allocations are insufficient to equalize sectoral rates of return. Furthermore, firms' demands for skills may be unsatisfied if the stock of potential trainables is insufficient to meet training investment levels that would equalize rates of return economywide. In short, capital market disequilibrium may well be a permanent attribute of our economy.

3. DYNAMICS: ACCUMULATION AND TECHNOLOGICAL PROGRESS

Current net investment is equal to total gross investment minus depreciation, where depreciation is taken to be proportional to the capital stock. Thus, aggregate productive physical capital stocks and unproductive housing stocks are given by

$$K_i = (1 - \delta_i)K_i(-1) + I_{i,M}(-1), \qquad i = A, M, KS \qquad (99)-(101)$$

$$H_j = (1 - \delta_{H,j})H_j(-1) + I_{H,j}(-1), \qquad j = US, RS, KS \qquad (102)-(104)$$

where the depreciation rates are allowed to vary not only between productive capital (containing equipment of shorter life) and housing (containing structures only), but also between housing of different types (luxury housing presumably having the longer life). Urban and farm land are assumed to grow at exogenous rates.

Factor-augmenting and disembodied technical progress are both present in our model. The factor-augmenting rates are given exogenously by

$$x = x(-1)e^{\lambda_K} \tag{105}$$

$$y = y(-1)e^{\lambda_S} \tag{106}$$

$$z = z(-1)e^{\lambda_L} \tag{107}$$

while the disembodied rates (assumed to be zero in rural housing and in both informal service sectors) are given by

$$A_i = A_i(-1)e^{\lambda_i}, \qquad\qquad i = M, KS, A \quad (108)\text{--}(110)$$

$$A_{H,j} = A_{H,j}(-1)e^{\lambda_{H,j}}, \qquad j = US, KS \quad (111)\text{--}(112)$$

While these propositions appear somewhat arbitrary at first glance, Appendix C.1 shows that they are consistent with important stylized facts regarding the factor-saving bias of technical progress, the unbalanced rate of technical progress across sectors, and the economywide rate of total-factor productivity growth. The first two of these attributes of technical progress factor-saving bias and unbalanced total-factor productivity growth—have become key stylized facts in development and they are central to debate over economic growth and distribution in the Third World. As a result, they require elaboration.

The output-raising effect of technical change has come to be known in the literature as total-factor productivity growth. These sectoral rates of total-factor productivity growth, $\overset{*}{T}_i(t)$, define the percentage rise in output, given fixed inputs, as

$$\overset{*}{T}_i(t) = \frac{\partial Q_i(t)}{\partial t}\frac{1}{Q_i(t)}, \qquad i = A, RS, US, KS, M$$

Total-factor productivity growth rates can be written for each of our eight sectors as

$$\overset{*}{T}_A = \lambda_A + \alpha_{A,K}\lambda_K + \alpha_{A,L}\lambda_L$$

$$\overset{*}{T}_M(t) = \lambda_M + \alpha_{M,K}(t)\lambda_K + \alpha_{M,L}(t)\lambda_L + \alpha_{M,S}(t)\lambda_S$$

$$\overset{*}{T}_{KS}(t) = \lambda_{KS} + \alpha_{KS,K}(t)\lambda_K + \alpha_{KS,L}(t)\lambda_L + \alpha_{KS,S}(t)\lambda_S$$

$$\overset{*}{T}_{RS} = \alpha_{RS}\lambda_L$$

$$\overset{*}{T}_{US} = \alpha_{US}\lambda_L$$

$$\overset{*}{T}_{H,j} = \lambda_{H,j}, \qquad j = US, KS$$

and

$$\overset{*}{T}_{H,RS} = 0$$

where the $\alpha_{i,j}$ are output elasticities or factor payment shares. In agriculture, the $\alpha_{i,j}$ have no time subscripts because the production function is Cobb–Douglas and output elasticities are constant. Furthermore, land is absent there since, by assumption, land does not enjoy augmentation through technical progress.

Both modern sectors exhibit variable output shares over time because the CES production functions yield such variability as long as modern-sector inputs grow at different rates. The traditional labor-intensive service sectors have the unskilled labor augmentation rate multiplied by α_i since diminishing returns prevail there (e.g., $\alpha_i < 1$). The housing sectors are restricted to constant disembodied rates, and the empirical evidence may well warrant our setting $\lambda_{H,j} = 0$ for all sectors, not just rural housing.

These expressions make it possible for sectoral rates of total-factor productivity growth to diverge, a result we shall label *unbalanced productivity advance*. There seems to have been early agreement in the literature (Massel, 1961; Kendrick, 1961, 1973; Baumol, 1967; Uneo and Kinoshita, 1968; Watanabe, 1968) that the modern sectors exhibit the most rapid total-factor productivity growth, with agriculture lagging behind in spite of Green Revolutions (or agricultural revolutions, to use an older phrase), and with traditional services almost stagnant. Certainly this has long been conventional wisdom among historians of past industrial revolutions (see, for example, Williamson and Lindert, 1980). The characterization is also central to the ability of Third World cities to grow, relative urban productivity advance pulling migrants to urban employment (Beier et. al., 1976). Indeed, we suspect that unbalanced productivity advance favoring urban-based sectors is a far more important determinant of urbanization than are the Engel effects stressed by urban economists (Artle, 1972; Mohan, 1979, p. 7). Our model is fully capable of replicating unbalanced productivity advance of this sort.

However, even better documentation is available for the *overall* rate of total-factor productivity growth for Third World economies (for recent estimates, see Christensen and Cummings, 1974; Elias, 1978; Levy, 1978; Colosio, 1979) and this aggregate rate can be written as

$$\overset{*}{T}(t) = \sum_i \omega_i(t)\overset{*}{T}_i(t) + \overset{*}{T}_{RA}(t)$$

where $\omega_i(t)$ represents sectoral value-added shares in GNP.

It should be apparent that this economywide rate need not be constant over time, even with the λ's in equations (110)–(112) held constant. Indeed, economywide, total-factor productivity growth has two parts, both of which are endogenous. The first part, $\sum_i \omega_i(t)\overset{*}{T}_i(t)$, is known in the literature as *intraindustry* total-factor productivity growth. Given unbalanced total-factor productivity growth, those sectors with the favored rates tend to undergo the most dramatic decline in supply price and therefore tend to enjoy relative output expansion. It follows (under price-elastic demand conditions) that sectors with the highest $\overset{*}{T}_i(t)$ tend to enjoy rising ω's over time. $\overset{*}{T}$ tends to rise over time as a result. In this sense, the economywide total factor productivity growth rate in our model is *partially embodied*. The empirical significance of this form of embodiment depends, of course, on the speed of change in output mix, $d\omega_i$. As it turns out, the influence is not very important (Appendix C.1 and Chapter 4).

The second part, $\overset{*}{T}_{RA}(t)$, is known in the literature as *interindustry* total-factor productivity growth. Interindustry total-factor productivity growth results from improved resource allocation between sectors, a source of growth of which much has been made in the development literature. Central to the labor surplus model, for example, is the premise that institutional factors tend to produce a gap in labor's marginal product between traditional agriculture and modern industry (Lewis, 1954; Fei and Ranis, 1961). Labor migration and labor absorption, therefore, tend to create economywide productivity gains as resources are allocated to uses of higher marginal productivity. Suppose we denote the relative share of interindustry total-factor productivity growth in the aggregate rate by the variable z. Then

$$\overset{*}{T}(t) = \sum_i \omega_i(t)\overset{*}{T}_i(t) + z(t)\overset{*}{T}(t)$$

or

$$\overset{*}{T}(t) = [1 - z(t)]^{-1} \sum_i \omega_i(t)\overset{*}{T}_i(t)$$

What do we know about the size of z? It is a function of factor-market disequilibrium since the initial size of the discrepancies between sectoral marginal productivities influences the magnitude of the gains from improved resource allocation. It is also a function of the speed of resource reallocation. Since the latter is very much constrained by the rate of accumulation in both the real world and in our model, we have a second reason to suspect partial embodiment in our model. As in the case of *intraindustry* total-factor productivity growth effects, however, these *interindustry* influences can only be resolved in empirical analysis. (Appendix C.1 discusses this issue at length.)

Factor-saving can take two forms. First, a shift in the output mix may favor one or a group of inputs at the expense of others. For example, the expansion of the manufacturing sector will tend to increase demands for the two inputs used relatively intensively there, capital and skills. In other words, unskilled labor is "saved" economywide by this shift in output. Such "compositional" effects are likely to have important implications for income distribution, causing a relative decline in the unskilled wage and concomitant inequality trends. To the extent that such compositional changes are induced by the character of technical change itself, they can be classified unambiguously as factor-saving technological progress. Unbalanced rates of total-factor productivity growth favoring the capital-cum-skill intensive sectors, thus inducing a shift in output to those sectors enjoying the relatively rapid rates of cost reduction, would be exactly the kind of technical progress yielding that result.

The second form of factor-saving technological progress can be analyzed conveniently in terms of the Hicksian concept of neutrality. Technical progress is neutral if it leaves the capital-labor ratio unaltered at a constant ratio of factor prices. The Hicksian factor-saving bias, $B_i(t)$, is defined to be the proportionate rate of change in the marginal rate of factor substitution in that sector. In the simple two-factor case,

$$B_i(t) = \frac{\partial F_K^i}{\partial t} \frac{1}{F_K^i} - \frac{\partial F_L^i}{\partial t} \frac{1}{F_L^i}$$

where F_K^i and F_L^i are the marginal products of capital and labor, respectively. For any given capital-labor ratio in the ith sector at time t, technical progress is labor-saving in the Hicksian sense if $B_i(t) > 0$. It can be shown that the bias can also be written as

$$B_i(t) = \frac{(\lambda_L - \lambda_K)(1 - \sigma_i)}{\sigma_i}$$

Thus, the bias depends on the difference between the rates of factor augmentation through technical change and on the elasticity of factor substitution.

There is accumulating empirical evidence supporting the view that technological progress in the modern sector is non-neutral. Indeed, this has become one of the stylized facts of contemporary development in the Third World. (For a review see Morawetz, 1974; Cline,

1975; and the following econometric studies: David and Van de Klundert, 1965; Williamson, 1971; Binswanger, 1974; Levy, 1978.) There is no need to review the explanations of the labor-saving bias in modern sectors in the Third World, but the bias has explicit implications for factor augmentation rates through technical change in our model. Since elasticities of substitution are less than unity in both the manufacturing and the modern-service sector, it follows that labor-saving can be captured by the restriction $\lambda_L > \lambda_K$. This restriction also implies another aspect of technological dualism thought to be relevant in the Third World. Namely, while labor-saving is typical of the modern sectors, it is not characteristic of traditional activities. The model is fully consistent with this asymmetry since, for example, the Cobb–Douglas production function in agriculture implies $B(t) = 0$.

In short, our model appears to capture the two central attributes of technical progress thought to be stylized facts in the Third World: it can deal effectively with both unbalanced as well as labor-saving productivity advance. It also offers, at least in part, an endogenous treatment of economywide total factor productivity advance.

4. Where Do We Go from Here?

Our model of Third World urbanization and economic growth has been developed and defended. Appendix B and Appendix C deal with problems of estimation. Chapter 3 attempts to validate the model on Third World time series from 1960 to the early 1970s and the OPEC crunch. Having convinced ourselves (and the reader) that the model is not pure fiction, but is capable of fairly effective prediction, the remainder of the book is free to raise the questions that motivated our inquiry at the start: What are the sources of urbanization and city growth? Are there limits to city growth? How sensitive is city growth in the Third World to such changing environmental conditions as fuel scarcity, technological slowdown, capital transfer austerity, and population dynamics?

CHAPTER THREE

Fact or Fiction?

1. INTRODUCTION

How well does our model of Third World urbanization account for observed experience over the past two decades? Can it account for trends in overall growth and structural change? Does it replicate the macro dimensions of urban in-migration and city growth, urban land scarcity and land use, housing and social overhead, city cost-of-living and density-related quality of life?

The model developed in Chapter 2 was motivated by quantitative issues raised in the literature and by dialogue between Third World analysts and policymakers. But what empirical reality was it designed to confront? We have two choices: the case study of a single country, or the analysis of a "prototype" economy. We have adopted the latter approach in this book, using the experience of a group of forty developing countries to form our data base. Having made this decision, our next step was to estimate the model's parameters and to establish the prototype economy's initial output, employment, and national accounts in terms of some benchmark date. As anyone who has worked with large, interdependent systems is aware, successful estimation hardly insures a macro model's ability to replicate some historic time-path. The next step, therefore, was to simulate the prototype economy over time and to confront this fictional history with the historical record. Fact or fiction? This is the crucial question in evaluating the model's plausibility.

Section 2 defends the prototype approach and defines the forty-country data base underlying the estimation. Much of the detail is allocated to Appendix B. Section 3 establishes the ground rules for evaluating the empirical validity of the model, including the time dimension for the tests. There we argue the wisdom of decomposing recent Third World development experience into two periods, pre-OPEC and post-OPEC, that is, 1960–1973 and 1973 to the present. As we shall see, the evaluation dwells on the pre-OPEC period and is organized around two sets of endogenous variables. Section 4 deals with general aspects of economywide growth, accumulation, and inequality. Although the remainder of the book focuses on urbanization and city growth issues, sections 4 and 6 first establish the plausibility of predictions on general development performance which any model of economic dynamics must confront. Section 5 turns to the problems of specific interest: migration, urbanization, land scarcity, and housing-cum-social overhead supply. We conclude that the model is quite successful in replicating the long-run development and urbanization experience of the forty-country group up to 1973.

2. PROTOTYPE MODELS AND THE REPRESENTATIVE DEVELOPING COUNTRY

The RDC Prototype

Based on numerous time-series and cross-section studies (Clark, 1957; Kuznets, 1957, 1966; Chenery and Syrquin, 1975; Chenery, 1979), the existence of a typical pattern of development has now been well established, so much so that we now speak freely of the "stylized facts" of development. This typical pattern is characterized by predictable shifts in output mix (industrialization), population growth (demographic transition), city growth (urbanization), the structure of demand (Engel's Law), the size of government (Wagner's Law), trade patterns (import substitution), inequality (the Kuznets Curve), and the like. While single-country deviations are numerous, statistical regularity is pervasive. Given this evidence and our desire to generalize about Third World urbanization, we have elected to employ what we call the "representative developing country" (RDC) as the data base upon which the model is calibrated and validated. Like Alfred Marshall's "representative firm," the RDC is a fictional economy embodying the experience of developing countries on five continents. While some analysts use the term "archetype developing economies" (de Melo and Robinson, 1982) and others use the term "prototype," our use of the RDC is motivated by the same issues: a desire to generalize *before* turning to the detail of country studies; and the fact that data is far more accessible for a forty-country group than for a single country.

The RDC is constructed in three steps. First, a group of developing countries is drawn to generate the data base; second, this development experience is summarized; and third, a relevant starting point or post-World War II benchmark date is selected. The criteria employed for selecting the developing countries are taken up below. The early 1960s are taken as the starting point. This benchmark represents the earliest year for which a fairly complete data set is available, and one that still provides a period long enough to evaluate development trends.

In selecting a statistical procedure for summarizing the development record of forty countries, we have elected to compute an unweighted average of each variable of interest. It is, after all, the record of individual countries that constitutes the unit of analysis. Furthermore, they form the basis of the evidence that has produced the stylized facts of development. The application of weights to construct the RDC would imply that some countries are in some sense more representative than others. We do not know enough about the development process to specify such weights on an a priori basis.

Selecting the RDC Group

Three criteria were used to select the RDC group: data availability, low per capita income, and the extent to which the country conformed to the model's most important assumptions.

Beginning with the list of 101 developing countries provided in the *World Tables 1976*, 24 countries were eliminated that failed to supply two or more major categories of sectoral production data for 1960. Five more countries were eliminated that had per capita incomes in excess of $500 (in 1960 prices). In addition, we excluded countries with a share of mineral exports in 1960 gross domestic product exceeding 20 percent, with a net deficit in the foreign trade account exceeding 10 percent of gross domestic product in 1960–1965, and with per capita income growth during the 1960s falling short of 1 percent per annum. Thus, three criteria were applied to yield these exclusions: data deficiencies (24); too developed (5); and lack of conformity to the model's most important assumptions (32). The third criterion may require some elaboration.

The model does not possess a detailed trade specification, but it was designed to examine those nations whose exports in 1960 were dominated by primary products and whose imports were composed largely of manufactures and industrial raw materials. However, a significant group of developing countries were and are heavily committed to mineral exports, oil producers included. In the 1970s, the latter were also price-setters, behavior at variance with the model's small-country, price-taker specification. Thus, we have excluded those nations that have been significantly dependent on mineral exports. Furthermore, we have excluded those countries that have been heavily dependent on foreign capital. (See Appendix B, section B.1.)

A total of forty nations remain to form the RDC group (Table 3.1). To obtain some perspective on the representativeness of this

TABLE 3.1
The Forty-Country RDC Group

Algeria	El Salvador	Malaysia	Portugal
Bangladesh	Ethiopia	Mexico	Sri Lanka
Brazil	Gambia	Morocco	Swaziland
Cameroon	Guatemala	Nicaragua	Syria
Chile	Honduras	Nigeria	Taiwan
Colombia	India	Pakistan	Thailand
Costa Rica	Indonesia	Panama	Togo
Dominican Republic	Ivory Coast	Paraguay	Turkey
Ecuador	Kenya	Peru	Uganda
Egypt	Korea	Philippines	Yugoslavia

group, Appendix B compares their key attributes with the larger group analyzed by Chenery and Syrquin in their *Patterns of Development* (1975). There we show that the two groups are quite similar in average population size, regional distribution, and trade orientation, although the RDC group is slightly larger, a bit more Latin, and has a trade orientation geared toward "large" (in contrast with the Chenery–Syrquin categories "small primary," "small balanced," and "small industry"). Finally, and perhaps most important, the RDC group contains *all* of the eleven largest developing countries excluding China. Given that exception, eleven of our RDC countries account for 71 percent of the population among the ninety-one less developed countries equal to or greater than 1 million in size: India, Indonesia, Brazil, Bangladesh, Pakistan, Nigeria, Mexico, the Philippines, Thailand, Turkey, and Egypt. In short, the RDC group covers more than 80 percent of the developing countries' population excluding China, and includes all of the eleven most populous.

Estimating the System

Estimating the RDC model in 1960 is no small task. After all, there are seventy-eight parameters estimated for the comparative static model alone (Appendix B, Tables B.13 and B.14). Some of these were estimated directly on the RDC data base, some were drawn from the econometric work of others, and some were part of the initial solution of the model itself. Appendix B supplies the relevant details.

Parameter estimation is only one part of the task in converting the model to quantitative analysis. In addition, it must conform to the initial conditions of the 1960 RDC group as closely as possible. For example, it should conform to the RDC group's structure of demand observed in 1960, its industrial output mix, labor force and capital stock distribution, urbanization level, and the sources and uses of saving. Obviously, if these input, output, and demand attributes of the 1960 RDC group are faithfully replicated by the model in its initial period, it follows that the model should also capture sectoral labor productivity differentials, relative capital output ratios, and other structural features of the low-income economy. Three tables follow which serve to summarize the results of the exercise, although the specialist may wish to consult the more comprehensive discussion in Appendix B.

The complete 1960 RDC national accounts are presented in Table 3.2. The far right-hand column of the table describes the RDC's initial output mix in 1960 (shares in GDP at factor cost). The economy was, of course, dominated by agriculture (36.6 percent, where the A-sector corresponds to the UN ISIC categories "agriculture, livestock, forestry, fishing, and hunting"), although industry already accounted for 15.9 percent of GDP in 1960 (UN ISIC categories "manufacturing, mining, and quarrying"). Perhaps more surprising is the fact that the KS-sector (our modern service sector including UN ISIC categories "construction, electricity, gas and water, trans-

TABLE 3.2

The 1960 RDC National Accounts: Industrial Structure and Aggregate Demand Mix

| | Investment Demand | | | HH | Gov't | Intermediate De | |
| | | Productive | Skills | Final | Final | | |
Sector	Housing	Capital	Training	Demand	Demand	A	M
A	—	—	—	29.50	—	—	3.58
M	—	12.80	—	11.79	—	3.49	—
KS	0.83	—	2.30	9.72	13.65	3.05	2.75
US	1.04	—	—	4.48	—	—	—
RS	0.93	—	—	1.86	—	—	—
H, KS	—	—	—	2.79	—	—	—
H, US	—	—	—	2.11	—	—	—
H, RS	—	—	—	2.61	—	—	—
TOTAL	2.80	12.80	2.30	64.86	13.65	6.54	6.33
Indirect Taxes	—	—	—	6.58	—	—	—
GDP (market prices)	.	15.6	2.30	71.44	13.65	—	—

SOURCE: Appendix B, sections B.3-B.7

portation, banking and real estate, public administration" and por-
tions of "commerce and trade") accounted for 29.6 percent of GDP.
Of the remainder, housing services accounted for 8.5 percent, about
equally distributed among rural, urban squatter, and urban luxury
housing, while informal services accounted for 9.4 percent.

Aggregate demand composition can be read along the bottom
row of Table 3.2 as shares in GDP (market prices). The investment
share in GDP (excluding firms' training investment) was 15.6 percent, about one-fifth of which was housing investment, the latter
already heavily influenced by urban squatter housing (more than a
third of total housing investment). The merchandise trade balance
deficit was 3 percent of GDP, while household final demand comprised 71 percent of aggregate demand. Reading down the household final demand column, we note that 41 percent of household
expenditures was devoted to food, 12 percent to housing (including
imputed owner-occupied rents and property taxes), 24 percent to
manufactures (inflated by sales taxes), and the remainder to services
of all kinds (23 percent). Government current expenditures were
already almost 14 percent of aggregate demand in 1960.

Table 3.3 summarizes input distribution in 1960. The last column
documents capital-stock use across sectors. It appears that one-
quarter of the RDC's capital stock was devoted to housing in 1960.

Trade in Competitive Goods Export (+) Import (−)	Intermediate Inputs				Value Added	Shares in GDP at Factor Cost (%)
	Z Non-Competitive Imports	A	M	KS		
6.28	0.67	—	3.49	3.05	32.38	36.60
−11.02	2.14	3.58	—	2.75	14.07	15.90
—	0.39	0.23	5.48	—	26.20	29.60
—	—	—	—	—	5.52	6.24
—	—	—	—	—	2.79	3.16
—	—	—	—	—	2.79 ⎫	
—	—	—	—	—	2.11 ⎬	8.50
—	—	—	—	—	2.61 ⎭	
−4.74	3.20	3.81	8.97	5.80	88.48	100.00
4.94	—	—	—	—	11.52	—
−3.00		—	—	—	100.00	—

TABLE 3.3
Labor Force and Capital Stock Distribution by Sector in the 1960 RDC

Sector	Labor Force Distribution (%)			Value of Capital Stock (1960 Prices)
	Unskilled (L)	Skilled (S)	Total (L + S)	
Agriculture (A)	60.1	—	60.1	36.75
Rural Informal Services (RS)	7.3	—	7.3	—
Total Rural	67.4	—	67.4	36.75
Manufacturing and Mining (M)	9.7	2.5	12.2	25.81
"Modern" Services (KS)	2.9	7.5	10.4	104.44
Urban Informal Services (US)	10.0	—	10.0	—
Total Urban	22.6	10.0	32.6	130.25
Housing	—	—	—	54.30
TOTAL	90.0	10.0	100.0	221.30

SOURCES: Appendix B, Tables B.6 and B.7

Of the remaining productive capital stock, 22 percent was in agriculture, 15 percent in manufacturing, and the vast majority, 65 percent, in the modern service sector. Given the sectoral employment
figures in Table 3.3, this capital stock distribution implies relative
factor intensities consistent with the stylized facts of development:
the capital-labor ratio in the A-sector was .61 in 1960 (36.75/60.1),
while the figures were 2.12 and 9.67 in M and KS. At a higher level
of aggregation, the productive capital to labor ratio in rural areas
was .54, while it was 4.01 in urban areas. The discrepancy was even
higher when housing is included in the capital stock totals. City-
building in our RDC group was already very capital-intensive by
1960.

The 1960 employment distribution is also displayed in Table 3.3.
By that date, 32.6 percent of the employed population was urban,
and 60.1 percent were either landed or landless farm workers. Skilled
workers accounted for only 10 percent of the labor force, three-
quarters of which were employed in the modern service sector.
Tables 3.2 and 3.3 also imply sectoral labor productivities consistent
with the stylized facts of development: taking agriculture and informal services as a base, labor productivity was more than twice that
level in manufacturing and four-and-a-half times that level in the
modern service sector.

Table 3.4 offers a final snapshot of the 1960 RDC economy where
the sources and uses of saving are summarized. These figures seem
to conform to the stylized facts of Third World accumulation.
Households financed all of the housing investment, and low-income

TABLE 3.4

Sources and Uses of Saving in the 1960 RDC (GDP = 100)

	(1)	(2)	(3)	(4)	(5)	(6)
			Uses			*1960 Average Saving Rate Out of Sources'*
		Productive				
Sources	*Housing*	*Investment*	*Subtotal*	*Training*	*Total*	*Disposable Income*
Households	2.80	3.41	6.21	—	6.21	8.0%
Skilled,						
Capitalists,						
and Landlords	0.83	3.13	3.96	—	3.96	12.0
Unskilled Urban	1.04	0.02	1.06	—	1.06	6.5
Rural	0.93	0.27	1.20	—	1.20	4.2
Corporations	—	4.94	4.94	2.30	7.24	30.2
Government	—	4.45	4.45	—	4.45	24.6
TOTAL	2.80	12.80	15.60	2.30	17.90	17.9

SOURCE: See Appendix B, section B.7

NOTE: Foreign capital inflows are assumed to be dominated by governmental bilateral and multilateral loans and aid, flowing directly to augment government revenue, and thus indirectly to "government saving."

families had very little surplus remaining to help finance productive accumulation in other sectors. Indeed, only property income recipients (the skilled, the capitalists, and the landlords) had excess savings after meeting housing investment demand. Productive investment was, therefore, financed mainly by corporate reinvestment (39 percent, or 4.94/15.6) and government saving (35 percent, including foreign capital), while households accounted for the minority claim (27 percent). The average saving rate out of household disposable income was 8 percent, although the rate ranged widely across income classes, from 4.2 to 12 percent. The government saving rate out of total revenues was 24.6 percent, while the corporate reinvestment rate from after-tax profits was 30.2 percent. Both rates were far in excess of the households' average saving rate (although the same was not necessarily true of *marginal* saving rates).

3. FACT OR FICTION? SOME GROUND RULES

Documenting Endogenous Variables

Our model of Third World urbanization generates predictions on more than a hundred endogenous variables (Appendix A). Most of these reflect general attributes of growth, distribution, and accumulation, while only some are directly related to urban issues, and only three motivate this book—urbanization, city growth, and rural-urban migration rates. Some of these—sectoral rates of return, land rents, rural-urban cost-of-living differentials—cannot be quantified by the historical accounts of the RDC group, although some—the relative rise in urban land scarcity—can be documented qualitatively. Given the quality of the historical data, what follows will focus on the variables for which we have relatively good time series evidence. If the model successfully replicates trends in those variables for which we have good documentation, we shall at least be encouraged to infer that the remainder of the model's predictions are reasonably accurate, even in the absence of hard evidence. But the reader should be aware that some variables are so closely influenced by the estimation itself—e.g., GDP per capita growth is greatly influenced by exogenous rates of total factor productivity and labor force growth—that comparison of prediction and fact may not constitute a severe test of the model's ability to replicate recent historical experience. Other variables offer a tougher test of the model's plausibility—e.g., migration rates, aggregate demand mix, employment distribution, sectoral output shares, and accumulation rates by asset type.

Finally, we should emphasize that urbanization is just one manifestation of many attributes of development. While Third World urbanization and city growth is our prime interest, the validity of the remainder of the model must be established first before the urban dimensions are to be taken seriously. Thus, we begin in section 4 with growth, accumulation, and inequality before turning to urbanization patterns in section 5.

What Kind of Test?

How are the tests to be performed? Perhaps "test" is the wrong word since many of the standard econometric procedures are simply inappropriate when applied to the predictions of a long-run general equilibrium model. After all, the data base is weak since several variables have no documentation whatsoever. Furthermore, the model is only a stylized abstraction of what is a very complex social process. Nor is it obvious that everyone would agree as to which variables are in some sense the most important. Yet, we are reluctant to embark on a detailed inquiry into the sources of Third World urbanization without some assurance that the model generates a plausible description of the development process. In short, what follows is an effort to establish the model as a plausible description of the patterns and rates of development in our forty-country RDC group, no more or less. We leave the more detailed testing of the model's performance for future case study applications.

The Time Dimension

The model was not designed to deal with short-run or even medium-term macroeconomic events. Indeed, the general equilibrium system was built to abstract from short-run structural problems. Prices and wages are flexible, most markets clear, and substitution elasticities are high in production and consumption— all attributes of an economy that has sufficient time to adjust to economic and demographic shocks. Thus, the model can hardly be expected to replicate macroeconomic events over a year or two. Instead, we can only hope that the model replicates historical trends over a period of a decade or more. Given those constraints, the model is evaluated over the decade of the 1960s and into the early 1970s—from 1960 to the 1973 OPEC watershed. An assessment of the more recent experience of post-OPEC structural adjustment is postponed until Chapter 5.

4. Fact or Fiction? Pre-OPEC Growth, Accumulation, and Inequality

Aggregate Growth and Trend Acceleration

Table 3.5 summarizes the model's aggregate growth performance over the pre-OPEC period, 1960–1973. The model is a fairly fast grower, averaging 6.26 percent per annum for GDP in constant prices, while GDP per worker growth rates average 3.58 percent per annum. Furthermore, the model exhibits significant trend acceleration, rising from 5.92 percent per annum 1960–1965 to 6.60 percent per annum 1968–1973. Panel B of Table 3.5 compares these predictions with the pre-OPEC history generated by the RDC group. Both series exhibit trend acceleration, although the model exhibits a somewhat steeper rise in GDP growth rates. Indeed, the steeper trend acceleration in the model's performance would appear to account for its somewhat faster growth over these thirteen years than the forty-country RDC group. While the model could have been calibrated to replicate the RDC history more closely, the effort strikes us as marginal given the quality of the data base, and given that we have made no effort to allow exogenous dynamic parameters

TABLE 3.5

Aggregate Growth Performance, 1960–1973: Model's Prediction and RDC History

A. *Model's Predictions: Levels and Annual Growth (%)*

	Levels		Annual Growth Rates	
Year	GDP (Constant Price)	GDP per Worker (Constant Price)	GDP (Constant Price)	GDP per Worker (Constant Price)
1960	100.0	1.00	5.83	3.18
1961	105.8	1.03	5.91	3.25
1962	112.0	1.07	5.85	3.20
1963	118.6	1.10	5.96	3.30
1964	125.7	1.14	6.02	3.36
1965	133.3	1.17	6.14	3.48
1966	141.5	1.21	6.25	3.58
1967	150.3	1.26	6.36	3.69
1968	159.9	1.30	6.47	3.80
1969	170.2	1.35	6.54	3.87
1970	181.3	1.41	6.56	3.88
1971	193.2	1.46	6.66	3.98
1972	206.1	1.52	6.81	4.13
1973	220.1	1.58		

B. *Model's Predictions and RDC History: Annual Growth (%)*

	GDP (Constant Price)		GDP per Worker (Constant Price)	
Period	Model	History	Model	History
1960–1965	5.92	5.78	3.19	3.24
1968–1973	6.60	6.12	3.98	3.58
1960–1973	6.26	5.80	3.58	3.26

SOURCES: The RDC history is taken from the IBRD *World Tables, 1976* and the ILO *Yearbooks.* See Appendix B

to reflect short-run influences, but rather have let total-factor productivity growth, labor force expansion, land augmentation, foreign capital inflows, and domestic prices of tradeables simply capture average trends over the period as a whole. Under these conditions, the correspondence between model's trajectory and history seems close enough to establish the model's plausibility at the most aggregative level.

Table 3.6 tells us more about the components of this trend acceleration. The source is certainly *not* exogenous total-factor productivity growth since it hardly varies over the period. Rather, the

TABLE 3.6
Aggregate Input Growth Rates, 1960–1973: Model's Predictions (%)

Variable	Period		
	1960–65	*1968–73*	*1960–73*
"Productive" Capital Stock (K): Endogenous	4.84	6.14	5.50
Housing Stock (H): Endogenous	4.47	5.63	5.07
Skilled Labor Force (S): Endogenous	3.64	4.59	4.06
Unskilled Labor Force (L): Endogenous	2.45	2.31	2.39
Rural Labor Force $(L_A + L_{RS})$: Endogenous	1.58	0.72	1.20
Urban Labor Force $(L + S - L_A - L_{RS})$: Endogenous	4.50	5.32	4.86
Total Labor Force $(L + S)$: Exogenous	2.54	2.54	2.54
Urban Land Stock (R_U): Exogenous	1.00	1.00	1.00
Farmland Stock (R_A): Exogenous	1.00	1.00	1.00
"Productive" Capital per Worker $(K/L + S)$	2.30	3.60	2.96
Housing Stock per Worker $(H/L + S)$	1.93	3.09	2.53
Skilled Labor per Worker $(S/L + S)$	1.10	2.05	1.52
Urban Land Stock per Urban Worker $(R_U/L + S - L_A - L_{RS})$	−3.50	−4.32	−3.86
Farmland Stock per Rural Worker $(R_A/L_A + L_{RS})$	−0.58	0.27	−0.20
Total Factor Productivity Growth: Exogenous	1.80	1.76	1.78

source of the trend acceleration lies with human and physical capital accumulation.

While there is little evidence to confirm the accumulation rates reported in Table 3.6, they appear to be consistent with qualitative accounts of this period. Both human and physical capital underwent deepening up to 1973, but capital stock (excluding housing) accumulation rates far exceeded those for skills, 5.50 versus 4.06 percent per annum, respectively. Capital and skills per worker both grew at substantial rates as a result, 2.96 and 1.52 percent per annum. This pattern of relatively more rapid rates of accumulation in non-human capital appears to be consistent with the conventional wisdom that relatively rapid rates of human capital accumulation tend to be an attribute of more advanced development.

What is especially attractive about the results summarized in Table 3.6 is the evidence that the trend acceleration in GDP growth is attributable to trend acceleration in accumulation rates. These rates are endogenous to the model. That is, since there are no exogenous shifts in corporate reinvestment rates, government saving rates, or foreign capital inflows embedded in the simulation, the model captures trend acceleration without any reliance on exogenous changes in saving behavior or rates of technological progress.

Productive capital per worker growth rates rise from 2.30 to 3.60 percent per annum between 1960–1965 and 1968–1973, while skills per worker growth rates rise from 1.10 to 2.05 percent per annum over the same period. All of this takes place in spite of a trend acceleration in housing stocks, total and per capita.

Unbalanced Growth and Industrialization

Table 3.7 summarizes industrialization experience in terms of shifts in output mix over time. The model replicates the RDC group's history exceptionally well. The M-goods sector underwent relatively rapid growth in the RDC group, rising from 15.9 percent of GDP at factor cost (current prices) in 1960 to 20.8 in 1973. The model generates almost identical trends with the M-sector share rising from 15.9 to 20.9 percent over the same period. The service sector underwent a more modest rise in the RDC group, from 47.5 to 50.6 percent of GDP at a factor cost. The model captures these trends too, rising from 47.5 to 50.9 percent. Finally, the relative decline in agricultural production predicted by our model closely corresponds to RDC historical experience: the model predicts a decline in the A-goods share from 36.6 to 28.2 percent in 1960–1973, while in fact the average decline in the forty-country RDC group was from 36.6 to 28.6 percent.

TABLE 3.7

Output Mix, 1960–1973: Model Predictions and RDC History (%)

	1960		1970		1973	
Sector	*Model*	*History*	*Model*	*History*	*Model*	*History*
Agriculture (*A*)	36.6	36.6	30.4	30.9	28.2	28.6
Manufacturing and Mining (*M*)	15.9	15.9	19.3	19.2	20.9	20.8
Modern Capital-Intensive Services (*KS*)	29.6	29.6	30.4	n.a.	30.8	n.a.
Urban Informal Services (*US*)	6.2	6.2	6.9	n.a.	7.2	n.a.
Rural Informal Services (*RS*)	3.2	3.2	3.1	n.a.	2.8	n.a.
Housing, All Sectors (*H*)	8.5	8.5	9.9	n.a.	10.1	n.a.
All Services Combined (*KS* + *US* + *RS* + *H*)	47.5	47.5	50.3	49.9	50.9	50.6

SOURCES: Share in GDP. The RDC history is taken from the IBRD *World Tables, 1976*. See Appendix B

Unbalanced sectoral output growth is a stylized fact of development which has attracted more of the economic historians' and development economists' interest than any other since Britain began the first Industrial Revolution. While any effective development model should be able to generate industrialization, it is satisfying that our model replicates the quantitative record so closely. After all, the task is difficult. The general equilibrium system must not only account for the aggregate rates of factor stock growth, but it must also deal with the allocation of those stocks between the various sectors of use, each with different factor intensities and each subjected to different patterns of demand. Of all the endogenous forces at work in the model, these unbalanced rates of output expansion (summarized in Table 3.7) are perhaps the most central. The model does very well on this score too.

The model is less effective in capturing changes in labor force distribution over time (Table 3.8). The distribution of employment between rural and urban activities is not the problem, which is fortunate given our primary interest in Third World urbanization and city growth. That is, while the ILO *Yearbooks* document a decline in the employment share in *A*-goods production from 60.1 percent of the total labor force in 1960 to 52.4 percent in 1970, the model predicts an almost identical decline from 60.1 to 52.5 percent. The problem appears instead in the distribution of the *urban* labor force. Thus, while the ILO *Yearbooks* document a modest rise in *M*-sector

TABLE 3.8
Labor Force Distribution, 1960–1973: Model's Predictions and RDC History (%)

Sector	1960 Model	1960 History	1970 Model	1970 History	1973 Model
Agriculture (*A*)	60.1	60.1	52.5	52.4	49.7
Manufacturing and Mining (*M*)	12.2	12.2	16.2	13.4	18.1
Modern Capital-Intensive Services (*KS*)	10.4	10.4	11.5	n.a.	12.0
Urban Informal Services (*US*)	10.0	10.0	12.2	n.a.	13.3
Rural Informal Services (*RS*)	7.3	7.3	7.6	n.a.	6.8
All Services Combined (*KS* + *US* + *RS*)	27.7	27.7	31.3	34.2	32.1

SOURCE: The RDC history is taken from ILO *Yearbooks*. See Appendix B

TABLE 3.9

Average Labor Productivities, 1960–1973: Model's Predictions

Sector	Average Labor Productivity (*Economywide = 1.00*)		1960–1973 Average Labor Productivity Growth per annum
	1960	*1973*	
Agriculture (*A*)	0.66	0.62	3.09%
Manufacturing and Mining (*M*)	1.85	1.81	3.41
Modern Capital-Intensive Services (*KS*)	3.10	2.90	3.05
All Informal Services (*US + RS*)	0.48	0.36	1.33
Economywide	1.00	1.00	1.00

SOURCE: Derived from Tables 3.7 and 3.8

employment shares from 12.2 to 13.4 percent over the 1960s, the model predicts a rise to 16.2 percent. Since the model captures historical output shares accurately (Table 3.7), it seems that we may have understated the labor-saving forces at work in manufacturing across the 1960s. Symmetrically, Table 3.8 suggests that we may have overstated the rates of labor-saving in services. We have not repaired this flaw in the model's predictions, and we should keep this in mind when making an overall assessment of the model's plausibility.

Table 3.9 combines the employment and output data in the previous two tables to summarize trends in sectoral average labor productivities. The economywide growth rate exceeds all of the sectoral rates since employment shifted toward the more capital-cum-skills intensive sectors over the period. Apart from that influence, the leading sector appears to have been manufacturing, while informal services lagged far behind.

Investment Allocation and Sources of Finance

Gross domestic investment as a share in GDP increased markedly in the RDC group between 1960 and 1973, from 15.6 to 19.5 percent (Table 3.10). The model also generates a rise in the investment share, although not at quite the same rate (15.6 to 18.4 percent of GDP). Total investment shares, including training investment, also drift upward in the model, a prediction that conventional national ac-

TABLE 3.10

Gross Domestic Investment and Sources of Saving, 1960–1973: Model's Predictions and RDC History (Share in GDP, %)

	1960		1973	
Variable	Model	History	Model	History
Total Private Saving	11.2 (71.5)	11.0 (70.7)	12.2 (66.3)	12.8 (66.0)
Gross Corporate Reinvestment in M and KS	4.9 (31.7)	n.a.	4.9 (26.6)	n.a.
Household Saving	6.2 (39.8)	n.a.	7.2 (39.7)	n.a.
Government Saving (including F)	4.5 (28.5)	4.6 (29.3)	6.1 (33.7)	6.6 (34.0)
Corporate Training Investment in M and KS	2.3	n.a.	2.2	n.a.
Gross Domestic Investment (market prices)	15.6 (100.0)	15.6 (100.0)	18.4 (100.0)	19.5 (100.0)
Total Investment (market prices)	17.9	n.a.	20.5	n.a.

SOURCES: The RDC history is taken from the IBRD *World Tables, 1976*, but only twenty-eight of the forty RDC countries have the required data which underlie "History" in the table above. See also Appendix B. Figures may not add up due to rounding

NOTES: All entries are percentage shares in GDP (market prices). Figures in parentheses are shares in gross domestic investment, excluding training.

counts cannot document. While the aggregate investment share was drifting upward over the period, however, the model suggests that the distribution of investment was remarkably stable.

Investment allocation by sector and type is poorly documented for the pre-OPEC period; as a result, Table 3.11 deals only with the model's predictions. Investment in plant and equipment remains stable at 72 percent of total investment, housing investment rises only modestly from 16 to 17 percent, and investment in training declines from 13 to 11 percent. The shifts by sector are a bit more marked, but even here the changes in investment distribution are modest: the M-sector increases its share from 15 to 18 percent at the expense of the KS-sector, whose share falls from 48 percent to 45 percent; and urban squatter housing investment increases its share from 6 to 8 percent at the expense of rural housing investment. Apart from these changes, the distribution of investment across sector and type is quite stable over the thirteen years.

This stability in investment mix is certainly not true of the sources of saving. Table 3.10 reports the model's predictions and RDC history for the 1960–1973 period, although there are serious problems of comparability between them. The *World Tables* normally only reports total private saving, and does not separate household savings from firm (corporate) reinvestment. While the distinction may be fuzzy in the economies being analyzed, the two sources of

TABLE 3.11

Investment Allocation, 1960–1973: Model's Predictions (Share in GDP, %)

Investment Use	1960		1973	
Plant and Equipment Investment (I_M)	12.8	(72)	14.8	(72)
Manufacturing and Mining ($I_{M,M}$)	2.6	(15)	3.6	(18)
Modern Capital-Intensive Services ($I_{KS,M}$)	8.6	(48)	9.3	(45)
Agriculture ($I_{A,M}$)	1.6	(9)	1.9	(9)
Housing Investment (I_H)	2.8	(16)	3.5	(17)
Formal Urban Luxury Housing ($I_{H,KS}$)	0.8	(5)	1.1	(5)
Informal Urban Squatter Housing ($I_{H,US}$)	1.0	(6)	1.6	(8)
Rural Housing ($I_{H,RS}$)	0.9	(5)	0.8	(4)
Total Gross Domestic Investment	15.6	(87)	18.3	(89)
Investment in Training ($I_{S,KS}$)	2.3	(13)	2.2	(11)
Total Investment	17.9	(100)	20.5	(100)

NOTE: Investment entries are percentage shares in GDP. Figures in parentheses are shares in total investment, including training. Figures may not add up due to rounding

saving are quite distinct in the model and are thus reported separately. Furthermore, what the model identifies as "training investment" is embedded in private and government consumption in the RDC national accounts. In spite of these problems of comparability, the results in Table 3.10 do provide some reassurance that the model generates plausible historical trends in the pre-OPEC period. The shift from private to public saving is certainly captured by the model: while the share of gross domestic investment financed by public saving rose in the RDC group from 29.3 to 34 percent, the model predicts a rise from 28.5 to 33.4 percent, both shares rising by about 5 percentage points. Furthermore, the model reveals that the fall in the private share of finance was not so much lagging household saving, but rather gross corporate saving whose share in gross domestic investment declines from 31.7 to 27.1 percent.

Investment allocation is probably the most difficult activity to model, perhaps explaining why so many multisectoral models choose to treat it as exogenous, often dictated solely by historic shares. In contrast, Chapter 2 devoted considerable attention to the endogenous determinants of investment allocation by type and sector, since we think they are crucial to understanding Third World growth and urbanization in the long run. Judging by the results summarized in Tables 3.10 and 3.11, it appears that the model has performed quite well in replicating this aspect of the pre-OPEC period.

Income Inequality and Wage Patterns

Our model was not designed to confront income distribution issues in detail. Since there are only four classes of wage earners—rural landless, unskilled urban in informal services, unskilled urban in modern sectors, and skilled workers, and property income recipients holding two kinds of market assets—shareholders and landlords, it would be false precision to report full-size distributions. Yet the model does have something to say about factor incomes and factor shares. To the extent that factor incomes are at the core of inequality *trends*, the model's predictions are certainly relevant. But even if they were not, the development literature has devoted enough attention to the operation of labor markets and the structure of pay to warrant a critical look at this aspect of the model's quantitative behavior. Table 3.12 supplies the ingredients for such an assessment.

Panel A of Table 3.12 presents size distributions both for the model and for an average of some eighteen of the RDC countries for which data exists. While we are well aware of the limitations of

TABLE 3.12

Inequality Indicators, 1960–1973: Model's Predictions and RDC History

	A. *Size Distribution: National Income Shares*					
	1960		1970		$\Delta = 1970–1960$	
jth Income Class	*Model*	*History*	*Model*	*History*	*Model*	*History*
95–100%	27.46	28.78	24.36	26.22	−3.10	−2.56
90–95%	9.29	n.a.	9.04	n.a.	−0.26	n.a.
60–90%	43.75	n.a.	47.48	n.a.	+3.73	n.a.
40–95%	53.04	n.a.	56.52	n.a.	+3.48	n.a.
20–95%	62.79	65.91	66.08	68.75	+3.29	+2.85
0–40%	19.05	n.a.	19.12	n.a.	+0.07	n.a.
0–20%	9.75	5.31	9.56	5.02	−0.19	−0.29

	B. *Urban Skilled Wage Premium*		
		Model 1960	*Model 1973*
$\text{Premium} = \dfrac{\text{Urban Unskilled Wage} - \text{Skilled Wage}}{\text{Urban Unskilled Wage}}$		1.50	1.74

SOURCES: The size distribution is taken from the IBRD *World Tables, 1976*, available for eighteen of the forty-country RDC group

NOTE: The model's predictions include imputed rental income from housing. The urban skilled wage premium is the ratio of the urban skilled wage differential to informal unskilled wages using the top 5 percent and bottom 20 percent national income shares reported in the *World Tables*, the similarity in trends between the model's predictions and history is impressive. First, the *World Tables* cannot be used to establish an unambiguous rise in inequality. True, the bottom 20 percent underwent further erosion, but the data suggests that the top 5 percent underwent an even more dramatic erosion in their income share. Clearly, the middle classes increased their share at the expense of both the very rich and the very poor. These are exactly the conditions under which Lorenz Curves intersect, and when inequality inferences are impossible without imposing value weights on various social classes (see Atkinson, 1970). It is impressive that the model exhibits the same behavior. While the model predicts a 3.1 percent decline in the top 5 percent's share of national income, RDC history documents a decline of 2.6 percent; and while the bottom 20 percent found their share declining by 0.3 percent, the model predicts a fall of 0.2 percent. Furthermore, the model shows who in the middle gained the most: the group in the 60–90 percent range increase their share by 3.7 percent.

Panel A in Table 3.12 seems to replicate the main outlines of RDC inequality trends in the pre-OPEC period. It also implies that the source of the inequality trends lies with increased *earnings* inequality. After all, in our model the classes which fall in the 60–90 percent range are urban skilled and unskilled in the formal sectors. The model, therefore, generates wage inequality.

Panel B offers more evidence on the source of inequality trends. Here we present one summary statistic for the whole wage structure, the wage premium on skills. The model predicts a rise in the index from 1.5 to 1.74 over the pre-OPEC period. While we are unaware of historical evidence from the RDC group which would make it possible to confront this prediction, it is clear that the model generates skill scarcity. To the extent that skill scarcities are price signals of inadequate human capital accumulation, the wage and income inequality trends reported in Table 3.12 are attributes of dynamic disequilibrium which even a neoclassical model of wage and price flexibility is capable of replicating.

5. FACT OR FICTION? PRE-OPEC URBANIZATION,
   LAND SCARCITY, AND HOUSING

The previous section has established the model's plausibility in a general sense: it appears to replicate the overall dimensions of growth, accumulation, and inequality in the RDC group between 1960 and 1973. But what about urbanization? Does the model replicate rapid city growth, heavy in-migration to the cities, squatter settlement sprawl, rising urban land values, housing scarcity, and rising costs of city life? Each of these variables is endogenous to the overall development process and each plays a role in the model developed in Chapter 2.

Migration, Urbanization, and City Growth

Table 3.13 documents four key aspects of urban development: the share of the population urban, city growth rates, net rural out-migration rates (as a percent of the rural population), and net urban

TABLE 3.13

Migration, Urbanization, and City Growth, 1960–1973: Model's Predictions and RDC History

			A. Model's Predictions: Annual, 1960–1973	
Year	% Urban	City Growth	Net Rural Out-Migration Rate	Net Urban In-Migration Rate
1960	32.60%	—	—	—
1961	33.55	5.56%	1.41%	2.91%
1962	34.30	4.87	1.13	2.24
1963	34.73	3.85	0.65	1.25
1964	35.25	4.13	0.81	1.51
1965	35.78	4.11	0.82	1.50
1966	36.49	4.60	1.10	1.98
1967	37.23	4.61	1.16	2.01
1968	38.07	4.90	1.35	2.27
1969	38.95	4.91	1.42	2.31
1970	39.93	5.15	1.60	2.51
1971	40.96	5.22	1.71	2.58
1972	42.15	5.56	2.02	2.91
1973	43.45	5.72	2.21	3.07

B. *Model's Predictions and RDC History: Period Averages, 1960–1970*

Variable	Model	History
(1) City Growth, per Annum (compounded)	4.67%	4.60%
(2) Total Increase in Share Urban	7.33	5.30
(3) Increase in Share Urban, Percent per Annum	0.73	0.53
(4) Net In-migrant Share of Urban Population Increase	45.0	(39.3, 40, 42, 49)
(5) Net In-migration Rate	2.09	(1.81, 1.84, 1.93, 2.26)
(6) Net Out-Migration Rate	1.10	(.97, .99, 1.03, 1.21)

SOURCES: The RDC history figures in (1), (2), and (3) are taken from the IBRD *World Tables, 1976.* Preston (1979, p. 198), Renaud (1979, Annex Tables 2.2 and 2.3), Linn (1979, p. 73), and Keyfitz (1980, p. 151) supply the various estimates in (4). Item (5) is derived from the preceding entries, as is item (6), taking 1970 as a base

in-migration rates (as a percent of the urban population). Once
again, there are problems with the data. While the model makes
predictions about labor force distribution, the historical data are
taken from demographic sources (summarized in the *World Tables*)
which deal with the spatial distribution of population. Furthermore,
comparisons across countries are fraught with problems of census
quality and conflicting definitions of urban units. Yet, *trends* in any
given statistic are less likely to be affected by such problems of comparability than are levels, and it is the former that interests us here.

There are two panels in Table 3.13: the first reports trends predicted by the model over the full pre-OPEC period; the second compares model and history for period averages. It would appear that
the qualitative dimensions of Third World urbanization are reproduced by the model in Panel A. The urbanization level rises over
time. While the 1960–1973 period is far too short to make inferences
about long-run urbanization patterns, there is, nonetheless, clear
evidence that the model is predicting rising or accelerating rates of
urbanization, conforming to the pre-inflexion point phase along
logistic urbanization curves commonly found in Third World time
series (Preston, 1979; Ledent, 1980). That is, in the first five years
of the simulation (1960–1965) urbanization levels rise by 3.18 percentage points, while in the last five years (1968–1973) they rise by
5.38 percentage points. Similarly, city growth rates rise over time,
conforming to the trends reported in the *World Tables, 1976* (Table
2, "Social Indicators") between 1960 and 1970. Rural-urban migration rates rise over time as well.

Panel B supplies a more detailed assessment of the model's performance. While city growth rates in the RDC group were 4.6 percent per annum over the 1960s, the model predicts a rate of 4.7
percent, certainly a close correspondence. True, the rate of urbanization is somewhat faster in the model than in the RDC's history
(a 7.3 versus a 5.3 percentage point increase), but we choose to
downplay the discrepancy given that the model predicts changes in
spatial employment distribution while "history" deals with population distribution. Panel B also reports in-migration and out-
migration rates for the decade as a whole. Once again, the model
appears to conform to the quantitative averages generated by the
RDC history across the 1960s: while the model predicts a rural out-
migration rate of 1.1 percent per annum, the estimates offered in
the literature range from .97 to 1.21 percent per annum; and while
the predicted urban in-migration rate is 2.1 percent per annum, the
estimates offered in the literature range from 1.81 to 2.26 percent
per annum. Finally, Panel B reports that 45 percent of the increase

in city population is accounted for by in-migration in the model. This figure falls between Preston's (1979) estimate of 39 percent based on twenty-nine developing countries, and Keyfitz's (1980, p. 151) regional estimate of 49 percent. It is also close to the 42 percent figure for less developed countries reported by Linn (1979, p. 73) for 1970–1975, and the 40 percent figure for twenty-two of our forty RDC countries reported by Renaud (1979, Annex Table 2.2 and 2.3) for the same period.

In summary, the model has successfully replicated the quantitative outlines of Third World urbanization in the pre-OPEC period.

Urban Land Use, Density, and Land Scarcity

Table 3.14 reports attributes of urban land use and scarcity predicted by the model in the pre-OPEC period. First, the share of urban land devoted to squatter settlements rises sharply over time, an attribute which has attracted the attention of many observers (Simmons, 1979; Davis, 1975; P. R. Shaw, 1978; Mohan, 1979; Beier et al., 1976). Competition for land use generates increasing land scarcity: the shadow site rent on urban land almost doubled between 1960 and 1970, reaching a level in 1973 about 2.3 times that of 1960. Urban land values (deflated by the general price level) surge apace, the index rising from a base of 100 in 1960 to 195.2 in 1970 and 239.7 in 1973. These trends in urban land values imply the very rapid growth of 7 percent per annum, exactly the sharp rises that were singled out at the UN Habitat Conference in 1976. With increasing scarcity of urban land, urban densities rise everywhere in our model, but apparently they rise most dramatically in luxury housing where the relative price of new units (compared to land rents) falls more sharply, encouraging land-saving and greater density.

TABLE 3.14
Urban Land Use, Density, and Land Scarcity, 1960–1973:
The Model's Predictions

Variable	1960	1970	1973
Share of Urban Land in Squatter Settlements (%)	43.0	52.2	53.9
Urban Land Density, Persons ÷ Area (1960 = 100)			
Luxury Housing Areas	100.0	152.0	172.7
Squatter Settlements	100.0	121.4	141.7
Shadow Site Rent on Urban Land (1960 = 100)	100.0	183.3	233.3
Shadow Price on Urban Land (1960 = 100)	100.0	195.2	239.7

Housing Scarcity and Cost-of-Living Differentials

Land scarcity is only one component of high urban cost of living since excess demand for housing units in the short run, and rising costs of housing construction in the long run, can also serve to inflate the cost (or deflate the quality) of city life. Table 3.15 summarizes these influences. The excess housing demand index is derived from the economics embedded in Chapter 2. Recall that the capital market segmentation assumption excludes intersectoral loans for housing investment finance: each socioeconomic class must rely on its own internally generated current saving to finance desired housing investment. Table 3.15 reports the gap between desired housing investment and saving by class. It appears that the saving constraint is never binding for rural households, nor is it binding for the skilled and property income recipients who consume higher quality urban luxury housing. However, for squatter settlements—the faster growing sector—the saving constraint is binding very early in the period, thus generating short-run excess demands for low quality dwelling units. This excess demand and increasing urban land scarcity insures a rapid upward drift in (shadow) rents within urban squatter settlements. The urban/rural cost-of-living index rises as a result. The rise is only 12 percent over the whole pre-OPEC period, since rents constitute but a small share of low-income urban households'

TABLE 3.15

Housing Scarcity and Rural-Urban Cost-Of-Living Differentials, 1960–1973: The Model's Predictions

Variable	1960	1970	1973
Excess Housing Investment Demand: Desired Housing Investment Demand − Household Saving ÷ Desired Housing Investment Demand			
Urban Luxury Housing	−3.77	−2.55	−2.67
Urban Squatter Settlements	−0.02	+0.37	+0.28
Rural Housing	−0.29	−0.58	−0.89
House Rent Index			
Urban Luxury Housing	1.00	1.35	1.46
Urban Squatter Settlements	1.00	1.72	1.90
Rural Housing	1.00	1.38	1.45
Urban Squatter ÷ Rural	1.00	1.25	1.31
Cost-of-Living Index			
Urban ÷ Rural	1.00	1.09	1.12

budgets. This may be enough, however, to discourage immigration to the city.

6. FACT OR FICTION? MODEL FORECASTS

Up to this point the model's predictions have been compared with actual historical experience over the period 1960–1973. Chapter 5 will, in addition, attempt to account for the structural adjustment that took place following OPEC. But what of the future? Can we expect a model that has performed well over the past two decades to do as well over the next two decades?

We can attempt an answer to this question by comparing our model's forecasts with those implied by the Chenery and Syrquin econometric estimates of the past stylized facts of development. Chenery and Syrquin (C–S) estimate multiple regressions describing the association between various structural features and two explanatory variables, per capita income and population. The resulting patterns of development are based on the combined cross-section and time series data for 101 developing countries over the period 1950–1979. It would be instructive to compare our model's predictions with those implied by the C–S regressions. Does the RDC model perform like the past empirical record when the RDC advances through the full range of development experience of the complete C–S cross-section? First, we computed predicted C–S values for six dependent variables of special interest. These calculations required the conversion of the RDC units measuring per capita income and population into those underlying the Chenery and Syrquin data.[1] After this conversion was completed, the actual growth of our RDC over the period 1960–2000 yielded the independent variables inserted into the C–S regressions,[2] producing forecasts of the dependent variables of interest. These forecasts are then compared with the model's predictions in Table 3.16.

---

[1] This is performed by linking the C–S average to the 1965 RDC values (Chenery and Syrquin, 1975, pp. 70–73). These 1965 values now in C–S units were pushed back to 1960 using the RDC's actual growth experience for that five-year period, yielding a 1960 per capita income and population of $180.8 and 18.4 million, respectively. (India was dropped from the sample since its population size is atypical of the RDC.) Following our previous methodology, each country should receive a roughly equal weight in the total.

[2] While many functional forms were subjected to examination in their statistical analysis, the double log form with each of the independent variables represented in its untransformed and squared terms provided the best overall fit. We use it in Table 3.16 as well.

TABLE 3.16
Comparison of Model Predictions with the Chenery and Syrquin "Patterns":
1960–2000

Variable	Date	Model Prediction	Chenery & Syrquin Prediction
Agricultural Output	1960	36.6%	34.2%
Share in GDP	2000	14.5	14.1
	Δ1960–2000	−22.1	−20.1
Manufacturing Output	1960	15.9	20.9
Share in GDP	2000	32.8	34.2
	Δ1960–2000	+16.9	+13.3
Investment	1960	17.9	18.6
Share in GDP*	2000	23.8	24.3
	Δ1960–2000	+5.9	+5.7
Government Current	1960	13.7	13.9
Spending Share in GDP	2000	14.2	14.8
	Δ1960–2000	+0.5	+0.9
Agricultural Employment	1960	60.1	57.2
Share in Total Labor Force	2000	27.5	28.9
	Δ1960–2000	−32.6	−28.3
Manufacturing Employment	1960	12.2	15.4
Share in Total Labor Force	2000	33.2	30.6
	Δ1960–2000	+21.0	+15.2

* Including training investment in the model's prediction

For sectoral output shares, final demand shares, and labor force distribution, the correspondence for the year 2000 is fairly high. True, manufacturing output and employment shares seem to have increased more slowly in the real world. Overall, however, the results provide some confirmation of our judgment that the RDC model will yield relevant forecasts—at least as judged by the "patterns of development" estimated by Chenery and Syrquin.

7. FACT OR FICTION? AN ASSESSMENT

The literature dealing with the application of computable general equilibrium models to Third World problems has rapidly grown in size over the past decade. In spite of its increasing sophistication in technique and novelty of application, this literature offers very few examples of model validation. Typically, the researcher passes from model construction, to estimation, and to analysis with little but a passing nod to validation. This may be explained in part by absence of the necessary time series, but we doubt it. More likely, this state of affairs is to be explained by the fact that most of the computable general equilibrium applications have little of interest to say about dynamics. Perhaps because of our interest and training in economic history, the present authors have broken with this tradition.

We believe that our model has replicated Third World growth, accumulation, distribution, and urban change very closely indeed. That conclusion was not guided by econometric precision, to be sure, but the evidence certainly suggests that ours is a plausible paradigm of long-run city growth for Third World economies passing through the transition to modernization. Of course, we have no way of knowing whether the structural parameters embedded in the model will remain relatively stable over the next two decades. To the extent that they do, we believe we have an empirically relevant paradigm which can now be used for three critical purposes: first, to better understand to what shocks Third World urban experience is most sensitive (Chapter 4); second, to isolate the key sources of rapid Third World city growth in the recent past (Chapter 5); and third, to explore the likely sources and direction of Third World city growth in the future (Chapter 6).

CHAPTER FOUR

How the Model Works:
Short-run Impact Multipliers

1. INTRODUCTION

Which exogenous variables and which policy parameters have had the greatest impact on past Third World city growth? Which are least likely to account for future trends? Any answer to these questions can be decomposed into three parts: (1) the size of past and future changes in exogenous variables thought to influence endogenous rates of city growth; (2) the short-run comparative static impact of each exogenous variable; and (3), the long-run forces set in motion by the short-run comparative static impact. This chapter will focus on short-run comparative static elasticities, although at points the discussion will be motivated by speculations regarding the size of each exogenous variable's historical change. After all, a small elasticity may hide a large dynamic impact, due either to major shocks in the exogenous variable of interest or to potent dynamic influences.

Section 2 explores the impact of five key macro events on urban growth: unbalanced productivity advance, world market conditions and price policy, capital accumulation, demographic change, and land scarcity. The short-run impact multipliers that guide the analysis are conventional elasticities, although in contrast with the partial equilibrium elasticities commonly used in the literature, our impact multipliers reflect full general equilibrium influences. These elasticities measure the response of some endogenous variable of interest (e.g., share of population in urban areas, city in-migration rates, city growth rates, urban land scarcity, housing demands, cost-of-living differentials) to some exogenous variable thought to have been important in driving past Third World urbanization (e.g., pre-OPEC cheap fuel, a favorable market for exportables, unbalanced productivity advance favoring urban sectors, population pressure, rapid capital accumulation). Each of these elasticities is computed with reference to the initial conditions of the RDC economy in 1970, that is, just prior to the 1973–1974 OPEC watershed to which the world economy has been adjusting since. Section 3 then asks whether these responses were unique to the early 1970s. Was the RDC less or more sensitive to some shocks in 1970 than in 1980? What about the year 2000? Which aspects of urbanization are most affected? Which types of shocks were most important? Section 3 helps identify the influence of an economy's economic structure and stage of development on the urban impact multipliers of greatest interest.

This chapter explores two types of short-run multipliers, both of which restrict structural adjustment in capital markets. That is, while labor markets are allowed to adjust through migration, and while urban land markets are allowed to seek an optimal land use solution, capital markets are severely constrained. Old capital, of course, cannot migrate in response to disequilibrium. In addition, new capital goods and newly trained skilled workers are not added to sectoral capacity in either of the measured short-run responses. The critical difference between the two short-run multipliers, however, lies with the treatment of *investment* response. Sections 2 and 3 deal with the "very short-run," where recent historical experience with sectoral investment allocation is assumed to persist, as entrepreneurs are slow to adjust to the new, shock-distorted rates of return. Following this analysis, we consider two additional questions. What happens when the current investment mix is allowed to respond to the shock-distorted rates of return? How does the subsequent short-run investment response influence the structure of demand, employment, and thus city in-migration and urbanization? Section 4 confronts these questions and finds investment responses to be an important component of short-run structural adjustment.

Finally, section 5 explores the impact of two policy variables, urban wage policy and government attitude toward urban squatter settlements.

2. WHAT DRIVES THIRD WORLD CITY GROWTH?

This section first examines the impact of unbalanced sectoral productivity advance on city growth. Unbalanced productivity advance is used as a vehicle to understand how the economy works in general, but it also reveals our prejudice that unbalanced productivity advance is *the* central force driving urbanization and city growth during any nation's industrial revolution. Second, we look for manifestations of short-run constraints on city growth in response to unbalanced productivity advance. Finally, we offer a brief comparative assessment of the sensitivity of Third World city growth to the remaining four key forces—world market conditions and price policy, accumulation, demographic change, and land scarcity.

Unbalanced Productivity Advance

If output demand is relatively price-elastic, then sectoral total-factor productivity growth tends to generate an elastic supply response rather than a relative price decline. This distinction is important since cost-reducing innovations will be passed on to users by falling prices in the inelastic demand case. Thus, the rise in the marginal physical productivity of factors used in a technologically dynamic sector will be partially offset by price declines, so that marginal *value* products rise by less, and resource shifts to the technologically dynamic sector are minimized, and this includes employment. If, on average, urban sectors tend to have relatively high rates of total-factor productivity growth, and if the demand for urban output is price-elastic, final demand shifts toward the dynamic urban sectors, the derived demand for urban employment is augmented, urban job vacancies are created, migration responds, and city growth takes place. The higher are price elasticities of demand for urban output, the greater is the city growth impact of unbalanced productivity advance favoring the modern sectors.

The role of demand elasticities can be seen in Table 4.1. Disembodied total-factor productivity improvements ($\overset{*}{A}_j$, in rates of change) in agriculture and manufacturing exert a much greater impact on urbanization experience than do productivity improvements in any of the three service sectors. The explanation is now apparent: P_A and P_M are exogenously determined and fixed by invoking the small-country case of infinite price elasticity. Services are nontradeables with far lower price elasticities of demand, sufficiently low, in fact, that the productivity-induced declines in service sector prices ($\overset{*}{P}_{KS}$, $\overset{*}{P}_{US}$, $\overset{*}{P}_{RS}$ in response to $\overset{*}{A}_{KS}$, $\overset{*}{A}_{US}$, and $\overset{*}{A}_{RS}$, respectively) imply stable marginal value products and thus trivial employment and city growth effects. While productivity advance in manufacturing represents an important potential determinant of Third World urbanization, rapid productivity advance in agriculture tends to forestall out-migration to the city. This result stands in stark contrast with the *closed* dual economy model where productivity advance in agriculture meets with demand absorption problems, a declining farm terms of trade, and thus a "labor surplus" which out-migrates to glut urban labor markets. Immiserizing agricultural growth of this type is not an attribute of our open-economy model.

It follows that unbalanced rates of total-factor productivity growth (TFPG) favoring manufacturing ($\overset{*}{A}_M - \overset{*}{A}_A > 0$) could well have been a key determinant of rapid in-migration and city growth throughout the Third World since the late 1950s. Not only are the

TABLE 4.1

The Comparative Static Impact of Unbalanced Productivity Advance on Third World City Growth (1970 Elasticities)

Endogenous Variable	Tradeable Commodities		Nontradeable Services		
	A_M	A_A	A_{KS}	A_{US}	A_{RS}
A. City Growth Attributes					
% Urban	.50	−.26	.03	−.01	−.03
City Growth Rate	10.29	−5.33	.68	−.26	−.67
In-migration Rate	20.57	−10.65	1.36	−.52	−1.33
Squatter House Rents	3.57	−.73	.40	0	−.14
COL Differential (Urban-Rural)	1.49	−.80	.12	−.11	.01
B. Some Economywide Attributes					
P_{KS}	.82	.22	−.91	.03	0
P_{US}	1.03	.24	.15	−1.09	0
P_{RS}	.02	1.17	.09	−.01	−1.03
Q_M	2.34	−.57	.24	.08	−.09
Q_{KS}	.02	.17	.99	.01	0
Q_{US}	.23	0	.02	.75	−.01
Q_A	−.34	1.31	.07	0	.07
Q_{RS}	−.11	.32	−.01	0	.60
L_M	1.36	−.84	.10	.18	−.09
L_{KS}	−.18	.15	−.07	.11	0
L_{US}	.24	0	.02	−.26	−.01
L_A	−.37	.15	−.02	.01	.08
L_{RS}	−.11	.34	−.01	0	−.41
Skill Premium	.41	−.24	−.03	.21	0

comparative static elasticities in Table 4.1 consistent with that position, but limited evidence suggests that annual rates of TFPG in manufacturing have been relatively high in most successful Third World economies. Indeed, Appendix C (Table C.8) confirms an unbalanced rate of productivity advance favoring manufacturing for sixteen LDCs during the 1960s, most of which also underwent rapid rates of urbanization. Note, however, that *both* the unbalancedness in sectoral TFPG growth rates *and* the levels themselves matter. The levels of TFPG matter primarily through various GNP-augmenting effects, tax-augmenting effects, and inequality effects, all of which favor city growth on the demand side.

While technological advance tends to be lower in the service sectors, and especially the informal service sectors (see Appendix C, Table C.8), Table 4.1 suggests that rapid TFPG in those sectors has had little impact on urbanization experience, for the demand elasticity reasons already offered. If rapid TFPG even in the modern capital-cum-skill intensive KS sector has little effect on urbanization, then it must follow that lagging productivity advance in the service sectors also matters little. It might prove helpful to dwell on this point. It is believed that urban social overhead is crucial to the profitability and viability of urban firms. In our model, KS activities serve that role (e.g., transportation, communications, electricity, gas, water, public administration, education, and health services), and Table 4.1 confirms that productivity advance there serves to augment KS services supplied in short-run equilibrium (Q_{KS}). However, almost all of those productivity gains are passed on to users elsewhere in the economy (P_{KS} declines), so that employment in KS itself (L_{KS}) changes very little. Who gains? Final demand consumers of KS services gain, and they tend to be the urban rich (Appendix B, Table B.10). But what about intermediate input demands? A major user of KS services is manufacturing, and thus employment (L_M) rises there as a result. The net effect on urbanization is, however, small and indirect.

Short-run Constraints on the City Growth Response

Productivity advance favoring modern sectors *does* foster urbanization. But in the short-run the city growth response is constrained, partly by output absorption problems on the demand side, partly by short-run capacity constraints and skill bottlenecks on the supply side, and partly by a rising supply price of unskilled labor in the cities. Table 4.2 outlines these short-run limits to city growth, focusing on urban labor's rising supply price. Urban job creation fosters an in-migration response, but note the following: while urban land use shifts to squatter settlements to accommodate rising density there, urban rents continue to rise steeply in the face of migrant influx; since the new in-migrants are unskilled and poor, rents in squatter settlements rise far more sharply than do luxury house rents, the former reflecting excess housing and site demands, and the latter mostly reflecting increased land scarcity as the poor's needs are partially accommodated by shifting land use; and the rural areas' cost-of-living advantage rises sharply as a result. (Presumably, disamenity aspects of crowding serve to reinforce these effects.) All of these short-run constraints on housing and urban land serve to raise the average unskilled wage in the cities, tending to choke off city growth in the short run. Other bottlenecks also limit

TABLE 4.2

*Short-run Constraints on the City Growth Response to
Unbalanced Productivity Advance (1970 Elasticities)*

Endogenous Variable	A_M	A_{KS}
A. *City Growth Attributes*		
City Growth Rate	10.29	.68
In-migration Rate	20.57	1.36
B. *"Congestion" Indicators*		
% Urban Land in Squatter Settlements	1.25	.13
Squatter House Rents	3.57	.40
Luxury House Rents	1.16	.15
COL Differential (Urban-Rural)	1.49	.12
C. *Factor Market Disequilibrium Indicators, the City*		
Average Urban Unskilled Wage	1.03	.15
Rural Unskilled Wage	.02	.09
Urban Skilled Wage	1.28	.13
Return to Capital in M	2.34	.27
Return to Capital in KS	.80	.07
Return to Capital in A	−.30	.06

city growth in the short run: job creation is constrained by skill
bottlenecks (the skilled wage rises) and by capital scarcity (the return to capital in manufacturing rises far above its return in other
uses). This suggests that the impact of unbalanced productivity advance on city growth may be far greater in the longer run.

Fuel and Imported Raw Material Scarcity

Since urban-based manufacturing is raw-material-intensive (Appendix Table B.8), any increase in the price of imported Z goods
serves to penalize manufacturing directly and other urban activities
indirectly, thus inhibiting urban job creation and city growth. Table
4.3 summarizes these effects. Since the model admits the possibility
of substitution away from the more expensive imported fuels and
raw materials, the amount of Z demanded in the aggregate diminishes. (The impact multiplier is a bit in excess of unity.) In-migration
and city growth are both choked off by imported fuel and raw
material scarcity, the former with an elasticity of −1.77 and the
latter with an elasticity of −.89. While these elasticities are significant, they are far lower than those reported for productivity advance
in Table 4.1 or for the other two exogenous prices reported in

TABLE 4.3

The Comparative Static Impact of World Market Conditions and Price Policy on Third World City Growth (1970 Elasticities)

Endogenous Variable	Domestic Price		
	P_Z	P_M	P_A
A. *Imported Fuel and Raw Materials*			
Z	−1.15	1.76	−.38
B. *City Growth Attributes*			
% Urban	−.04	.54	−.32
City Growth Rate	−.89	11.13	−6.51
In-migration Rate	−1.77	22.23	−13.01
Squatter House Rents	−.31	3.57	−1.58
% Urban Land in Squatter Settlements	−.11	1.33	−.90
COL Differential (Urban-Rural)	−.12	1.51	−1.11
C. *Economywide Attributes*			
Q_M	−.20	1.38	−.85
Q_{KS}	−.01	−.17	.10
Q_{US}	−.02	.23	−.10
Q_A	0	−.48	.41
Q_{RS}	.05	−.15	−.15
Skill Premium	−.05	.46	−.27

Table 4.3. At first glance, this may suggest that the sensitivity of Third World urbanization to fuel-cum-raw-material scarcity has been overdrawn in the literature, a conclusion that we share with Michael Bruno (1982). Given what we know about the historical record since 1960, however, one must be cautious in leaping to that conclusion. After all, P_Z soared in the 1970s after a period of stability during the 1960s. Thus, P_Z may have been a dominant influence on Third World urbanization over the past two decades in spite of the modest elasticities reported in Table 4.3. The issue is confronted again in Chapter 5.

Domestic Price Policy and World Market Conditions

Table 4.3 also reports the short-run impact multipliers for prices of *A* and *M*, both of which compete in world markets, although these prices are usually heavily distorted by Third World external and internal price policy. Table 4.3 makes it clear that Third World city growth is far more sensitive to P_A and P_M than to P_Z. Any effort to understand the sources of past and future city growth in

TABLE 4.4

The Comparative Static Impact of Accumulation on Third World City Growth
(1970 Elasticities)

	Productive Capital			Unproductive Capital		
Endogenous Variable	K_M	K_{KS}	K_A	H_{KS}	H_{US}	H_{RS}
A. City Growth Attributes						
% Urban	.09	.02	−.03	0	.39	−.13
City Growth Rate	1.82	.40	−.68	.07	7.92	−2.75
In-migration Rate	3.63	.81	−1.35	.15	15.83	−5.50
Squatter House Rents	.61	.19	−.11	0	−1.54	−.41
Luxury House Rents	.19	.01	.04	−1.02	.04	−.06
COL Differential (Urban-Rural)	.25	.06	−.10	0	−.52	.18
B. Employment Effects						
L_M	.24	.07	−.11	.01	.72	−.25
L_{KS}	−.03	−.02	.02	0	.35	−.13
L_{US}	.05	0	0	0	.40	−.13
L_A	−.08	−.05	.04	−.01	−.25	.09
L_{RS}	.10	.28	−.08	.02	−.32	.07
C. Wage Impact						
Average Urban Unskilled Wage	.18	.07	.02	0	−.30	.10
Rural Unskilled Wage	.01	.05	.12	0	.07	−.02
Skill Premium	.12	.13	0	0	.77	−.27

the Third World must sort out these relative price conditions with
care, including the impact of past liberalization and future protectionist trends in the industrialized countries, as well as the influence
of various price-distorting policy regimes in the Third World itself.

Accumulation, Capacity, and Job Creation

Table 4.4 summarizes the impact of productive capital accumulation and population-sensitive unproductive capital accumulation on
employment demand, urban job creation, and city growth. Some of
the qualitative results are certainly predictable: accumulation in
either of the modern urban sectors fosters job creation; and an investment policy that favors manufacturing at agriculture's expense
fosters urbanization. But some of the results in Table 4.4 may come
as a surprise. In spite of the fact that the initial capital stock in KS far
exceeds that of M (Appendix Table B.7), aggregate urban employment creation is far less sensitive to accumulation in KS than it is to

M. The explanation lies with two influences. First, the modern service sector is more capital-cum-skill intensive than is manufacturing and second, in contrast with manufacturing, capacity expansion in KS is met with demand absorption problems and output price decline, no increase in labor's marginal *value* product, and thus no *direct* employment impact in KS itself. Yet, the accumulation in KS does have a modest *indirect* employment effect on manufacturing, since the latter is a user of modern (social overhead) services.

Most surprising is the finding that the accumulation of urban squatter housing has the most potent short-run impact on urban job creation and city growth. We were unprepared for the result. After all, these impact multipliers are limited to the very short run and thus exclude whatever employment effects might be associated with the formation of these stocks through investment. In the very short run, housing stock accumulation has no *direct* employment impact since, by assumption, housing services are produced with only land and structures, and no labor. The relatively large urban employment effects associated with the accumulation of squatter housing are therefore all *indirect:* house rents are lowered due to the augmented supply of dwelling space, relative cost of living in the cities declines, in-migration is fostered, nominal wages of the unskilled are lowered by the temporary labor glut, and employment expands throughout the city as a result, especially in manufacturing. In contrast with Coale and Hoover's (1958) emphasis on the tension between unproductive and productive capital accumulation on city growth, Table 4.4 suggests no conflict: of the six alternative modes of accumulation listed, accumulation of H_{US} yields the highest urban job creation and city growth effects. A major goal for the remainder of this book is to assess whether this conclusion holds for the longer run as well.

Land and Labor

Popular accounts of rapid Third World urbanization emphasize that high population growth lies at the core of the problem. Table 4.5 suggests that this is simply not the case, although the degree to which the popular account requires modification depends on which aspect of urbanization and city growth is of interest. Consider urbanization first.

W. Arthur Lewis (1977) has stressed just how capital-intensive the cities are. Our model conforms to that reality (Table 3.3) since urban activities are, on average, far less labor-intensive than rural activities. We also know from the Rybczynski Theorem in trade

TABLE 4.5

The Comparative Static Impact of Land Endowments and Population Growth on Third World City Growth (1970 Elasticities)

	Land Endowment		
Endogenous Variable	Agriculture R_A	Urban R_U	Population Pressure L
A. *City Growth Attributes*			
% Urban	−.03	.04	−.57
City Growth Rate	−.69	.88	6.38
In-migration Rate	−1.38	1.77	12.75
Squatter House Rents	−.10	−.18	1.00
COL Differential			
(Urban-Rural)	−.10	−.06	.07
B. *Employment Effects*			
L_M	−.11	.08	.33
L_{KS}	.02	.04	.59
L_{US}	0	.04	.50
L_A	.02	−.03	1.32
L_{RS}	.04	−.04	.93
C. *Wage Effects*			
Average Urban			
Unskilled Wage	.03	−.04	−.23
Rural Unskilled Wage	.15	.01	−.40

theory that an increased endowment of any given factor of production should favor the expansion of those sectors that use the now-more-abundant factor most intensively. Thus, whatever its source, population-induced labor force growth should foster the relative expansion of rural activities and suppress the percent of total population urban. Based on this analysis, population growth does *not* offer an explanation for increased rates of urbanization, and the negative impact multiplier in Table 4.5 (% Urban, −.57) confirms the point.

But what about in-migration and city growth? Table 4.5 reports a more conventional result since here the impact multipliers are positive and large. We shall have more to say below on the issue of whether these impact multipliers are sufficiently large to warrant support for the popular view that rapid population growth lies at the core of the Third World city growth problem.

Let us trace through the city growth impact of an exogenous rise in the economywide unskilled labor force, induced by some previous demographic event. The economic theory underlying migration decisions in our model applies to "movers" and "stayers" alike. Furthermore, subject to cost-of-living differentials and employment expectations, real earnings are everywhere equated among these homogenous unskilled workers. Thus, the spatial source of the economywide labor force growth does not matter—it may well be centered in rural areas where fertility rates are higher. How do labor markets absorb this demographically-induced event? As we suggested above, the rural labor-intensive sectors expand most dramatically, a result consistent with Rybczynski's Theorem. But the theorem is reinforced by short-run city growth constraints. That is, rising urban densities breed land scarcity, a relative rise in squatter house rents follows as a consequence, city cost of living rises relative to the countryside, and thus in short-run equilibrium the nominal wage falls by more in rural areas. The rise in the nominal wage gap tends to foster a greater labor absorption rate in rural areas, reinforcing the Rybczynski Theorem.

What about land endowments? Conventional wisdom argues that agricultural land scarcity has tended to push labor into cities. While an extension of the arable land stock would certainly increase the retention of labor in rural areas, thus retarding urbanization, the size of the impact reported in Table 4.5 is very small. Changes in the agricultural land endowment are not an important part of the city growth tale. Indeed, Table 4.5 suggests that the relative scarcity or abundance of *urban* land is a more important factor in city growth; although here too the impact multipliers are small.

Looking for the Sources of City Growth:
A Comparative Assessment

Table 4.6 summarizes our results thus far, with attention focused on three aspects of urban growth—the percentage urban, the city growth rate, and the in-migration rate—and nineteen exogenous variables. Urban growth appears to be most sensitive to nine of these variables: prices and productivity change in manufacturing and agriculture, labor force growth, capital accumulation in manufacturing, accumulation of rural and urban housing stocks for the poor, and skills. With few exceptions, these nine exogenous variables are the likely sources of Third World urbanization, past, present, and future. The exceptions, of course, would include those variables with far lower impact multipliers, but ones which we know to have undergone very large variation—fuel and raw material prices being two prime examples.

TABLE 4.6

What Drives Third World City Growth? A Comparative Assessment (1970 Elasticities)

Exogenous Variable	Endogenous Urbanization Variable		
	% Urban	City Growth Rate	In-migration Rate
A. *Land and Labor*			
R_A	−.03	−.69	−1.38
R_U	.04	.88	1.77
L	−.57	6.38	12.75
B. *Accumulation*			
K_M	.09	1.82	3.63
K_{KS}	.02	.40	.81
K_A	−.03	−.68	−1.35
H_{KS}	0	.07	.15
H_{US}	.39	7.92	15.83
H_{RS}	−.13	−2.75	−5.50
C. *Prices*			
P_Z	−.04	−.89	−1.77
P_M	.54	11.13	22.23
P_A	−.32	−6.51	−13.01
D. *Productivity Advance*			
A_M	.50	10.29	20.57
A_A	−.26	−5.33	−10.65
A_{KS}	.03	.68	1.36
A_{US}	−.01	−.26	−.52
A_{RS}	−.03	−.67	−1.33
E. *Other Forces*			
Skilled Labor Force: S	.23	6.96	13.90
Foreign Capital: F	0	−.03	−.06

3. DO INITIAL CONDITIONS MATTER? STRUCTURAL EVOLUTION OF CITY GROWTH FORCES

The sensitivity of city growth to external shocks is determined by two sets of influences—the parameters describing the economy's behavior, and its initial conditions. For example, a rise in the scarcity of fuel will have a greater negative impact on city growth the more fuel-intensive are city production activities relative to the countryside and the lower are the elasticities of substitution between energy and non-energy inputs. That is, production parameters matter. But initial conditions may matter as well, since if cities have evolved toward a product mix that favors energy-intensive processing (and away from personal services), a rise in fuel prices will have a more potent contractionary impact on city employment and city growth.

While parameters are fixed over time in our model, the economy's structure is not. As we have seen in Chapter 3 and as we shall see below in Chapter 6, our simulated RDC economy undergoes systematic change over time. In the three decades between 1970 and 2000, per capita income increases by about three-and-a-half times, the economy switches from a net export of primary products to a net export of manufactures, imported fuel consumption rises from 3.5 to 5 percent of GDP, the share of population in the cities surges from a little less than 40 percent to about 68 percent, the share of the labor force skilled increases from 11 to 24 percent, and manufacturing as a share of total urban employment rises from 41 to 49 percent. Clearly, this developing prototype economy has a different economic structure in the year 2000 than it does in 1970. It follows that city growth may well exhibit somewhat different sensitivity to external shocks in 2000 than in 1970.

If we compute short-run impact multipliers at various points in time, what do we expect to find? The answers aren't obvious, but one result seems likely: an agrarian nation with a relatively small urban enclave is *more* likely to be urban-responsive to urban-specific shocks than is the highly urbanized system, since the latter will find it more difficult to shift the structural adjustment onto the remainder of the economy. Apart from this generalization, theoretical inferences are impossible. Numerical analysis is the only way to sort out these general equilibrium complexities.

Table 4.7 reports short-run impact multipliers at four "census" dates from 1970 to 2000. To simplify, the table presents only three endogenous urbanization variables—total city population (or labor force), the city growth rate, and the rate of city in-migration. The short-run impact multipliers are calculated for each of the exogenous variables found to have been important influences on city growth in the previous section, variables that reflect the impact of the five key macro events on urban growth—unbalanced productivity advance, world market conditions and price policy, capital accumulation, demographic change, and land scarcity.

In general, three morals emerge from Table 4.7. First, the size of the short-run impact multipliers appear to be highest around 1980 for those exogenous variables that matter most. That is, city growth is currently more sensitive to exogenous shocks than it will be in the year 2000, or than it was in 1970. In most cases, the differences are

TABLE 4.7
Structural Evaluation of City Growth Forces: Short-run Impact
Multipliers, 1970–2000

| | | Endogenous Urbanization Variable | | |
		City Population	City Growth Rate	In-Migration Rate
A. Capital, Housing, and Skills				
K_M	1970	.09	1.82	3.63
	1980	.08	1.98	5.86
	1990	.05	1.06	2.71
	2000	.03	.71	2.61
K_{KS}	1970	.02	.40	.81
	1980	.01	.24	.71
	1990	.01	.11	.29
	2000	0	−.03	−.13
K_A	1970	−.03	−.68	−1.35
	1980	−.04	−1.05	−3.10
	1990	−.02	−.54	−1.37
	2000	−.02	−.47	−1.73
H_{US}	1970	.39	7.92	15.83
	1980	.31	7.95	23.50
	1990	.38	8.46	21.61
	2000	.36	9.37	34.27
H_{RS}	1970	−.13	−2.75	−5.50
	1980	−.19	−4.76	−14.08
	1990	−.13	−2.87	−7.33
	2000	−.11	−2.86	−10.46
S	1970	.34	6.96	13.90
	1980	.33	8.42	24.89
	1990	.33	7.48	19.10
	2000	.36	9.33	34.12
B. Prices				
P_Z	1970	−.04	−.89	−1.77
	1980	−.05	−1.37	−4.06
	1990	−.02	−.51	−1.31
	2000	−.01	−.36	−1.30
P_M	1970	.54	11.13	22.23
	1980	.52	13.20	39.05
	1990	.31	6.98	17.83
	2000	.20	5.24	19.15
P_A	1970	−.32	−6.51	−13.01
	1980	−.35	−8.84	−26.15
	1990	−.22	−4.94	−12.60
	2000	−.15	−3.96	−14.50

(continued)

TABLE 4.7 *(continued)*
Structural Evaluation of City Growth Forces: Short-run Impact
Multipliers, 1970–2000

		Endogenous Urbanization Variable		
Exogenous Variable		*City Population*	*City Growth Rate*	*In-Migration Rate*
C. *Productivity Advance*				
A_M	1970	.50	10.29	20.57
	1980	.49	12.33	36.47
	1990	.27	6.02	15.35
	2000	.16	4.20	15.36
A_A	1970	−.26	−5.33	−10.65
	1980	−.28	−7.13	−21.08
	1990	−.21	−4.67	−11.91
	2000	−.15	−4.06	−14.85
A_{KS}	1970	.03	.68	1.36
	1980	.02	.60	1.76
	1990	.01	.18	.46
	2000	0	−.03	−.12
D. *Land and Labor*				
R_A	1970	−.03	−.69	−1.38
	1980	−.05	−1.19	−3.51
	1990	−.03	−.62	−1.58
	2000	−.02	−.55	−2.00
R_U	1970	.04	.88	1.77
	1980	.02	.63	1.86
	1990	.04	.94	2.39
	2000	.04	1.02	3.75
L	1970	.31	6.38	12.75
	1980	.41	10.39	30.72
	1990	.37	8.26	21.09
	2000	.36	9.37	34.29

pronounced. For example, the elasticity of city in-migration rates with respect to the price of manufactures (P_M) is 39.05 in 1980, while 22.23 and 19.15 in 1970 and 2000, respectively. Second, the size of the short-run impact multipliers appear to drift downwards over time, especially when 1980 and 2000 are compared. For example, the elasticity of city in-migration rates with respect to productivity advance in manufacturing (A_M) declines from 36.47 in 1980 to 15.36 in the year 2000; the elasticity of city growth with respect to the nationwide unskilled labor force (L) declines from 10.39 in 1980 to 9.37 in the year 2000; and the elasticity of city population with respect to the price of manufactures (P_M) declines from .52 in 1980 to

.20 in the year 2000. Third, rarely does the sign of the impact change over time. Indeed, only in the case of capital accumulation and productivity advance in *KS* do the impact multipliers switch sign, explained here by the eventual dominance of declining price effects discussed in section 2.

In summary, initial conditions *do* matter. Urban performance of countries in intermediate stages of development appear to be more sensitive to exogenous shocks than are those at very low or very high levels of development. This statement holds, of course, only for *urban* attributes. While Table 4.7 does not display the evidence, aggregate economic indicators—like GDP per capita—are increasingly sensitive to those exogenous shocks to which urban attributes themselves are sensitive, the more advanced the economy. The explanation is not hard to find: advanced economies are more specialized in urban activities and thus urban-specific shocks have a larger impact on them.

4. The Importance of Investment Response

Current investment allocation can have an important comparative static impact on the RDC through the composition of aggregate demand. As Chapter 2 points out, there are several accumulation modes in our model. This implies that there are, in effect, several capital-goods producing sectors, not just one. Since each of these capital goods sectors has different employment intensities, and since all but one are nontradeable services, the *structure* of capital goods demands may matter to the net city growth impact. While none of these capital goods sectors is specialized solely in the production of investment goods, they can be assigned to investment type in the following way: the *KS* sector satisfies investment demand in skills training as well as new construction of urban luxury housing. The *M* sector satisfies (as do imports) investment demand for producer durables and other capital formation activities in the three capital-using sectors, *M*, *KS*, and *A*. The informal urban service sector satisfies new construction requirements in urban squatter settlements. The informal rural service sector satisfies new construction requirements for rural dwellings.

The important point to remember is that there are several capital goods sectors, and each possesses different factor-intensity and locational attributes. Low-rent housing construction is highly labor-intensive; urban luxury housing and social overhead construction is more capital- and skill-intensive; so too is the production of producer durables and skill formation. Thus, any economic/demographic event that serves to change investment allocation among these activities will also have an impact on the structure of aggregate demand and thus on urban employment and city growth.

Table 4.8 sorts out these influences. Short-run impact multipliers are reported there under two assumptions. Those in parentheses simply repeat the multipliers that were discussed in the previous sections, although these refer to 1980 rather than 1970 initial conditions. Here, the investment mix is assumed stable, motivated by the belief that in the very short-run entrepreneurs rely on the recent past before making adjustments to profit distortions induced by some exogenous shock. In this case, any change in a given investment component in the table is the result of changes in the total saving pools only, thus explaining the low (and identical) impact multipliers recorded in parentheses in the last five columns of Table 4.8. The second impact multiplier allows investment to respond to the shock-distorted change in the structure of profit rates. These, of course, are far higher in those last five columns, but the key motivation for this exercise is to isolate the impact of investment response on city growth, and for this we can focus on the first column of Table 4.8.

While there are a few interesting exceptions, Table 4.8 suggests that the comparative static impact of economic/demographic shocks on city growth are almost always higher when the investment response is considered. That is, the short-run impact of the shock is augmented by investment response. Some examples might be instructive.

Consider a rise in P_Z, the relative price of imported fuels and raw materials, which, for simplicity, we shall continue to abbreviate as "fuel price shocks." An exogenous increase in the price of imported fuels slows down city growth significantly, but the impact is even greater when short-run investment responses are included. As we have already seen in section 2, fuel-intensive city production activities contract in the face of rising fuel scarcity, even though fuel-saving occurs throughout the economy. As employment contracts in manufacturing and modern urban services—both relatively fuel-intensive urban activities—city jobs dry up. In addition, these employment effects are augmented as falling urban aggregate demand spills over into urban informal services. A key source of these spillover effects is low-rent housing. Since the derived demand for low-rent dwellings slacks off with the employment contraction in manufacturing and modern services, urban squatter settlement house rents decline, and new construction investment in the squatter settlements diminishes. This spillover causes output and employment in informal urban services to decline. Since the latter is highly

TABLE 4.8
Exploring Short-run Investment Response (1980 Elasticities: Short-run Investment Mix Variable vs. Short-run Investment Mix Fixed in Parentheses)

| | | | | Investment Component | | |
| | | | | | Housing Investment in: | |
Exogenous Variable	City Growth Rate	Plant and Equipment (I_M)	Training (I_{SKS})	Urban Squatter (I_{HUS})	Luxury (I_{HKS})	Rural (I_{HRS})
A. Capital, Housing, and Skills						
K_M	1.46 (1.98)	−.36 (.16)	3.65 (.16)	.33 (.16)	.08 (.16)	−1.07 (.16)
K_{KS}	.12 (.24)	−1.27 (.07)	9.93 (.07)	.15 (.07)	.88 (.07)	.40 (.07)
K_A	−1.83 (−1.05)	−.23 (.03)	1.45 (.03)	−.50 (.03)	.14 (.03)	.30 (.03)
H_{US}	6.22 (7.95)	.38 (.03)	−.40 (.03)	−2.69 (.03)	.09 (.03)	−1.34 (.03)
H_{KS}	−.45 (−.16)	0 (−.01)	0 (−.01)	−.13 (−.01)	−1.64 (−.01)	−.20 (−.01)
H_{RS}	−5.04 (−4.76)	.25 (−.03)	−.04 (−.03)	−1.09 (−.03)	.05 (−.03)	−3.57 (−.03)
S	10.27 (8.42)	1.47 (.18)	−10.71 (.18)	1.84 (.18)	.64 (.18)	.94 (.18)
B. Prices						
P_Z	−2.35 (−1.37)	−.14 (−.09)	−.12 (−.09)	−.70 (−.09)	−.01 (−.09)	.16 (−.09)
P_M	14.14 (13.20)	−.94 (.87)	13.94 (.87)	4.01 (.87)	.21 (.87)	−5.29 (.87)
P_A	−10.09 (−8.84)	.69 (.09)	−3.39 (.09)	−2.86 (.09)	.21 (.09)	3.67 (.09)
C. Productivity Advance						
A_M	14.95 (12.33)	.71 (.84)	2.40 (.84)	4.44 (.84)	−.20 (.84)	−4.83 (.84)
A_A	−7.86 (−7.13)	.85 (.34)	−3.07 (.34)	−1.76 (.34)	.25 (.34)	3.84 (.33)
A_{KS}	1.66 (.60)	.14 (.12)	.26 (.12)	.61 (.12)	.70 (.12)	−.05 (.12)
D. Land and Labor						
R_A	−1.08 (−1.19)	.10 (.04)	−.36 (.04)	−.23 (.04)	.03 (.04)	.48 (.04)
R_U	.18 (.63)	−.01 (0)	.04 (0)	−.29 (0)	−.03 (0)	−.32 (0)
L	11.10 (10.39)	.36 (.32)	−3.66 (.32)	2.22 (.32)	.22 (.32)	4.46 (.32)

labor-intensive, city growth is choked off by far more when these investment responses are considered. Thus, the short-run impact multiplier reported in Table 4.8 *with* investment responses allowed is -2.35, while in the *absence* of investment responses the multiplier is only -1.37. While there are other investment responses that serve to reinforce the negative impact of fuel scarcity on city growth, the decline in new housing construction in urban squatter settlements appears to be doing most of the work.

Consider another example, productivity advance in manufacturing, $\overset{*}{A}_M$. Section 2 has already shown how this influence augments city growth rates, but the impact is even greater when investment responses are allowed. The structure of investment shifts sharply in favor of those sectors supplying capital goods in urban areas. Since manufacturing uses skills intensively, the demand for skills rises, thus encouraging investment in training and a derived demand for urban-based *KS* activities. The demand for capital rises in manufacturing, a more capital-intensive activity than agriculture, and this direct effect is reinforced by the indirect demand for capital in *KS*, an important supplier of intermediate inputs to manufacturing. As a result, investment in plant and equipment rises, further augmenting the demand for manufacturing output, and adding to city job creation. In-migration to the cities also creates new housing demand in urban squatter settlements, generating housing construction there, and offering additional jobs for those employed in urban informal services who construct those dwellings. Thus, the short-run impact multiplier reported in Table 4.8 *with* investment responses allowed is 14.95 while in the *absence* of investment responses the multiplier is 12.33. Once again, it appears that new housing construction for low-income households is doing most of the work in these aggregate investment demand spillovers.

Not all of the sixteen comparative static results reported in Table 4.8 are as straightforward as the two examples discussed above, and some are not reinforcing at all. Three that are offsetting are the accumulation of capital in manufacturing (K_M), the accumulation of capital in modern services (K_{KS}), and the accumulation of housing units in urban squatter settlements (H_{US}). In each of these cases, capital accumulation, *ceteris paribus*, tends to lower returns on new investment, suppress investment, diminish demand in urban capital goods sectors, and thus offset the urban/employment creating effects from the initial capacity expansion due to accumulation. These cases seem to be the exception to the rule, however.

In summary, Table 4.8 suggests that derived investment demand is an important aspect of the city's total employment and population growth response to various economic/demographic shocks that have driven Third World city growth in the past and that will drive it in the future. New housing investment is typically a critical part of that investment response, suggesting that urban employment spillovers through new residential construction are at the heart of the matter. In any case, for the remainder of the book we shall focus on impact multipliers that include these investment responses. They are too important to ignore.

5. EXPLORING THE IMPACT OF TWO URBAN POLICIES

Urban Wage Policy

The "Todaro model" has enjoyed considerable popularity since it was introduced in 1969. While the Todaro model was discussed in Chapter 2, it might prove useful to reproduce a version of it again in Figure 4.1. The Corden–Findlay (1975) version of the Todaro model assumes capital immobility, constant output prices, and only two (explicit) sectors, agriculture (A) and manufacturing (M). By ignoring cost-of-living differentials, by assuming wage equalization through migration, and by ignoring overt unemployment, equilibrium is achieved at E, where the two labor demand curves intersect (AA' and MM'). Corden and Findlay then incorporate the widely-held belief that the wage rate in Third World modern

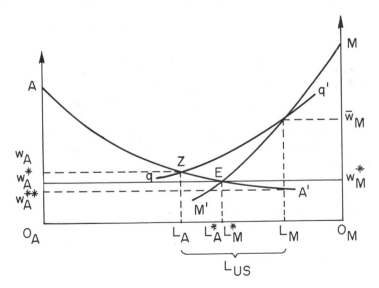

Figure 4.1 The Todaro–Corden–Findlay Model

sectors is pegged at artificially high levels, say at $\bar{w}_M$. Alternatively, one can view $\bar{w}_M$ as the result of a policy that attempts to raise the "wage gap" between the two sectors to $k = \bar{w}_M/w_A^{**}$, as we do in our model. If overt unemployment is assumed away, then all who fail to secure the favored jobs in M must accept the lower-paying jobs in A at w_A^{**}. In this situation, urban employment has been choked off by the wage policy, a conventional result which most labor economists will find appealing.

Rapid urban growth in the Third World has been accompanied by an impressive expansion in traditional or informal service sector (under)employment. Todaro explains this apparent conflict—in-migration in the face of urban underemployment—by developing a simple search model of spatial migration where employment expectations in the favored sector are central. Given the chance of employment at the favored pegged wage in M, at what rural wage would the potential migrant be indifferent between (under)employment in the traditional urban service sector and employment in agriculture? This is the essence of the qq' curve in Figure 4.1. Equilibrium in these two regional labor markets is given at Z, where the qq' curve intersects the AA' curve.

What does the Todaro–Corden–Findlay model tell us about the sources of city growth? Any urban wage policy that increases the pegged wage in the favored M sector, or widens the wage gap between the favored sector and alternative urban employment, will serve to *raise* the level of urbanization; that is, $O_A L_A^* > O_A L_A$ in Figure 4.1. This counterintuitive result follows from an empirical assumption that appears innocuous: since qq' can be shown to have an elasticity of unity, then the labor demand function in the favored sector (MM') must fall below qq' since the own-wage elasticity implied by MM' is surely less than 1. We have no objection to this elasticity characterization; in fact, it is an empirical attribute of our model as well.

In contrast with the Todaro–Corden–Findlay predictions, Table 4.9 shows that a rise in the wage gap, κ, serves to *lower* city population in our model (although the impact, $-.06$, is very small), to *lower* city in-migration rates, and to *lower* city growth rates. What accounts for the difference? Both models assume capital immobility in their comparative static analysis, both take the prices of *commodity* outputs as constant, and both assume that the expected wage dictates migration behavior (although our model allows for cost-of-living differentials while the Todaro–Corden–Findlay model does not).

TABLE 4.9

The Impact of Urban Wage Policy in Manufacturing and "Modern"
Services (1980 Elasticities)

Endogenous Variable	Rise in the Exogenous "Wage Gap": κ
A. *City Attributes*	
City Population	$-.06$
City Growth Rate	-1.73
In-migration Rate	-5.11
B. *Urban Unskilled Employment in:*	
Manufacturing (M)	$-.50$
Modern Services (KS)	$-.22$
Informal Services (US)	.44
C. *Urban Unskilled Wages*	
"Favored" Employment (w_{ML})	.21
Informal Sector Employment (w_{US})	$-.78$
Expected Urban Wage (w_U)	$-.14$

The source of the difference between the two models' predictions lies with their treatment of the urban informal service sector. For Todaro–Corden–Findlay, the informal service sector passively accepts all workers who wish to wait there for employment selection by the favored sector. Wages do not fall in response to this labor glut, since the informal sector wage is already implicitly zero. Nor are labor demand conditions in the traditional or informal service sector of any importance since any urban worker failing to secure employment in the M sector can always find a place in informal services at a fixed wage (zero). In short, labor absorption problems in the residual informal service sector are assumed away in the Todaro–Corden–Findlay model. We reject this view. Instead, we have adopted the position that traditional or informal service employment is determined by supply and demand forces just as in any other labor market that escapes formal government and union restrictions.

Table 4.9 should now make good sense. The urban wage policy is implemented as an increase in the wage gap, κ, between favored sector employment, w_{ML}, and informal sector employment, w_{US}. Since the experiment in Table 4.9 entails raising the gap by 1 percent, it is hardly surprising that the difference between the impacts on w_{ML} and w_{US} should sum to one [$.21 - (-).78 \cong 1$]. What *is* surprising, however, is the size of the decline in informal sector wage rates. Apparently, the labor absorption problem there is serious. The model thus relates the following narrative: a policy-induced rise in the wage gap favoring workers in the modern M and KS sectors chokes off employment there, these displaced workers glut the informal sector labor market, wages fall there, employment in the informal service sector rises as a consequence, but the expected urban wage facing potential migrants falls (the impact multiplier being $-.14$). In-migration declines, city growth rates fall, and the city population diminishes.

In summary, our model reveals that a policy that pegs formal sector wages above market levels will serve to choke off city growth; the opposite is true of the Todaro–Corden–Findlay model. The difference is not explained by the greater complexity of our general equilibrium model. Rather, the difference is explained by alternative interpretations of the informal service sector—its wage flexibility and absorptive capacity. Todaro's model was motivated by the apparent inconsistency between rising (under)employment in informal urban services and continued in-migration to the city. His explanation is based on the assumption of expectations of favored job-selection—the higher the pegged wage in the favored modern sector, the greater the in-migration by workers who hope to be selected from the informal sector queue. Informal service sector employment expands as a result. Our model offers a different, and more conventional, explanation. The higher pegged wage in the favored sectors displaces workers, swelling the ranks of those employed in informal urban services, and depressing wages there and elsewhere in the economy as a consequence.

Government Squatter Settlement Policy

Consider a misanthropic (and inefficient) government policy of eviction and razing in urban squatter settlements (represented by a decline in H_{US}), an inequitable policy motivated by the belief that city growth will be forestalled. The belief is certainly confirmed by the short-run impact multipliers reported in Table 4.10. The first effect of the policy, of course, is to create housing scarcity among the poor and thus raise (shadow) rents (the impact multiplier being 1.79). Housing scarcities serve to raise the urban/rural cost-of-living differential (.54), making the city less attractive to potential in-migrants. The resulting labor scarcity tends to inflate *nominal* wages for the city's unskilled (.37), but less than the cost-of-living increase so that real wages fall. Note that the rise in nominal wages serves to en-

TABLE 4.10

The Impact of a Government Squatter Settlement Eviction Policy
(*1980 Elasticities*)

Endogenous Variable	Settlement Housing Stock: H_{US}
A. *City Attributes*	
City Population	$-.25$
City Growth Rate	-6.22
In-migration Rate	-18.41
B. *Rents, Cost-of-Living, and Nominal Wage*	
Squatter Settlement House Rent, P_{HUS}	$+1.79$
COL Differential, Urban-Rural	$+.54$
Unskilled Urban Wage, w_{ML}	$+.37$
C. *Offsetting Investment Response*	
Squatter Settlement Construction Investment, I_{HUS}	$+2.69$
Informal Sector Output, Q_{US}	$+.25$
D. *Urban Unskilled Employment in:*	
Manufacturing, L_M	$-.84$
Modern Services, L_{KS}	$-.36$
Informal Services, L_{US}	$+.26$

courage firms in M and KS to curtail employment, but that employment in the informal service sector rises. The explanation for the puzzling service sector response is simple enough; housing scarcity fosters new low-rent housing construction, and this spillover is sufficient to actually raise output and employment in the informal service sector. The offset is not enough to deter achievement of the desired government intent: the city in-migration rate declines, the city growth rate falls off, and the city population is reduced.

Similar results are forthcoming from a policy of increased property taxation, especially if it falls heavily on residential housing in squatter settlements. If property taxation in that form seems foreign to current practices in the Third World, note the following: the stream of benefits to urban squatter settlements includes water supply, paved roads, police protection, and health clinics, while property taxes are typically non-existent. This amounts to a negative tax on (a positive transfer to) urban squatter settlements. A policy that lowers the benefit stream per low-income urban household serves to raise the effective tax.

6. AN OVERVIEW

We now have a clearer understanding of how our model responds in the short-run to various economic/demographic shocks, exogenous influences thought to have been important sources of Third World city growth since the early 1960s. The next step is to combine these short-run impact multipliers with measures of the actual historic behavior of these key exogenous influences from 1960 to 1980. Chapter 5 will do just that, isolating the sources of Third World urbanization and city growth, past and present.

CHAPTER FIVE

Past Sources of Third World City Growth

1. THE AGENDA

What explains rapid Third World city growth over the past two decades? What accounts for the modest city growth slowdown more recently? Were exogenous conditions unusually favorable for rapid city growth in the 1960s? Did these conditions dramatically reverse in the 1970s? Or can the city growth slowdown be explained by forces endogenous to Third World economies themselves?

There is no shortage of speculation on these questions. Almost all observers have stressed population pressure as *the* key source of unusually rapid city growth in the Third World since 1960. Furthermore, there seems to be agreement that cheap energy and relatively abundant raw material supply accounts for rapid city growth prior to OPEC, and that a reversal of those conditions explains the slowdown since. Some observers appear to suggest that arable land shortages have generated a powerful rural push, accounting for heavy rural emigration to Third World cities, at least by nineteenth-century European standards. Some analysts appeal to the enormous capital requirements of city building and foreign capital abundance as helping to account for unusually rapid city growth in the 1960s, while increasing foreign capital scarcity helps account for city growth slowdown more recently. And surely all observers believe that domestic policy has imparted an urban bias (Lipton, 1976), with import substitution policies in the 1960s having been reinforced by trade liberalization in the industrialized countries. While popular accounts are less explicit on the issue, unbalanced productivity advance in urban-based industry would also appear prominently on a list of the likely key forces driving rapid city growth in the Third World. And in *Patterns of Urban and Rural Population Growth* (UN, 1980, p. 30) we are told that the "basic engine of urbanization" has always been the combination of rising per capita income and income-inelastic demands for agricultural products.

Speculation is one thing, explicit hypothesis testing another. This chapter puts quantitative flesh on these speculations. Using our model of Third World city growth, we are equipped to sort out the quantitative importance of each of these competing forces. The analysis applies the historians' counterfactual (Fogel, 1964, 1967; Kelley and Williamson, 1974; Williamson, 1974). That is, we shall ask how Third World cities would have grown under alternative conditions. Section 2 will identify the changes in exogenous conditions in the pre- and post-OPEC "epochs" which might account for the city growth slowdown after 1973–1974. Sections 3 and 4 will then explore the contribution of those changing exogenous conditions to slowdown by asking what would have happened in their absence. Section 5 will attempt to uncover those conditions most important in producing the unusually rapid city growth up to the early-mid 1970s. This exercise turns out to be extremely relevant in guiding our expectations about the future.

2. Changes in the Growth Environment beyond OPEC

The changing growth environment in the aftermath of the OPEC price shock has been significant. Changes have been manifested mainly in relative prices, captured in our model by exogenous trends in P_A, P_M, and P_Z. The magnitude of these epochal price shocks is summarized in Table 5.1. Relative to primary exports from developing countries, the price of quality-adjusted manufactured goods declined at an annual rate of 0.7 percent up to 1973. The rate of decline accelerated thereafter, averaging 1.6 percent per annum up to 1979. In contrast, the relative price of imported raw materials (including fuels) rose by 5.2 percent per annum after 1973, while the same relative price exhibited long-run stability prior to 1973. As Appendix C points out, these price trends are conditional on the

TABLE 5.1

The Growth Environment, Pre-OPEC vs. Post-OPEC: Dynamic Parameters Assumed in the RDC Simulations

Exogenous Variable	Per Annum Growth	
(Dynamic Parameter)	*1960–1973*	*1973–1979*
Imported Raw Materials Price: P_Z	0%	5.2%
M-Goods Price: P_M	−0.7	−1.6
Agricultural Land Stock: R_A	1.0	0.5
Urban Land Stock: R_U	1.0	1.0
Total Labor Force: $L + S$	2.54	2.68

Source: Appendix C, section C.2

base periods selected, on averaging devices applied, and on the underlying price series themselves. But there can be little doubt about the epochal character of the post-OPEC price trends which the Third World faced in the 1970s.

Table 5.1 also summarizes one demographic attribute of the two epochs: the higher rate of labor force growth after 1973, although the acceleration was quite modest. Finally, the table documents our assumed rates of agricultural land stock growth, a decline that serves to capture the apparent disappearance of extramarginal land augmentation possibilities during the 1970s.

Clearly there were other—perhaps less important—non-price changes in the economic/demographic environment surrounding our developing RDC group after 1973. For that matter, not all of the epochal price trends were OPEC-related. Nonetheless, in what follows we shall invoke poetic license and label these two epochs as "pre-OPEC" and "post-OPEC."

3. City Growth Slowdown after OPEC

As every analyst knows, the world economy is undergoing painful adjustment to the price shocks associated with short-run OPEC policy and long-run raw material/fuel scarcities. Since the world economy was still digesting the impact of these disequilibrating shocks as late as 1979, it seems clear that a long-run general equilibrium model cannot be expected to account adequately for the short-run trends that Third World countries have undergone since 1973. Thus, we have made no effort to perform the same validation tests for the post-OPEC period that we performed on the pre-OPEC period in Chapter 3. However, we intend to illustrate just how sensitive our model is to such epochal shocks. These brief illustrations will serve to motivate much of the remainder of the book.

Tables 5.2 and 5.3 summarize the model's predictions, the first documenting overall growth performance, and the second focusing on urban growth. The tables offer three predictions: 1) a 1960–1973 prediction using the actual pre-OPEC economic/demographic environment, a model prediction that has already been compared with history in Chapter 3; 2) a 1973–1979 prediction using the actual post-OPEC economic/demographic environment discussed in section 4 and documented in Table 5.1; and 3) a counterfactual post-OPEC prediction. The third of these predictions simply allows the pre-OPEC environmental conditions to continue beyond 1973. The counterfactual experiment makes it possible to assess what the

TABLE 5.2
Predicted Growth Performance: Pre-OPEC vs. Post-OPEC

Variable	Per Annum Growth		
	1960–1973 Actual Pre-OPEC Environment	*1973–1979 Actual Post-OPEC Environment*	*1973–1979 Counterfactual Pre-OPEC Environment*
GDP (constant price)	6.26%	6.48%	7.12%
GDP (constant price) per Worker	3.72	3.80	4.58
"Productive" Capital Stock: K	5.50	5.66	6.74
Housing Stock: H	5.07	5.01	6.10
Skilled Labor Force: S	4.06	5.16	5.49
Unskilled Labor Force: L	2.39	2.36	2.14
Rural Labor Force:			
$(L_A + L_{RS}) = L_R$	1.20	1.10	−0.55
Urban Labor Force:			
$(L + S) − (L_A + L_{RS}) = L_U$	4.86	4.65	6.04
"Productive" Capital			
per Worker: $K/L + S$	2.96	2.98	4.20
Housing Stock			
per Worker: $H/L + S$	2.53	2.33	3.56
Skilled Labor			
per Worker: $S/L + S$	1.52	2.48	2.95
Urban Land Stock			
per Urban Worker: R_U/L_U	−3.86	−3.65	−5.04
Farmland Stock			
per Rural Worker: R_A/L_R	−0.20	−0.60	1.55
Output (constant price) in:			
Agriculture	4.23	4.35	2.98
Manufacturing and Mining	9.36	8.25	11.30
Modern Services	6.87	7.61	7.84
All Informal Services	5.14	4.60	5.17
Housing Services	3.90	4.86	5.01

NOTE: The 1973–1979 "counterfactual" results assume the 1960–1973 dynamic parameters to prevail after 1973. See Table 5.1

growth and urbanization experience would have been like in the absence of the post-OPEC epochal shocks.

The results reported in Table 5.2 are informative indeed. Any analyst examining the pre-1973 and post-1973 record predicted by the model might have concluded that the OPEC price shocks mattered little to aggregate growth performance in the late 1970s. GDP per worker growth did not fall off, and aggregate GDP growth actually rose from 6.26 to 6.48 percent per annum between 1960–1973 and 1973–1979. Furthermore, the rate of capital accumulation rose modestly from 5.50 to 5.66 percent per annum, and the skilled labor force growth rate climbed from 4.06 to 5.16 percent per annum over the same period.

The key issue, however, is what would have happened in the absence of those shocks. At an aggregate level, the OPEC impact appears primarily as a retardation in trend acceleration rates, not as a decline in the rates themselves. Thus, while the rate of accumulation of productive capital rose from 5.50 to 5.66 percent per annum, according to the model it would have risen to 6.74 percent per annum had the RDC economies not been beset by the epochal changes in economic/demographic conditions after 1973. Similar results are forthcoming for housing stock accumulation, GDP growth, and skills accumulation. For example, according to the model housing stocks would have accumulated at the per annum rate of 6.10 percent after 1973, rather than at the actual rate of 5.01 percent, which, as it turns out, was slightly lower than the pre-OPEC rate.

The most visible impact of the OPEC watershed, however, appears at the sectoral rather than at the aggregate level. While agricultural output growth (in constant prices) was higher in the post-1973 epoch than in the pre-1973 epoch, it would have been far lower under the counterfactual conditions. Moreover, while manufacturing and mining combined underwent retardation in output growth from 9.36 to 8.25 percent per annum, the post-1973 growth would have been considerably higher under the counterfactual conditions. And while informal service sector output growth collapsed from 5.14 to 4.60 percent per annum, it would have remained stable under the counterfactual conditions. In short, sectoral output growth exhibits more responsive behavior to the OPEC watershed, but with agriculture more heavily favored and manufacturing most heavily penalized.

If the post-1973 shocks had their largest impact at the sectoral level, then we should expect to find urbanization and city growth responsive as well. City growth slowdown is one such manifestation of post-1973 adjustment as documented in the IBRD *World Tables, 1980* (p. 437); the rate of urban population growth among all developing countries fell from 4.4 to 4.3 percent per annum between 1960–1970 and 1970–77. The model predicts a similar city growth retardation in the RDC group: Table 5.3 documents a predicted city growth slowdown from 4.86 to 4.65 percent per annum. But note

TABLE 5.3
Urban Adjustments to Post-OPEC: Model's Predictions

A. Post-OPEC Predictions: Annual, 1973–1979

	Actual Post-OPEC Environment				Counterfactual Pre-OPEC Environment			
Year	% Urban	City Growth	Net Rural Out-Migration Rate	Net Urban In-Migration Rate	% Urban	City Growth	Net Rural Out-Migration Rate	Net Urban In-Migration Rate
1973	43.45	5.72	2.24	3.07	43.45	5.72	2.24	3.07
1974	44.45	5.10	1.78	2.32	44.78	5.75	2.38	3.10
1975	45.22	4.48	1.38	1.72	46.25	5.92	2.65	3.27
1976	46.26	5.03	1.86	2.26	47.80	6.03	2.90	3.38
1977	47.05	4.52	1.51	1.76	49.46	6.14	3.18	3.47
1978	47.85	4.47	1.52	1.71	51.22	6.23	3.49	3.56
1979	48.58	4.29	1.40	1.53	53.03	6.16	3.67	3.49

B. *Period Averages, Pre-OPEC vs. Post-OPEC*

Variable	1960–1973 Actual Pre-OPEC Environment	1973–1979 Actual Post-OPEC Environment	1973–1979 Counterfactual Pre-OPEC Environment
City Growth, per Annum	4.86%	4.65%	6.04%
Total Increase in Share Urban	10.85	5.13	9.58
Increase in Share Urban, % Per Annum	0.83	0.86	1.60
Net In-Migration Share of Urban Population Increase	47.72	41.34	57.50
Net In-Migration Rate	2.35	1.83	3.30
Net Out-Migration Rate	1.37	1.60	3.13

NOTE: The 1973–1979 "counterfactual" results assume the 1960–1973 dynamic parameters to prevail after 1973. The net in-migration rate is calculated as the ratio of total immigrants per annum to the average urban population in all previous years. The net out-migration rate is calculated as the ratio of total emigrants (= immigrants) per annum to the average rural population in all previous years.

that the rate of city growth would have *surged* in the absence of those post-OPEC conditions. Under the counterfactual conditions, the rate of city growth would have been 6.04 rather than 4.65 percent per annum. Similarly, while the predicted city in-migration rate actually fell from 2.35 to 1.83 percent, it would have risen to 3.30 in the counterfactual environment. The same conclusions hold for the urban population share and rural out-migration rates.

It seems quite clear that exogenous economic/demographic conditions had a powerful impact on the rate of Third World urbanization during the 1970s. The city growth slowdown appears to have had little to do with the endogenous forces driving development. Rather, the slowdown was induced by a combination of unfavorable exogenous conditions that followed after the 1973–1974 watershed.

4. ISOLATING THE SOURCES OF CITY GROWTH SLOWDOWN

What were the most important forces accounting for the post-1973 city growth slowdown? Table 5.4 reports five counterfactual simulations which help supply some answers. Each of these counterfactuals generates a history across the mid-late 1970s, but the table presents only one of the model's predictions—rates of city growth. Each of these five counterfactuals should be compared with the "actual" 1973–1979 performance reproduced in the first column, which, along with column (2), has already been reported in Table 5.3. For example, the "fuel abundance" counterfactual in column (3) maintains all of the exogenous conditions underlying the "actual" in column (1) *except* fuel price behavior: while the OPEC-augmented "actual" $\overset{*}{P}_Z$ was 5.2 percent per annum between 1973 and 1979, the counterfactual assumes $\overset{*}{P}_Z = 0$, as was indeed the case up to 1973.

What were the main forces responsible for the Third World urban slowdown? It certainly had nothing to do with retarding agricultural land expansion or labor force growth, since these forces were pushing in the opposite direction. Rather, it appears that prices and world market conditions were doing all the work. Furthermore—and in spite of all the attention that it has received—rising fuel scarcity was nowhere near as important a source of city growth slowdown as was the accelerated decline in the relative price of manufactures (lower $\overset{*}{P}_M$). This finding supports the view that any future trend toward protectionism in the industrialized countries will play a very important role in shaping Third World city growth over the next two decades. The same might be said, of course, for the mix of internal policies that may alter the relative price of manufactures in the future.

TABLE 5.4

Sources of a City Growth Slow Down? Some Counterfactuals Applied to 1973–1979

			OPEC Watershed Counterfactuals, 1973–1979			
			Fuel Abundance	World Markets	Land Expansion	Population Pressure
	"Actual" 1973–1979	Total Pre-OPEC Environment	Pre-OPEC $\dot{P}_Z = 0$ Only	Pre-OPEC $\dot{P}_M$ Only	Pre-OPEC $\dot{R}_A$ Only	Pre-OPEC $\overline{(L+S)}$ Only
Year	(1)	(2)	(3)	(4)	(5)	(6)
1973	5.72	5.72	5.72	5.72	5.72	5.72
1974	5.10	5.75	5.35	5.59	5.09	5.06
1975	4.48	5.92	4.91	5.67	4.51	4.50
1976	5.03	6.03	5.28	5.90	4.95	4.96
1977	4.52	6.14	5.13	5.91	4.47	4.48
1978	4.47	6.23	5.05	5.96	4.36	4.36
1979	4.29	6.16	4.83	5.79	4.27	4.28
Average	4.65	6.04	5.09	5.80	4.61	4.60

NOTE: Each entry refers to the per annum rate of city growth, and the bottom row supplies the average growth rate for the period 1973–1979 as a whole. The six cases make the following assumptions about six key exogenous variables (see Table 5.1 and text), where "*" denotes growth rates:

Variable	1	2	3	4	5	6
$\dot{P}_Z$, Fuel and Raw Material Prices	5.2%	0	0	5.2%	5.2%	5.2%
$\dot{P}_M$, Domestic Price of Manufactures	−1.6	−0.7%	−1.6	−0.7	−1.6	−1.6
$\dot{R}_A$, Agricultural Land Stock	0.5	1.0	0.5	0.5	0.5	0.5
$\overline{(L+S)}$, Population (or Labor Force)	2.48	2.54	2.68	2.68	1.0	2.54
$\dot{F}$, Foreign Capital Inflow	$\longleftarrow$ $\dot{F}$ such that $F/GDP = 3\%$ $\longrightarrow$					
TFPG, Productivity Growth (Economywide)	1.8	1.8	1.8	1.8	1.8	1.8

5. How Favorable Were Pre-OPEC Conditions to City Growth?

The model replicates the Third World city growth slowdown across the mid-late 1970s. It also appears that the slowdown would not have taken place if the more favorable exogenous conditions of the 1960–1973 epoch continued through the 1970s; indeed, the pace of city growth would have quickened. Finally, the model suggests that city growth slowdown is explained largely by sharp changes in the relative price of tradeables and imported intermediate inputs.

If post-1973 economic/demographic conditions generated a city growth slowdown, can it also be argued that pre-1973 conditions were unusually favorable for rapid Third World city growth? The answers are important since they will be helpful in guiding any predictions about the future. We attack the problem by posing a wide variety of demographic, price, and technological counterfactuals which are more likely to prevail in the future or were experienced by countries whose past city growth performance is often used to gauge whether the present Third World has "over-urbanized."

Table 5.5 reports ten counterfactuals that have been motivated by allegations in the literature. Two of these are demographic (2 and 3); five are technological (6 through 10); one deals with arable land (11); one deals with foreign capital conditions (4); and one deals with the state of foreign markets (5). To make the comparisons as sharp as possible, Table 5.5 is restricted to predictions about city growth performance. Whatever insights the model offers there can be readily extended to other aspects of urban experience as well.

Can the high rates of population growth in the Third World account for rapid city growth there? Certainly the conventional literature would suggest so: a World Bank team recently told us that "the increase in population growth of the twentieth century is the single most important factor distinguishing present and past urbanization" (Beier et al., 1976, p. 365); Samuel Preston (1979, p. 204) has told us that "the rate of population growth in the nation in which a city is located has a powerful effect on a city's growth rate"; and similar comments can be found sprinkled elsewhere in the literature. The argument certainly seems plausible on the face of it. After all,

While Europe was urbanizing, national population growth rates were typically around 0.5 percent a year. In contrast, the rates for developing countries today are usually around 2.5 and 3.0 percent a year. These much higher growth rates have resulted in both larger absolute population movements to the cities and larger natural population increase within the cities. [Beier, 1976, p. 4]

Table 5.5 explores the contribution of Third World population explosions to the "unusually" rapid city growth up to 1973 in two ways. First, it challenges the view that it *was* "unusual," by exploring the impact on city growth had the Third World been burdened with the rate of population growth that prevailed in nineteenth-century America. Between 1820 and 1900, the rate of population growth in America was 2.61 percent per annum. At the nineteenth-century American rate, but holding all other pre-OPEC conditions constant, the counterfactual rate of city growth would have been 4.87 percent per annum. Not only is this counterfactual rate almost exactly what the RDC group recorded, but it is almost exactly the rate that America herself recorded across the nineteenth century, 4.83 percent per annum! (US Bureau of the Census, 1975, pp. 11–12.) Compared with America, there is nothing unusual about Third World city growth. But what about nineteenth-century Europe? Column (2) in Table 5.5 reports a counterfactual that may be even more relevant. It asks: How fast would Third World city growth have been had the far lower population growth in the industrialized countries across the 1960s prevailed? The demographic counterfactual being posed is dramatic, to be sure: according to the IBRD *World Tables, 1980* (p. 437) the rate among industrialized countries was 0.9 percent per annum, in contrast with the RDC rate of 2.54 percent per annum. This makes the counterfactual result reported in Table 5.5 all the more striking: under these far "less favorable" demographic conditions, the rate of city growth would have been reduced to 4.64 percent per annum, hardly a great diminution from the "actual" 1960–1973 rate of 4.86 percent.

We emerge from these demographic counterfactuals with two morals. First, there was nothing "unusual" about Third World city growth prior to OPEC, at least compared with nineteenth-century America. Second, a far lower rate of population growth would have mattered little to Third World urban experience. It appears that the role of population pressure has been greatly overdrawn as a source of Third World city growth in the recent past.

The Third World was, of course, a heavy recipient of foreign capital during the 1960s and 1970s, reaching on average about 3 percent of GDP in our RDC group. How would city growth have been affected under more austere financial transfer conditions and less philanthropic motives? Suppose there had been *no* net capital

TABLE 5.5

City Growth: Some Alternative Counterfactuals Applied to 1960—1973

		Other More Distant Counterfactuals			
		Demographic		Foreign	Stable
				Capital	World
		No Population	19th C. U.S.	Austerity	Market.
	"Actual"	Pressure Developed	Population	$F = 0$	$\dot{P}_M = 0$
	1960 1973	Countries Rate	Growth Rate		
Year	(1)	(2)	(3)	(4)	(5)
1961	5.56	4.99	5.59	5.73	6.26
1962	4.87	4.65	4.84	6.46	6.17
1963	3.85	3.82	3.88	3.13	4.91
1964	4.13	4.01	4.06	3.71	5.21
1965	4.11	4.14	4.18	3.92	5.12
1966	4.60	4.48	4.55	4.50	5.50
1967	4.64	4.57	4.67	4.58	5.53
1968	4.90	4.72	4.91	4.81	5.83
1969	4.94	4.76	4.95	4.82	5.84
1970	5.15	4.87	5.16	5.00	6.08
1971	5.22	4.93	5.23	5.06	6.17
1972	5.56	5.17	5.61	5.49	6.51
1973	5.72	5.20	5.66	5.55	6.58
Average	4.86	4.64	4.87	4.82	5.82

NOTE: Each entry refers to the per annum rate of city growth, and the bottom row supplies average growth rate for the period 1960–1973 as a whole. The eleven cases make the follow assumptions about eight key exogenous variables (see Table 5.1 and text), where "*" den growth rates:

Variable	1	2	3	4
$\dot{P}_Z$, Fuel and Raw Material Prices	0	0	0	0
$\dot{P}_M$, Domestic Price of Manufactures	−0.7%	−0.7%	−0.7%	−0.7%
$\dot{R}_A$, Agricultural Land Stock	1.0	1.0	1.0	1.0
$\overline{(L + S)}$, Population (or Labor Force)	2.54	0.9	2.61	2.54
$\dot{F}$, Foreign Capital Inflow	←$\dot{F}$ such that F/GDP = 3%→			F = 0
TFPG, Productivity Growth (Economywide)	1.8	1.8	1.8	1.8
$\dot{T}_A/\dot{T}_M$, Unbalanced TFPG (A relative to M)	0.8	0.8	0.8	0.8
$\dot{T}_{KS}/\dot{T}_M$, Unbalanced TFPG (KS relative to M)	0.5	0.5	0.5	0.5

Other More Distant Counterfactuals

		Technological			
chnological lowdown: FPG Falls rom 1.8 to 1% p.a.	Technological Speedup: TFPG Rises from 1.8 to 3% p.a.	Balanced TFP Growth	More Unbalanced TFP Growth	Very Unbalanced TFP Growth	Fixed Land Endowment $\overset{*}{R}_A = 0$
(6)	(7)	(8)	(9)	(10)	(11)
5.01	6.40	5.04	6.21	7.70	5.59
4.28	5.57	4.30	5.78	7.42	4.97
3.62	4.00	3.37	4.85	6.11	4.00
3.72	4.40	3.52	5.10	6.01	4.21
3.69	4.64	3.65	5.18	5.95	4.31
3.92	5.31	3.99	5.51	6.12	4.69
3.97	5.51	4.05	5.63	6.30	4.80
4.07	5.94	4.34	5.86	6.55	5.00
4.08	6.04	4.39	5.98	6.78	5.09
4.17	6.40	4.60	6.18	7.00	5.26
4.22	6.61	4.67	6.35	7.20	5.36
4.47	7.07	5.13	6.68	7.52	5.69
4.53	7.71	5.18	6.82	7.67	5.79
4.14	5.77	4.32	5.86	6.79	4.98

6	7	8	9	10	11
0	0	0	0	0	0
−0.7%	−0.7%	−0.7%	−0.7%	−0.7%	−0.7%
1.0	1.0	1.0	1.0	1.0	$\boxed{0}$
2.54	2.54	2.54	2.54	2.54	2.54
		$\longleftarrow \dot{F}$ such that $F/\text{GDP} = 3\%$ $\longrightarrow$			
$\boxed{1.0}$	$\boxed{3.0}$	1.8	1.8	1.8	1.8
0.8	0.8	$\boxed{1.0}$	$\boxed{0.5}$	$\boxed{0.25}$	0.8
0.5	0.5	$\boxed{1.0}$	$\boxed{0.5}$	$\boxed{0.25}$	0.5

transfers to the Third World between 1960 and 1973? This counterfactual regime of "foreign capital austerity" is reported in column (4). The short-run impact would have been to foster urbanization, apparently because domestic manufactures would have had to expand to replace shrinking imports and because urban-based nontradeable services would have been favored. But the long-run forces would have dominated over the period as whole, the saving constraint would have been affected, and declining rates of capital formation would have caused a contraction in city growth. This result may seem conventional at first sight, but note the magnitudes reported in Table 5.5. In spite of W. Arthur Lewis's emphasis (Lewis, 1977) on the capital-intensity of the cities, and in spite of the belief that urban growth tends to breed foreign capital dependence, foreign capital austerity would not have altered city growth performance in the Third World by much.

It is commonly believed that agricultural land scarcity has played an important role in pushing labor into Third World cities. The "fixed land endowment" counterfactual reported in column (11) suggests the contrary. This counterfactual poses the following question: By how much would city growth have been raised had the arable land stock not grown at all between 1960 and 1973? Push effects would have been augmented, to be sure: the counterfactual city growth rate is 4.98 percent per annum, compared with the "actual" rate of 4.86 percent. But the difference is much too small to suggest that arable land stock growth mattered much to city growth experience in the past.

Thus far we have rejected population pressure, foreign capital conditions, and arable land stock growth as important ingredients of recent Third World city growth. None of these seems to have been a key driving force, and they certainly do not add up to "unusually favorable" city growth conditions. The more important influences appear to have been world markets and technological change.

Table 5.4 has already confirmed that imported fuel and raw material abundance helps explain the rapid city growth in the Third World up to the OPEC watershed and the slowdown thereafter. Similarly, Table 5.4 also confirmed that world market conditions for manufactures were also highly favorable forces contributing to high rates of city growth in the pre-OPEC period, the reversal of those conditions accounting for much of the slowdown thereafter. Indeed, Table 5.4 suggests that world market conditions for manufactures were a more important ingredient of rapid city growth up to 1973 than was the relative abundance of fuel and raw materials.

Table 5.5 explores this issue further. Column (4) poses the following counterfactual: By how much would Third World city growth have been raised had the relative price of manufactures remained stable between 1960 and 1973, rather than undergoing the 0.7 percent per annum decline that in fact characterized the period? The model suggests that the rate of city growth would have been far higher than the "unusually rapid" rate actually achieved, 5.82 rather than 4.86 percent per annum. Compared with the post-OPEC period, world market conditions *were* very favorable to Third World city growth in the 1960s and early 1970s. They would have been even more favorable under stable world market conditions. Once again, these findings reinforce the view that protectionist or liberalization trends over the next two decades, especially in the industrialized nations, will play a very important role in dictating the speed of urbanization and city growth in the Third World.

The final set of counterfactuals in Table 5.5 deals with the rate and character of technological change. Two of these counterfactuals deal with the aggregate rate of total-factor productivity growth (TFPG). The counterfactuals maintain the relative rates of unbalanced TFPG across sectors, while changing only the aggregate rate. Column (6) reports the impact on city growth stemming from an economywide productivity slowdown from the measured rate of 1.8 percent per annum assumed in the model's "actual" predictions, to a counterfactual rate of 1 percent per annum. Column (7) considers the opposite case, a technological speedup from 1.8 to 3 percent per annum. This range—from 1 to 3 percent per annum—captures the performance of eight out of thirteen Asian and Latin American countries for which we have documentation (Appendix C, Tables C.2 and C.4), so the counterfactuals are certainly relevant alternatives. The predicted rates of city growth are very responsive to these alternatives, suggesting that rapid rates of city growth in the Third World are in large measure technologically determined. The counterfactual experiments also suggest that any future slowdown in TFPG performance in the Third World will have a potent impact on city growth performance.

The remaining three technological counterfactuals focus on the character rather than the rate of TFPG. These experiments maintain the "actual" rate of aggregate TFPG, 1.8 percent per annum, while changing sectoral unbalancedness. For example, column (8) explores the counterfactual impact of balanced TFPG, where the sectoral rates are the same in A, M, and KS. Column (9), in contrast, augments the unbalancedness by increasing the extent to which agriculture lags behind: that is, agriculture's rate is taken as half that of manufacturing, rather than 80 percent of manufacturing as was in fact the case up to 1973. Column (10) does the same, but makes sectoral unbalancedness even more extreme. This range seems to capture most of the country experience documented in Appendix C.

These unbalanced-productivity-advance counterfactuals reported in Table 5.5 suggest that the unbalanced character of technological progress is a critical force driving Third World city growth. Had sectoral TFPG been "balanced" across the 1960s and early 1970s, the rate of city growth would have been lower, 4.32 versus 4.86 percent per annum. To the extent that technological change was biased in favor of urban-based sectors, especially manufacturing, then conditions were especially favorable to Third World city growth in the pre-OPEC period. Of course, these conditions were even more conducive to city growth in fast-growing economies like Korea and Taiwan where unbalancedness was more pronounced (as in column 10). Finally, to the extent that the technological slowdown currently besetting the industrialized countries gets transferred to the Third World over the next two decades, a city growth slowdown is also assured since urban-based industrial sectors are surely going to be hit hardest.

6. USING THE PAST TO LOOK AT THE FUTURE

Chapter 3 reported a test of our model's ability to replicate growth, accumulation, distribution, and city growth in the Third World up to the 1973 watershed. It appeared to replicate the experience well, encouraging the view that the model could be used to uncover the sources of that urban growth during the 1960s and the early 1970s, as well as during the difficult period of structural adjustment since. This chapter has done just that, using counterfactual analysis as a tool for digging insights out of the recent past.

Some key morals have emerged from this counterfactual exercise. First, rapid rates of population growth are not the central influence driving Third World city growth, as a reading of the popular literature would suggest. Nor does it appear that capital transfers to the Third World played a very significant role. In addition, arable land scarcity exerted only a very modest impact in pushing labor to the cities. Second, the most potent influences on Third World city growth appear to have been the rate and unbalancedness of sectoral productivity advance—technological events that have favored the urban modern sectors, and relative prices. Third, OPEC-induced fuel scarcity has been less important in driving city growth than the state of world markets for manufactures.

These findings have been helpful in understanding two aspects of Third World city growth experience over the past two decades. First, they appear to account for the city growth slowdown since 1973. While rising fuel and raw material scarcity mattered, an increasingly unfavorable world market for manufactures seems to have mattered far more. Second, they appear to help understand whether and to what extent Third World city growth was "unusually fast" up to 1973. Technology and prices seem to have been doing most of the work in accounting for the pre-OPEC city growth, but whether these technology and price conditions were unusual can only be assessed as the remainder of the twentieth century unfolds.

What, then, can we expect from the future? These results from the past will serve to guide our look into the future, an effort that follows in Chapter 6.

CHAPTER SIX

Projections to the Year 2000

1. PREDICTIONS, PROJECTIONS, AND COUNTERFACTUAL ANALYSIS

What will the year 2000 be like?

Demographers have certainly supplied answers to this question. Under various assumptions about migration rates and urban-rural birth and mortality differentials, Keyfitz (1980), Rogers (1977, 1982), Ledent (1980, 1982), and the United Nations (1980) have offered a number of projections of Third World urbanization and city growth over the next two decades. Some of these projections assume a constant migration rate and some allow it to vary, but all take the migration rate to be exogenous. That is, the demographic projections are made in the absence of any model in which economic forces are allowed to have an impact on migration rates to the city. Since demographic projections typically contain no endogenous forces driving rural emigration or urban immigration rates, city growth must be viewed as exogenous in these demographic projections.[1]

Since our model endogenizes rural-urban migration flows, we are in a position to learn far more about the future, although our predictions for the year 2000 need not be any more accurate than those of the demographers'. First, we can explore long-run patterns of migration, city growth, and urbanization in a stable economic/demographic environment where exogenous prices, technological change, labor force growth, land expansion rates, and foreign capital inflows all exhibit smooth trends, shielded from the disturbances of demographic transition, OPEC price shocks, productivity slowdown and rising foreign capital austerity. By isolating these influences, we will, in effect, be able to explore a counterfactual world of urbanization and economic development where endogenous

---

[1] Demographers might take issue with this critique. Migration as a constant fraction of population in the rural sending region, for example, results in a diminishing number of migrants per period. Thus, some demographers might argue that an exogenous and constant rural emigration *rate* implies endogenous flows and perhaps even an endogenous city immigration rate. The issue, however, is the extent to which there is behavioral content in the migration specification. In the demographers' models, migrants do not respond to economic events. In the Kelley–Williamson model, they do.

forces of growth and development are allowed to have their unfettered impact on the spatial redistribution of population. What would our model predict under such conditions? A smooth logistic or *S*-curve? If so, where would the point of inflexion be? 1970? The year 2000? Second, we can explore long-run patterns of migration and city growth in an economic/demographic environment that experts think is most likely to prevail over the next two decades. This BASELINE projection can then be compared with the STABLE projection to examine the impact of a changing economic/demographic environment over the next two decades. The gap between the two projections should yield insight into the role of these future economic/demographic environmental changes, especially since we can use the model to disaggregate the impact of each event separately by use of the counterfactual.

Section 2 defines the most likely economic/demographic environment over the next two decades which underlies the BASELINE. It then explores the projections to the year 2000, comparing BASELINE with STABLE conditions. Our projections of migration and city growth are then compared with the demographers'. Section 3 turns to the sources of Third World city growth where we assess the relative importance of various forces driving future city growth performance.

2. USING THE MODEL TO PROJECT THE FUTURE

Defining the BASELINE

Table 6.1 summarizes the values of the dynamic parameters underlying the model's projections to the year 2000. It repeats the "actual" environmental conditions used in Chapters 3 and 5 to analyze the pre-OPEC and post-OPEC periods. It also reports the BASELINE and STABLE values assumed for the two decades following 1980. The STABLE values simply assume that the pre-OPEC conditions persisted through the 1970s and will continue to hold for the next two decades. We do not view these post-1980 trends as very likely events, but that is not the purpose of the exercise. Rather, the STABLE values simply offer a useful benchmark by which to explore the urban transition in a developing country under the idealized circumstances of a stable exogenous economic and demographic environment. The BASELINE values are a different matter entirely.

As Appendix C points out, the ILO (1977) offers projections of labor force growth for each of the forty countries comprising our

TABLE 6.1
Dynamic Parameters Assumed in Projections to the Year 2000

Variable (per annum growth)	BASELINE or Actual				STABLE
	1960–1973	1974–1980	1981–1990	1991–2000	1960–2000
$\dot{P}_Z$, Relative price, fuels and raw materials	0	+5.2%	+1.5%	+1.5%	0
$\dot{P}_M$, Relative price, manufactures	−0.7%	−1.6	−0.6	−0.6	−0.7%
$\dot{R}_A$, Agricultural land stock	+1.0	+0.5	0	0	+1.0
$\dot{R}_U$, Urban land stock	+1.0	+1.0	+1.0	+1.0	+1.0
$\overline{L + S}$, Population and labor force	+2.54	+2.68	+2.79	+2.84	+2.54
$\dot{F}$, Foreign capital inflow	F/GDP = 3%		F/GDP declines linearly to 2.4% in 2000		F/GDP = 3%
TFPG, Economywide total-factor productivity	1.8	1.8	1.8	1.8	1.8

SOURCE: See text and Appendix C

RDC group. Table 6.1 reports the average growth rates for the 1980s and 1990s implied by the ILO projections. There is no evidence of retardation in labor force growth implied by the ILO figures; instead, their "middle" projection underlying the BASELINE suggests a slight acceleration to the year 2000. By comparing the city growth projections under conditions of accelerating labor force growth rates with the somewhat lower and constant rates in the STABLE experiment, we should be able to assess the role of population growth on future migration and urbanization.

Relative price projections are, needless to say, hazardous. Yet Table 6.1 reports what experts at the World Bank believe to be most likely. They do not foresee the same dramatic increase in the relative price of fuels and raw materials which took place during the 1970s, but they do project an upward drift in P_Z at the brisk rate of 1.5 percent per annum. They also predict a persistent decline in the relative price of manufactures at the rate of 0.6 percent per annum, much like the trends typical of the pre-OPEC epoch. Appendix C discusses these relative price predictions in some detail, but the reader should be reminded that we are far less interested in what truly *will* happen to relative prices to the year 2000 than in *what might happen under alternative relative price scenarios*. Given that qualification, the experts' guesses will serve to establish a BASELINE around which counterfactual alternatives can be evaluated.

Foreign capital inflows are even more difficult to project. They will certainly be dependent on real income growth and fiscal austerity in the lending countries of the industrialized North. They will also be dependent upon OPEC price policy and financial surpluses thereby generated in the oil-surplus nations. Nonetheless, the World Bank has projected the most likely "resource gaps" in the oil-importing Third World, and these imply the BASELINE trends in F/GDP reported in Table 6.1. The most likely case seems to be a steady decline in F/GDP from an average of 3 percent in the 1970s to 2.4 percent by the year 2000. These projected time series on F/GDP are, incidentally, quite similar to those estimated by Chenery and Syrquin (1975, Table 3, pp. 20–21) based on cross-section data, and ranging over a comparable per capita income spread among low-income countries.

Apparently, there are no expert opinions on the likely future trends in total-factor productivity growth and in the land stock. The qualitative literature suggests the wisdom of assuming the complete disappearance of an extensive margin in agriculture, thus motivating the BASELINE assumption of zero growth in R_A. The assumption of urban land growing at 1 percent per annum is reasonable but purely guesswork. Since we have no research on total-factor productivity growth in the late 1970s, let alone for the next two decades, we have assumed that the 1.8 percent estimated for the pre-OPEC period will continue to the year 2000. There has, of course, been a productivity slowdown in the industrialized North for some time now (Hulten and Nishimizu, 1982), but we do not have any hard evidence confirming similar long-run trends in the Third World. And those Third World countries that do offer some evidence fail to suggest any consistent trend in the late 1970s, let alone whether those trends are temporary aspects of structural adjustment. (Yugoslavia [Nishimizu and Robinson, 1982 ongoing, Table 10.2] and Singapore [Tsao, 1982, Table 9, p. 46] show some evidence of recent slowdown, but Korea [Nishimizu and Robinson, 1982 ongoing, Table 10.2] appears to have maintained the pace of total-factor productivity growth quite well through the 1970s.) To repeat, there is simply not enough evidence to assume anything other than the constant rate of total-factor productivity growth underlying the BASELINE projections to the year 2000.

Growth, Accumulation, and Structural Change in the Long Run

Table 6.2 summarizes the BASELINE's growth performance over the four decades, 1960–2000. Since our interest is in urbanization and city growth, we shall not dwell on long-run aggregate growth, although there are some attributes worth noting.

As Chapter 4 pointed out, the model exhibits trend acceleration, although the structural adjustment problems of the 1970s interrupt that process. Thus, while GDP per capita growth rises between 1960 and 1990, the long-run trend acceleration halts temporarily in the 1970s. Furthermore, it appears that per capita GDP growth rates level off in the 1990s. The source of that trend acceleration is clearly related to accumulation patterns: skills per worker growth rates reach a peak in 1980, undergoing a slow retardation thereafter, and capital per worker growth rates level off in the 1990s. The explanation of the accumulation experience is, in turn, the conventional growth-theoretic one: diminishing returns to capital begins to set in late in the period (the capital-output ratio begins to rise after 1980), and the rise in the investment share in GDP fails to offset the forces of diminishing returns as that share's rise slows down late in the period.

Meanwhile, industrialization and structural change trace out the stylized "patterns of development," so that by the year 2000 only a

TABLE 6.2
Growth, Accumulation, and Structural Change: BASELINE, 1960–2000

Panel A: Growth and Accumulation

Year	GDP per Capita (Constant Price)	Investment Shares in GDP		Per Annum Growth			
		GDI	Total (incl. training)	GDP per Capita (Constant Price)	Capital Stock per Worker	Housing Stock per Worker	Skilled Labor Force, per Worker
1960	1.00	15.6%	17.9%	3.2%	1.7%	0.6%	2.7%
1965	1.17	17.3	19.0	3.4	2.8	2.8	0.3
1970	1.41	18.0	20.0	3.9	3.5	3.0	1.9
1975	1.70	18.5	20.9	3.5	3.0	2.7	1.5
1980	2.04	19.0	21.6	3.7	3.1	2.0	3.1
1985	2.49	19.3	22.2	4.2	4.3	3.0	2.4
1990	3.07	19.5	22.8	4.4	4.5	2.8	2.8
1995	3.79	19.7	23.3	4.4	4.5	2.7	2.6
2000	4.69	19.8	23.8	4.3	4.5	2.6	2.4

Panel B: Structural Change and Distribution

Year	Sectoral Output Shares in GDP					Labor Force Distribution				Index of Skilled Wage Premium
	A	M	KS	Housing	Other	A	M	KS	Other	
1960	36.6%	15.9%	29.6%	8.5%	9.4%	60.1%	12.2%	10.4%	17.3%	1.50
1965	33.3	17.7	29.6	9.5	9.9	56.1	14.1	10.7	19.1	1.58
1970	30.4	19.3	30.4	9.9	10.0	52.5	16.2	11.5	19.8	1.71
1975	27.5	21.4	31.0	10.0	10.1	47.7	19.0	12.4	20.9	1.76
1980	26.5	22.6	31.2	9.8	9.9	43.9	21.4	13.8	20.9	1.64
1985	23.3	25.3	31.6	10.0	9.8	39.7	24.4	14.9	21.0	1.49
1990	19.8	28.2	32.1	10.1	9.8	35.1	27.8	16.2	20.9	1.35
1995	16.9	30.8	32.5	10.2	9.6	31.0	30.8	17.6	20.6	1.19
2000	14.5	32.8	32.9	10.2	9.6	27.5	33.2	19.0	20.3	1.02

little more than a quarter of the labor force is still in agriculture, while about a third is in manufacturing.

Finally, we should note some evidence on earnings distribution trends. Panel B of Table 6.2 presents one summary statistic for the entire wage structure, the wage premium on skills. Chapter 4 pointed out that this index tended to rise over the pre-OPEC period, and this is repeated, of course, in the BASELINE 1960–1970/75. Thus, the model generates skill scarcity in its early phases of growth. And to repeat Chapter 4, if skill scarcities can be viewed as price signals in the wake of inadequate human capital accumulation, then the inequality trends reported in Table 3.12 are attributes of disequilibrium that even a neoclassical model is capable of replicating. But what about the future of skill scarcity and earnings inequality? Table 6.2 (Panel B) suggests that the disequilibrium is at its peak now and will recede in the future: the skilled wage premium index declines from 1975 to the year 2000, presumably in response to the very high rates of skill accumulation in the quarter century following 1975 (see Panel A, "per annum growth in skilled labor force per worker").

City Growth in the Long Run

Table 6.3 documents six key aspects of urban transition: the percentage population urban, city growth rates, net rural out-migration rates (as a percentage of the rural population), net urban in-migration rates (as a percentage of the urban population), the share of urban population increases accounted for by in-migration, and the labor force share in manufacturing as a ratio of the share of population urban. Each of these six statistics plays an important role in debates over city growth. Three of these are also reproduced in Figure 6.1, where the percentage urban, the city growth rate, and the city in-migration rate are all plotted for both the BASELINE and the STABLE case. The comparison is informative.

Consider Figure 6.1 first. The STABLE environment, the reader will recall, yields the model's prediction under conditions where the pre-OPEC environment is assumed to hold throughout the forty-year period. While such conditions are hardly realistic, they do serve the useful purpose of illustrating the stylized patterns of urban change in the absence of shifting macro economic/demographic conditions. The model appears to replicate the standard logistic curve, where the point of inflexion in the urbanization rate (the increase in the share urban) reaches a peak in the late 1970s. The rate of increase slows down thereafter. Indeed, the rates of city growth and

ABLE 6.3

Migration, Urbanization, and City Growth: BASELINE and STABLE, 1960–2000

Year	% Urban	% Labor Force in Mfg ÷ % Urban	City Growth	Net Rural Out-Migration Rate	Net Urban In-Migration Rate	Net In-Migrant Share of Urban Population Increase
			Panel A: BASELINE			
1960	32.6%	.374	5.56%	1.41%	2.91%	
1965	35.8	.394	4.11	0.82	1.50	45.1%
1970	39.9	.406	5.15	1.60	2.51	
1975	45.2	.420	4.48	1.38	1.72	48.1
1980	49.2	.435	4.10	1.28	1.35	
1985	54.3	.450	4.84	2.23	1.96	44.7
1990	59.7	.466	4.67	2.53	1.79	
1995	64.4	.478	4.33	2.45	1.41	35.6
2000	68.4	.486	3.97	2.21	1.05	
			Panel B: STABLE			
1960	32.6	.374	5.56	1.41	2.91	
1965	35.8	.394	4.11	0.82	1.50	45.1
1970	39.9	.406	5.15	1.60	2.51	
1975	46.2	.427	5.94	2.67	3.29	60.6
1980	54.8	.454	5.97	3.74	3.31	
1985	62.9	.480	4.98	3.75	2.35	53.0
1990	69.3	.493	4.32	3.64	1.70	
1995	74.2	.499	3.79	3.26	1.18	34.7
2000	77.9	.501	3.43	2.85	0.84	

city in-migration rise sharply through the 1960s and 1970s, peak in the late 1970s, and decline sharply thereafter, following Zelinsky's (1971, p. 233) hypothesis of mobility transition. (See also Ledent, 1980, 1982; Rogers, 1977, pp. 164–167; and UN, 1980, p. 29.) Thus, the STABLE scenario predicts a pronounced decline in city growth rates from a high of almost 6 percent per annum in 1980 to the much more modest rate of about 3.5 percent per annum by the year 2000.

Based on the STABLE model, it would also appear that the vast majority of the urban transition will be completed by the year 2000. This can be seen most clearly in Figure 6.2 where the STABLE model is allowed to grow over a full century (from 1960 to 2060). In the absence of any changes in the macro economic/demographic environmental conditions underlying the STABLE model, the equilibrium urban share is about 85 percent (America's current "urban

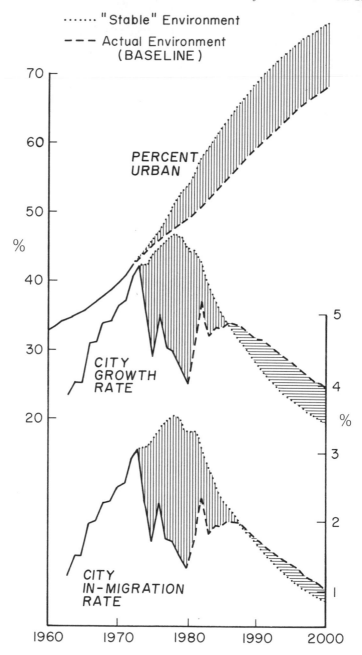

Figure 6.1 Migration, Urbanization, and City Growth:
BASELINE and STABLE 1960–2000

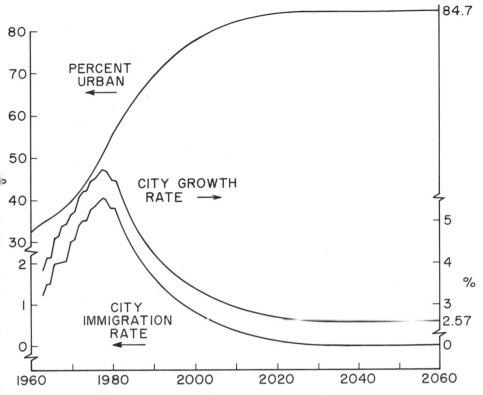

Figure 6.2 A Century of Migration, Urbanization, and City Growth: 1960–2060, STABLE

limit" from which it now appears to be retreating). The RDC economy would almost reach that level by 2020, the city in-migration
rate would be about zero by 2030, and the city growth rate would
match the national rate of population growth in that year as well.
Between 1960 and the end of the urban transition, the urban share
increases by 52.4 percentage points (from 32.6 percent in 1960 to
85 percent in equilibrium). By the year 2000, the STABLE model
has already undergone an increase of 45.3 percentage points. In
short, the economy has passed through almost nine-tenths of the
urban transition by the year 2000.

Figure 6.1 also plots the BASELINE trends. City growth rates
reach an earlier peak in the BASELINE, due to the city growth
slowdown induced by the post-OPEC conditions discussed at length
in Chapter 5. Furthermore, the gap between the BASELINE and
the STABLE predictions (indicated by the shaded area in Figure
6.1) is large indeed, confirming the analysis in Chapter 5 where

the city growth slowdown was analyzed by source. But note too that city growth rates, at least in part, tend to make up the lagging performance through the late 1980s and 1990s. Nevertheless, the BASELINE also predicts the same long-run decline in city growth rates: city growth rates decline from 5.15 percent per annum in 1970 to less than 4 percent per annum in the year 2000.

In short, whether we focus on the BASELINE or the STABLE model predictions, the model produces the conventional logistic curve with rising then falling city growth and in-migration rates. Based on the model, urban problems will be far less severe by the end of the century, even though there will be no serious diminution of Malthusian population pressure in the Third World over the remainder of the century. Presumably, we will hear fewer complaints from urban planners, the term "over-urbanization" will disappear from our lexicon, and pessimists' stress on urban environmental decay will lose its urgency. By the year 2000, it will be easier to cope with the far lower city growth rates.

Table 6.3 offers more information of interest to the urban analyst. Consider, for example, the debate on "over-urbanization" which was initiated by Bert Hoselitz in the 1950s. His thesis was that urbanization was outpacing industrialization in developing countries in the sense that urban population shares were large in relation to industrial employment shares, at least when compared with the historical performance of currently developed countries (UN, 1980, p. 17). While this view was confirmed by Hoselitz (1955, 1957) and others based on data from the 1950s, the UN (1980) has rejected it on more recent evidence. The thesis was tested by examining trends in such statistics as the percentage of the labor force in industry relative to the percentage of the population in urban areas. This statistic is also produced by the two scenarios in the second column of Table 6.3, although "industry" is limited to manufacturing alone. Comparing 1970 with 1950, the UN (1980, p. 17) concluded that "urban growth is no longer outpacing industrial growth: if anything, a slight reversal of the over-urbanization tendency has appeared." The BASELINE's predictions are consistent with the UN finding since the statistic rises, although at a declining rate, throughout the four decades. According to the UN findings, industrialization (or manufacturing employment growth) has been the "engine of urbanization" over the past two decades in the Third World, and, according to both the BASELINE and the STABLE scenarios, it will continue to be so in the future, although at a lesser rate.

When demographers discuss the sources of urban growth, they confine their attention to the statistical decomposition of that growth into its two components—the natural increase in the urban

population and in-migration flows. The debate between them has
been active enough to motivate a recent article by Nathan Keyfitz
(1980) entitled "Do Cities Grow by Natural Increase or by Migration?" The question is of interest to an economist only because the
in-migration rate is determined endogenously in any serious general
equilibrium model of development and city growth. The last column
of Table 6.3 offers the relevant statistic, the net in-migrant share of
urban population increase. For the 1960s, the model predicts 45.1
percent, a figure which we have already shown in Chapter 3 replicates the findings of the demographers for that period. The figure
falls between the UN (1980, Table 11, p. 25) estimate of 39.3 percent
and Keyfitz's (1980, p. 151) estimate of 49 percent. More to the point,
the model predicts a long-run decline in the relative importance of
in-migration as a "source" of urban population growth, from about
45 percent in the 1960s to about 35 percent in the 1990s (and close
to zero in the year 2020). These trends are fully consistent with the
work of Andrei Rogers (1982) and others. Yet, Table 6.3 illustrates
that the share rises to a peak in the 1970s before undergoing the
long-run decline, a temporal pattern consistent with the in-migration rate which remains at high levels until late in the 1970s in the
BASELINE case, or until the early 1980s in the STABLE case.

Tables 6.4 and 6.5 offer additional details on the urban transition.
Consider first the urban land use and land scarcity trends documented in Table 6.4. While urban land density and scarcity indices
continue to rise without interruption through the four decades, there
is evidence in both the BASELINE and STABLE cases that the rate
will slow down at the end of the century, more or less paralleling
the retardation in city growth. For example, the per annum rate of
increase in the shadow price of urban land rises from 6.9 percent in
the 1960s to peak rates ranging between 7.6 and 7.8 percent in the
1980s (the former in BASELINE, the latter in STABLE), falling to
7.1 percent in the 1990s (in both cases). A similar retardation is
apparent in the share of urban land devoted to low-quality housing
needed to satisfy the dwelling requirements of low-income urban
households. This share rises by 9.2 percentage points in the 1960s,
but it will rise by only 1.8 percent points in the 1990s according to
the BASELINE predictions, and will *fall* by 0.1 percentage points
in the 1990s according to the STABLE predictions. Consider next
the housing scarcity indicators and cost-of-living differentials documented in Table 6.5. It appears, for example, that the household
saving constraint is never binding on housing investment *except*
in low-cost squatter settlements, but even here the constraint is
binding only for the period of most rapid city growth. That is, the
constraint is binding up to the mid-1970s, the period of rising city

TABLE 6.4

Urban Land Use and Land Scarcity: BASELINE and STABLE, 1960–2000

Year	Share of Urban Land in Squatter Settlements	Land Density, Persons/Area		Urban Land	
		Luxury Housing Areas	Squatter Settlements	Shadow Site Rent	Shadow Price
		Panel A: BASELINE			
1960	43.0%	1.00	1.00	1.00	1.00
1965	49.3	1.27	1.06	1.33	1.41
1970	52.2	1.52	1.21	1.83	1.95
1975	53.1	1.81	1.55	2.50	2.60
1980	51.0	2.11	1.89	3.00	3.16
1985	54.0	2.71	2.13	4.33	4.59
1990	55.9	3.45	2.43	6.17	6.59
1995	57.1	4.22	2.83	8.50	9.37
2000	57.7	5.43	2.83	11.67	13.11
		Panel B: STABLE			
1960	43.0	1.00	1.00	1.00	1.00
1965	49.3	1.27	1.06	1.33	1.41
1970	52.2	1.52	1.21	1.83	1.95
1975	55.0	1.90	1.55	2.83	2.76
1980	56.7	2.37	1.89	4.00	3.90
1985	58.6	3.17	2.13	5.83	5.71
1990	59.3	4.22	2.49	8.17	8.29
1995	59.5	4.75	2.83	11.17	11.78
2000	59.2	6.33	3.40	14.83	16.43

growth rates and high in-migration rates in both the BASELINE and STABLE cases. In any case, urban house rents rise throughout the period, thus producing the upward drift in the urban-rural cost-of-living differential over time.

Comparisons with Purely Demographic Projections

The advantage of the Kelley-Williamson model of Third World urbanization lies with its endogenous treatment of city in-migration, a model in which economic events, including policy, play a role. This is not true, of course, of purely demographic models which have been used for projections to the year 2000. The accuracy of these competing projections is not at issue; even the most accurate demographic model suffers the weakness of being incapable of counterfactual analysis. Section 3 will illustrate the point by showing how

TABLE 6.5
Urban Housing Scarcity and Rural-Urban Cost-of-Living Differentials: BASELINE and STABLE, 1960–2000

Year	Excess Housing Investment Demand			House Rent Indices			COL Differential:
	Urban Luxury Housing	Urban Squatter Settlements	Rural Housing	Urban Luxury Housing	Urban Squatter Settlements	Rural Housing	Urban/Rural
			Panel A: BASELINE				
1960	-3.77	-0.02	-0.29	1.00	1.00	1.00	1.00
1965	-2.63	+0.42	-0.24	1.19	1.43	1.24	1.05
1970	-2.55	+0.37	-0.58	1.35	1.72	1.38	1.09
1975	-2.77	+0.12	-0.87	1.48	1.82	1.55	1.09
1980	-3.04	-0.27	-0.96	1.51	1.68	1.78	1.02
1985	-3.58	-0.33	-1.33	1.67	2.14	1.89	1.10
1990	-4.22	-0.50	-1.64	1.87	2.62	2.01	1.18
1995	-4.99	-0.68	-1.79	2.11	3.17	2.19	1.27
2000	-5.93	-0.88	-1.87	2.37	3.80	2.41	1.37
			Panel B: STABLE				
1960	-3.77	-0.02	-0.29	1.00	1.00	1.00	1.00
1965	-2.63	+0.42	-0.24	1.19	1.43	1.24	1.05
1970	-2.55	+0.37	-0.58	1.35	1.72	1.38	1.09
1975	-2.80	+0.19	-1.11	1.53	2.02	1.49	1.14
1980	-3.27	-0.13	-1.93	1.77	2.27	1.57	1.18
1985	-3.73	-0.38	-2.37	2.03	2.72	1.72	1.26
1990	-4.35	-0.60	-2.40	2.29	3.26	1.90	1.35
1995	-5.14	-0.81	-2.34	2.55	3.88	2.11	1.44
2000	-6.12	-1.00	-2.16	2.81	4.59	2.36	1.53

Third World urban experience over the next two decades might behave under alternative world market conditions, altered technical progress, unforeseen acceleration in demographic transition, new policy regimes, and the like. But before we turn to such experiments, how does the BASELINE prediction of the year 2000 compare with purely demographic projections?

Table 6.6 summarizes the projections of five demographic models. The first is a recent effort by Robert Schmidt (1983). The key elements of Schmidt's model are a roughly constant rate of total population growth very close to that assumed in the BASELINE (2.7 percent per annum) and a *constant* net rate of rural out-migration (a CMR equal to 1.13 percent per annum). Thus, not only is Schmidt's CMR exogenous, but it is held fixed at a rate far below

TABLE 6.6
Kelley–Williamson BASELINE and Demographic Projections to the Year 2000 Compared

Year	Kelley–Williamson BASELINE (Endogenous CMR)		Schmidt (Exogenous, Fixed CMR)		Ledent (Exogenous, Variable CM	
	% Urban	City Growth	% Urban	City Growth	% Urban	City Growth
1960	32.6%		31.9%		32.6%	
		4.7%		4.7%		4.8%
1970	39.9		38.9		40.5	
		4.8		4.3		4.7
1980	49.2		45.5		49.2	
		4.8		3.9		4.4
1990	59.7		51.0		57.2	
		4.3		na		3.9
2000	68.4		na		63.2	
Average Per Annum Δ	0.9		0.6		0.8	
Average Per Annum Growth		4.7		4.3		4.5

SOURCES: Schmidt (Exogenous, Fixed CMR): R. M. Schmidt (1983), Table 3, "medium" projection, and based on our forty-country RDC group for aggregate population growth projections. Crude migration rate fixed.

Ledent (Exogenous, Variable CMR): J. Ledent (1982), equation (20), p. 532 used to project the urban share based on the BASELINE's per capita GNP. The city growth rates are derived by applying the percentage urban to the BASELINE's population trends. Crude migration rate exogenous, but variable.

UN-Preston (LDC) (Exogenous, Variable CMR): United Nations (1980), Tables 4 and 8, pp. 11 and 16, where LDC = all less-developed regions. Crude migration rate that predicted by the BASELINE. In the BASELINE, the CMR surges from 1.41 percent in 1960 to a peak of 2.53 percent in 1990, and declines to 2.21 percent in the year 2000 (Table 6.3). The second demographic projection reported in Table 6.6 is that recently offered by Jacques Ledent (1982). As with all the other demographic models, Ledent views migration rates as exogenous although the CMR in his projections is allowed to vary. In Ledent's case, the CMR tends to pass through phases predicted by Zelinsky's mobility transition hypothesis, and much like those predicted endogenously by the BASELINE—namely, the first two decades are ones of a rising CMR while the last two decades are ones of a falling CMR. The timing is unlike that of the BASELINE, but the general configuration is at least similar. The third demographic projection

UN-Preston (LDC) (*Exogenous, Variable CMR*)		*UN-Preston (40 RDCs)* (*Exogenous, Variable CMR*)		*Rogers* (*Exogenous, Variable CMR*)	
% Urban	City Growth	% Urban	City Growth	% Urban	City Growth
21.9%		27.4%		30.9%	
	4.0%		4.4%		5.5%
25.8		32.8		40.9	
	4.1		4.3		4.6
30.5		38.3		51.7	
	4.1		4.4		3.7
36.5		44.4		61.0	
	3.8		4.3		2.8
43.5		50.9		67.8	
0.5		0.6		0.9	
	4.0		4.3		4.1

exogenous, but variable (UN, 1980, p. 10).

UN-Preston (40 RDCs) (Exogenous, Variable CMR): United Nations (1980), Table 50, pp. 159–161.

Rogers (Exogenous, Variable CMR): A. Rogers (1977), Table 10.11, p. 182, "scenario Bb," from his year 15 (yielding the percentage urban figure closest to our BASELINE's 1960 figure) to 55, forty years hence. This gives us the percentage urban projections. The city growth rates are derived from the same table, starting with the same year.

is supplied by Andrei Rogers (1977), who uses a spatial variant of Ansley Coale's (1969) classic analysis of Third World demographic trends. In Rogers's model, the exogenous CMR is allowed to rise over time. The fourth and fifth demographic projections have been generated by the UN (1980) under the guidance of Samuel Preston. The United Nations method relies on gravity-type migration flows and natural urban/rural increase differentials, both declining linearly with the urban share. Like the other demographic projections, the UN projection treats the CMR as exogenous, but in contrast with all the others, the CMR declines throughout. We find this assumption the least attractive, but, nevertheless, we report two UN projections in Table 6.6: one covers the "less-developed region" as a whole, while the other is limited to the countries comprising our RDC group.

How does the BASELINE with endogenous migration rates stack up against the demographers' projections with exogenous migration rates? First, the urban transformation is far more dramatic in the BASELINE. The average annual increase in the percentage urban is 0.9 percent in the BASELINE; only Rogers's projection matches that performance, the others recording far lower rates of urbanization over the four decades. The same is true of city growth rates, the BASELINE recording 4.7 percent per annum over the four decades, while the demographic projections range from 4 to 4.5 percent per annum. Second, all but one of the demographic projections predict a much earlier retardation in city growth than the BASELINE, and the retardation is more dramatic. (The exception is the UN–Preston [forty RDCs] projection.) The key explanation for these differences lies, of course, with the predicted behavior of migration in the Kelley–Williamson model. The latter suggests that Third World economic development embodies forces that are far more favorable to city in-migration than the purely demographic model would suggest. Since the endogenous forces of economic development tend to generate *increasing* city "pull" in the early stages of growth, the demographers' model fails to capture the forces driving the mobility transition. In contrast, the Kelley–Williamson model offers an endogenous explanation for both the urban and the mobility transition.

3. THE SOURCES OF FUTURE CITY GROWTH

Migration is at the heart of the urban transition and, in the absence of behavioral content behind the migration decision, a purely demographic model is inadequately equipped to explore the impact of endogenous events associated with long-run development on the relative attractiveness of the city and thus on changing migration rates. Our model, however, is fully equipped for the task. Furthermore, it is also able to assess the impact of *exogenous* price/technology/demographic shocks on Third World urban experience. Thus, we are ready to explore Third World urban experience to the year 2000 under alternative scenarios and policy regimes.

Which scenarios and which policy regimes? Based on past sources of city growth analyzed in Chapter 5, our examination of the sources of future city growth will be motivated by five key issues: 1) alternative views on fuel and natural resource scarcity over the next two decades; 2) alternative views on the likely trends in prices up to the year 2000, induced by world market conditions and/or domestic policy; 3) alternative views on the likely austerity of world capital markets; 4) alternative views on the future pace of productivity advance over the remainder of this century; and 5) alternative views on the speed of the demographic transition in the near future.

World Markets, Natural Resource Scarcity, and Prices

How sensitive are these long-run city growth predictions to alternative price scenarios? Table 6.7 summarizes five alternatives—four counterfactuals and the BASELINE itself. The case most favorable to urbanization is STABLE, where the relative prices of fuel and natural resource intermediates (P_Z), manufactures (P_M), and non-fuel primary products (P_A) are all held constant over the two projection decades, 1980–2000. The case least favorable to urbanization is POST-OPEC where the relative price trends of the 1973–1979 period are assumed to prevail to the year 2000. The remaining three cases—BASELINE, AVERAGE HISTORIC (actual trends 1960–1979), and PRE-OPEC (actual trends 1960–1973)—fall in the intermediate range.

Table 6.7 confirms that future price trends will matter a great deal to Third World urbanization over the next two decades. Were POST-OPEC conditions to prevail, the rate of urbanization would continue to slow down sharply during the 1980s, stopping entirely after the year 1990. That is, in spite of continued economywide growth and accumulation, the POST-OPEC price trends would simply be so deleterious to urbanization that the "urban transition" would halt: city growth rates would fall to the national rate of population growth by the early 1990s, and the net rate of city in-migration would first fall to zero before switching to a net out-migration

TABLE 6.7
City Growth Projections, 1980–2000: Alternative Price Scenarios ($\overset{*}{P}_Z$ and $\overset{*}{P}_M$ Varied)

		BASELINE	
Year	% Urban	City Growth	Net Urban In-migration Rate
1980	49.2%	4.10%	1.35%
1985	54.3	4.84	1.96
1990	59.7	4.67	1.79
1995	64.4	4.33	1.41
2000	68.4	3.97	1.05

		PRE-OPEC	
Year	% Urban	City Growth	Net Urban In-migration Rate
1980	49.2%	4.10%	1.35
1985	54.2	4.80	1.92
1990	59.6	4.67	1.79
1995	64.3	4.31	1.39
2000	68.2	3.95	1.04

		AVERAGE HISTORIC	
Year	% Urban	City Growth	Net Urban In-migration Rate
1980	49.2	4.10	1.35
1985	53.2	4.34	1.47
1990	57.1	4.23	1.36
1995	60.6	3.98	1.07
2000	63.5	3.74	0.84

		POST-OPEC	
Year	% Urban	City Growth	Net Urban In-migration Rate
1980	49.2	4.10	1.35
1985	50.9	3.26	0.41
1990	51.5	2.92	0.09
1995	51.3	2.71	−0.17
2000	50.5	2.50	−0.37

(continued)

TABLE 6.7 (*continued*)

		STABLE	
Year	% Urban	City Growth	Net Urban In-migration Rate
1980	49.2	4.10	1.35
1985	56.0	5.54	2.64
1990	63.5	5.26	2.36
1995	70.0	4.70	1.77
2000	75.3	4.19	1.27

NOTE: These counterfactuals assume the following over 1981–2000 for $\dot{P}_Z$ and $\dot{P}_M$ (BASELINE values for all other exogenous variables):

	$\dot{P}_Z$	$\dot{P}_M$
BASELINE	+1.51%	−0.6%
STABLE	0	0
PRE-OPEC	0	−0.7
POST-OPEC	+5.2	−1.6
AVERAGE HISTORIC	+1.7	−1.0

to rural areas. While this POST-OPEC case is unfavorable to urbanization in the extreme, and the less unfavorable relative price trends underlying BASELINE are thought by World Bank experts to be far more likely, nonetheless it *is* a relevant historical counterfactual which in fact has created so many structural adjustment problems in recent years.

The moral of the story is that relative price trends will have a potent impact on future urban experience in the Third World. Figure 6.3 offers the reader a visual impression of the large magnitudes involved. But *which* relative price trends will matter most?

Tables 6.8 and 6.9 decompose these price scenarios into their two component parts: Table 6.8 maintains all the BASELINE assumptions except assumptions about the relative scarcity of fuels and imported natural resources (P_Z relative to P_A); and Table 6.9 maintains all the BASELINE assumptions except assumptions about trends in the relative price of manufactures (P_M relative to P_A). Consistent with the findings in Chapters 4 and 5, the terms of trade between urban-based manufactures and rural-based primary products appears to be a far more critical determinant of future Third World urban performance than the relative price of imported fuels and natural resources. For example, in the BASELINE the urban share reaches 68.4 percent in the year 2000, but only 50.5 percent in the

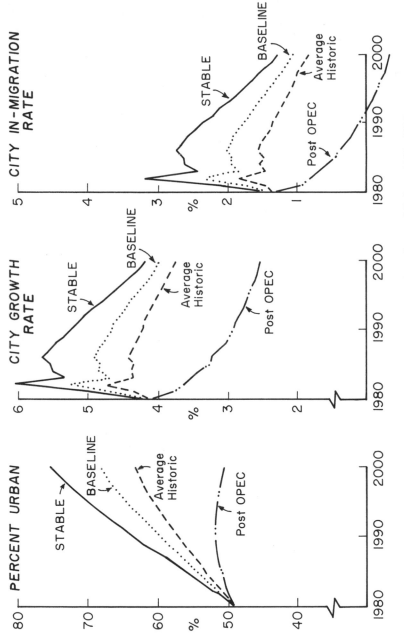

Figure 6.3 World Markets, Natural Resource Scarcity, and Prices, 1980–2000, Various Scenarios

TABLE 6.8

City Growth Projections, 1980–2000: Alternative Fuel and Natural Resource Scarcity Scenarios ($\overset{*}{P}_Z$ Varied)

BASELINE

Year	% Urban	City Growth	Net Urban In-migration Rate
1980	49.2%	4.10%	1.35%
1985	54.3	4.84	1.96
1990	59.7	4.67	1.79
1995	64.4	4.33	1.41
2000	68.4	3.97	1.05

PRE-OPEC

Year	% Urban	City Growth	Net Urban In-migration Rate
1980	49.2%	4.10%	1.35%
1985	54.5	4.91	2.03
1990	60.2	4.77	1.88
1995	65.2	4.38	1.46
2000	69.3	3.99	1.08

AVERAGE HISTORIC

Year	% Urban	City Growth	Net Urban In-migration Rate
1980	49.2	4.10	1.35
1985	54.2	4.85	1.96
1990	59.6	4.67	1.79
1995	64.3	4.32	1.40
2000	68.2	3.97	1.06

POST-OPEC

Year	% Urban	City Growth	Net Urban In-migration Rate
1980	49.2	4.10	1.35
1985	53.7	4.60	1.72
1990	58.3	4.43	1.56
1995	62.3	4.16	1.24
2000	65.7	3.86	0.95

(*continued*)

TABLE 6.8   (*continued*)

| | | STABLE | |
| | | | |
Year	% Urban	City Growth	Net Urban In-migration Rate
1980	49.2	4.10	1.35
1985	54.5	4.91	2.03
1990	60.2	4.77	1.88
1995	65.2	4.38	1.46
2000	69.3	3.99	1.08

NOTE: These counterfactuals assume the following over 1981–2000 for $\dot{P}_Z$ (BASELINE values for all other exogenous variables):

BASELINE	+1.51%
STABLE	0
PRE-OPEC	0
POST-OPEC	+5.2
AVERAGE HISTORIC	+1.7

TABLE 6.9
City Growth Projections, 1980–2000: Alternative World Market Scenarios ($\dot{P}_M$ Varied)

| | | BASELINE | |
| | | | |
Year	% Urban	City Growth	Net Urban In-migration Rate
1980	49.2%	4.10%	1.35%
1985	54.3	4.84	1.96
1990	59.7	4.67	1.79
1995	64.4	4.33	1.41
2000	68.4	3.97	1.05

| | | PRE-OPEC | |
| | | | |
Year	% Urban	City Growth	Net Urban In-migration Rate
1980	49.2%	4.10%	1.35%
1985	54.0	4.71	1.83
1990	59.0	4.58	1.70
1995	63.5	4.25	1.33
2000	67.2	3.93	1.02

(continued)

TABLE 6.9   (*continued*)

AVERAGE HISTORIC

Year	% Urban	City Growth	Net Urban In-migration Rate
1980	49.2	4.10	1.35
1985	53.2	4.36	1.49
1990	57.2	4.24	1.38
1995	60.7	4.00	1.08
2000	63.6	3.75	0.85

POST-OPEC

Year	% Urban	City Growth	Net Urban In-migration Rate
1980	49.2	4.10	1.35
1985	51.6	3.64	0.79
1995	53.3	3.42	0.57
1995	54.5	3.27	0.38
2000	55.3	3.12	0.23

STABLE

Year	% Urban	City Growth	Net Urban In-migration Rate
1980	49.2	4.10	1.35
1985	55.8	5.48	2.58
1990	63.1	5.21	2.31
1995	69.5	4.67	1.74
2000	74.6	4.18	1.26

NOTE: These counterfactuals assume the following over 1981–2000 for $\overset{*}{P}_M$ (BASELINE values for all other exogenous variables):

BASELINE	-0.6%
STABLE	0
PRE-OPEC	-0.7
POST-OPEC	-1.6
AVERAGE HISTORIC	-1.0

combined POST-OPEC case (Table 6.7). Were the POST-OPEC price scenarios restricted to the more severe fuel and natural resource scarcity trends only, the figure would be 65.7 percent (Table 6.8). Were the POST-OPEC price scenarios restricted to the less favorable relative price of manufactures trends only, the figure would be 55.3 percent (Table 6.9). In short, it appears that future Third World city growth will be far more sensitive to urban-based manufacture's terms of trade than to relative fuel and natural resource scarcities.

Labor Force Growth, Malthusian Pressures, and Demographic Transitions

What about future demographic scenarios? Table 6.10 and Figure 6.4 present four alternatives—three counterfactuals and the BASELINE itself. The BASELINE relies on the ILO's "middle" projection (of our RDC forty-country group) to the year 2000. The ILO also reports "high" and "low" labor force projection, and

TABLE 6.10

City Growth Projections, 1980–2000: Alternative Labor Force Growth Scenarios ($\overline{L + S}^*$ Varied)

		BASELINE	
Year	% Urban	City Growth	Net Urban In-migration Rate
1980	49.2%	4.10%	1.35%
1985	54.3	4.84	1.96
1990	59.7	4.67	1.79
1995	64.4	4.33	1.41
2000	68.4	3.97	1.05

		LOW GROWTH	
Year	% Urban	City Growth	Net Urban In-migration Rate
1980	49.2%	4.10%	1.35%
1985	54.3	4.83	2.01
1990	59.8	4.64	1.83
1995	64.9	4.22	1.50
2000	69.1	3.85	1.13

(continued)

TABLE 6.10   (*continued*)

VERY LOW GROWTH

Year	% Urban	City Growth	Net Urban In-migration Rate
1980	49.2	4.10	1.35
1985	54.7	4.71	2.12
1990	60.5	4.51	1.93
1995	66.2	4.00	1.64
2000	70.9	3.57	1.21

HIGH GROWTH

Year	% Urban	City Growth	Net Urban In-migration Rate
1980	49.2	4.10	1.35
1985	54.2	4.84	1.91
1990	59.5	4.70	1.78
1995	64.0	4.43	1.32
2000	67.7	4.07	0.98

NOTE: These counterfactuals assume the following for labor force growth, $\overline{L + \overset{*}{S}}$ (BASELINE values for all other exogenous variables):

	1981–1990	1991–2000
BASELINE	2.83%	2.88%
LOW GROWTH	2.77	2.69
VERY LOW GROWTH	2.50	2.30
HIGH GROWTH	2.87	3.07

these ILO assumptions underlie the HIGH GROWTH and LOW GROWTH cases reported in Table 6.10. That is, these two counterfactuals maintain all BASELINE assumptions except those dealing with labor force growth following the ILO's projections. Since it could be argued that the ILO has failed to capture the more recent evidence of demographic transition, Table 6.10 also considers a case of VERY LOW GROWTH, where the rate of labor force growth is allowed to decline very sharply from the 2.68 percent per annum rate in the late 1970s, to 2.5 percent per annum in the 1980s, and to 2.3 percent per annum in the 1990s. These demographic events underlying the VERY LOW GROWTH case appear overly optimistic to us, but they certainly will serve to place an outer bound on our counterfactual experiments.

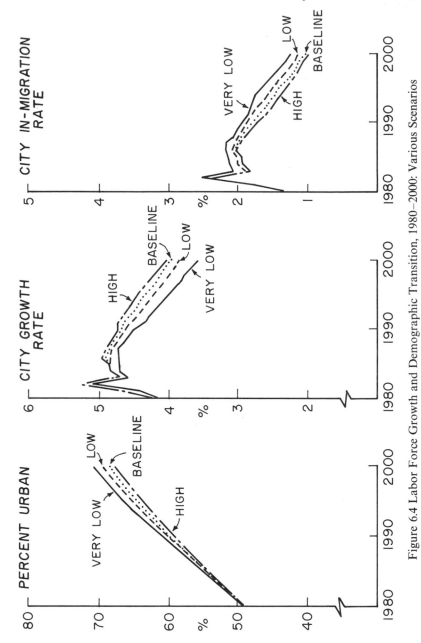

Figure 6.4 Labor Force Growth and Demographic Transition, 1980–2000: Various Scenarios

Which of these cases is most favorable for urban growth? As we pointed out in Chapter 4, the answer depends on the urban attribute of interest. Rapid rates of economywide labor force growth do indeed foster rapid rates of city growth, but they do *not* foster rapid rates of urbanization. In any case, what is most striking about the results presented in Table 6.10 is how little future Third World urban performance is influenced by the choice between the three ILO alternatives—BASELINE, LOW GROWTH, and HIGH GROWTH. Rates of city growth and in-migration peak in the mid-1980s in each case, each undergoes a pronounced retardation over the subsequent decade and a half, and they all reach similar values in the year 2000. For example, while the rate of city growth is 3.97 percent per annum in the year 2000 according to the BASELINE, the figure is only slightly lower according to LOW GROWTH (3.85 percent per annum), and only slightly higher according to HIGH GROWTH (4.07 percent per annum). Even under the unlikely demographic conditions underlying VERY LOW GROWTH, the contrasts with BASELINE are hardly spectacular: compared with BASELINE, VERY LOW GROWTH reaches 70.9 rather than 68.4 percent urban in the year 2000; city growth rates are 3.57 rather than 3.97 percent per annum; and the rate of city in-migration is 1.21 rather than 1.05 percent per annum.

In short, compared with the role of relative prices, Third World urban growth is unlikely to be very sensitive to any relevant range of alternative demographic and labor force growth scenarios, at least over the next two decades.

Foreign Capital Conditions

If changing demographic events are unlikely to influence Third World city growth trends by much up to the year 2000, foreign capital conditions are likely to be an even less significant influence. Table 6.11 reports only two alternatives, alternatives that the *World Development Report* (1981) characterizes as "high" and "low" bounds. The BASELINE assumes an optimistic case where the "resource gap share of GDP" (F/GDP) remains at the 3 percent level which prevailed, on average, over the 1970s. Indeed, BASELINE might well be labeled LARGESS. The second case, AUSTERITY, might be viewed as the more relevant alternative. Here the share is assumed to decline from 3 percent to 1.8 percent by the year 2000, following the *World Development Report*'s "low" projection, but a projection that they feel is more likely unless fuel-induced

TABLE 6.11

City Growth Projections, 1980–2000: Alternative
Foreign Capital Conditions Scenarios (F/GDP Varies)

BASELINE ≡ LARGESS

Year	% Urban	City Growth	Net Urban In-migration Rate
1980	49.2%	4.10%	1.35%
1985	54.3	4.84	1.96
1990	59.7	4.67	1.79
1995	64.4	4.33	1.41
2000	68.4	3.97	1.05

AUSTERITY

Year	% Urban	City Growth	Net Urban In-migration Rate
1980	49.2%	4.10%	1.35%
1985	54.3	4.82	1.94
1990	59.7	4.68	1.80
1995	64.4	4.32	1.40
2000	68.3	3.95	1.04

NOTE: The AUSTERITY counterfactual assumes BASELINE conditions for all but F/GDP (where $F/GDP = 3\%$ in BASELINE ≡ LARGESS):

Austerity		Austerity	
1981	2.90%	1986	2.64%
1982	2.88	1987	2.58
1983	2.81	1988	2.52
1984	2.76	1989	2.46
1985	2.70	1990	2.40
Austerity		Austerity	
1991	2.34	1996	2.04%
1992	2.28	1997	1.98
1993	2.22	1998	1.92
1994	2.16	1999	1.86
1995	2.10	2000	1.80

price shocks over the next two decades return to the dramatic path witnessed in the wake of 1973–74.

Table 6.11 can be summarized quickly. Whether foreign capital flows to the Third World will reflect conditions of LARGESS or AUSTERITY, future urban growth performance will not be significantly influenced. Relative prices and the state of world commodity markets simply overwhelm foreign capital conditions in importance.

Productivity Slowdown, Speedup, and Unbalancedness

As we pointed out earlier in this chapter, expert opinion offers no quantitative guidelines on the future of productivity advance in the Third World. As a result, the six alternative productivity growth scenarios in Table 6.12 should be viewed as sensitivity analysis only,

TABLE 6.12
City Growth Projections, 1980–2000: Alternative Productivity Growth Scenarios

		BASELINE	
Year	% Urban	City Growth	Net Urban In-migration Rate
1980	49.2%	4.10%	1.35%
1985	54.3	4.84	1.96
1990	59.7	4.67	1.79
1995	64.4	4.33	1.41
2000	68.4	3.97	1.05

		SLOWDOWN	
Year	% Urban	City Growth	Net Urban In-migration Rate
1980	49.2%	4.10%	1.35%
1985	53.9	4.73	1.84
1990	58.8	4.49	1.62
1995	63.0	4.19	1.27
2000	66.6	3.90	0.99

		SPEEDUP	
Year	% Urban	City Growth	Net Urban In-migration Rate
1980	49.2	4.10	1.35
1985	54.6	5.00	2.08
1990	60.5	4.80	1.92
1995	65.5	4.36	1.44
2000	69.6	3.93	1.02

(continued)

TABLE 6.12   (*continued*)

	BALANCED		
Year	% Urban	City Growth	Net Urban In-migration Rate
1980	49.2	4.10	1.35
1985	53.7	4.60	1.72
1990	58.4	4.51	1.64
1995	62.8	4.26	1.34
2000	66.5	3.96	1.05

	MORE UNBALANCED		
Year	% Urban	City Growth	Net Urban In-migration Rate
1980	49.2	4.10	1.35
1985	55.8	5.57	2.66
1990	63.5	5.32	2.43
1995	70.3	4.79	1.85
2000	76.0	4.30	1.38

	VERY UNBALANCED		
Year	% Urban	City Growth	Net Urban In-migration Rate
1980	49.2	4.10	1.35
1985	57.9	6.36	3.44
1990	67.8	5.82	2.91
1995	76.3	5.00	2.06
2000	82.9	4.35	1.43

NOTE: These counterfactuals assume the following over 1981–2000:

	TFPG	$\dot{T}_A/\dot{T}_M$	$\dot{T}_{KS}/\dot{T}_M$
BASELINE	1.8%	0.8	0.5
SLOWDOWN	1.0	0.8	0.5
SPEEDUP	3.0	0.8	0.5
BALANCED	1.8	1.0	1.0
MORE UNBALANCED	1.8	0.5	0.5
VERY UNBALANCED	1.8	0.25	0.25

although the qualitative dimensions will certainly be familiar to the informed reader. Following the research strategy of Chapter 5, Table 6.12 offers two kinds of experiments. The first changes the overall rate of total-factor productivity growth, while maintaining the *relative* rate (or unbalancedness) across sectors. Thus, SLOW-DOWN and SPEEDUP maintain all the assumptions of BASE-LINE except that the former lowers the aggregate rate of total-factor productivity growth to 1 percent per annum, while the latter raises it to 3 percent per annum, a range that covers the total-factor productivity experience through the early 1970s of half of the sixteen developing countries documented in Appendix C. The second holds the aggregate rate of total-factor productivity growth constant at the BASELINE rate of 1.8 percent per annum, but varies the degree of unbalancedness across sectors. These three cases—labeled BALANCED, MORE UNBALANCED, and VERY UNBAL-ANCED—are described in the notes to Table 6.12, but they can be summarized briefly here: BALANCED assumes that agriculture, manufacturing, and the *KS* sector all enjoy the same rates of total-factor productivity growth; MORE UNBALANCED assumes that agriculture and the *KS* sector lag behind at half the rate of manu-facturing; and VERY UNBALANCED assumes that these two sectors lag behind at one-quarter the rate of manufacturing.

Figure 6.5 summarizes the impact of the aggregate rate of total-factor productivity growth on urban performance, where projections to the year 2000 under SPEEDUP and SLOWDOWN assumptions are compared with BASELINE. The results are striking, and con-sistent with the findings of Chapters 4 and 5. While the share of the population urban in the year 2000 *is* responsive to the overall pace of total-factor productivity growth, the influence is far smaller than the literature would suggest. While the percentage urban in the year 2000 is 68.4 percent in BASELINE, it is not much higher in SPEED-UP (69.6 percent), nor all that lower in SLOWDOWN (66.6 per-cent). Furthermore, even those end-point differences seem to be the result of cumulative short-run influences in the first half of the pro-jection period: by the year 2000, the net urban in-migration rate is almost identical in the three cases, and the same is true of city growth rates.

In contrast, Figure 6.6 illustrates just how sensitive urban projec-tions are to the *unbalanced* rate of total-factor productivity growth across sectors. BASELINE captures a stylized fact of early phases of modern economic growth: the rate of technical change is usually far more rapid in the modern, urban-based manufacturing sectors

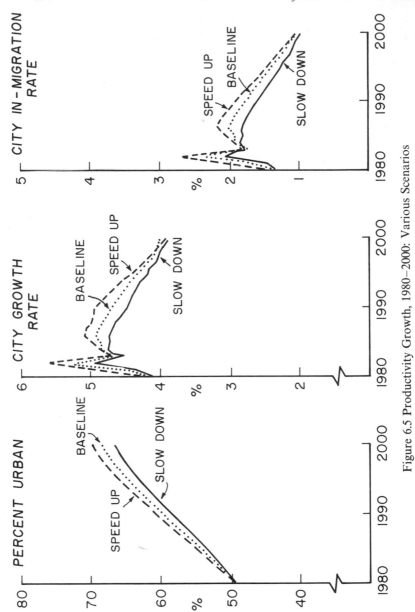

Figure 6.5 Productivity Growth, 1980–2000: Various Scenarios

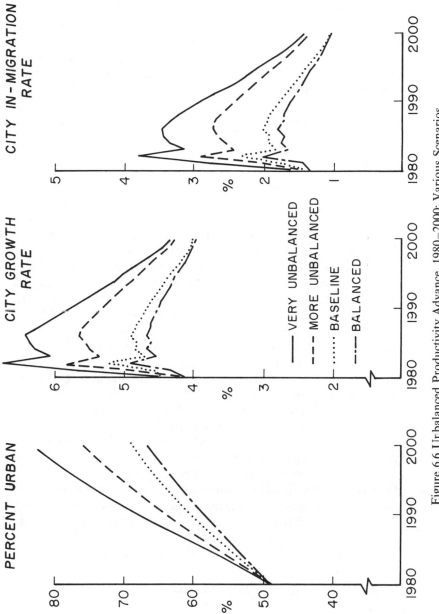

Figure 6.6 Urbalanced Productivity Advance, 1980–2000: Various Scenarios

than in the traditional, rural-based primary products sectors. Traditional service sectors, of course, also tend to lag behind. The size of the bias and the magnitude of the unbalancedness varies across nations, but it has been a technological fact of life since Britain's first Industrial Revolution, in spite of past agricultural revolutions and contemporary Green Revolutions. The BALANCED scenario asks us to imagine what future urbanization would be like if all sectors enjoyed the same rate of technical progress, that is, if unbalancedness disappeared from Third World experience. This case may seem unlikely, but it *would* be consistent with the technological slowdown in manufacturing which has characterized Japan and America in recent years (Hulten and Nishimizu, 1982). In fact, balanced sectoral productivity performance seems to have characterized American growth experience since the 1920s, as it passed into mature stages of growth (Williamson and Lindert, 1980). Perhaps BALANCED is not so unlikely after all. Or perhaps the MORE UNBALANCED and VERY UNBALANCED cases, typical of fast-growing success stories like Korea and Taiwan, are more likely to spread to the rest of the Third World over the next two decades. In short, any of these three cases—BALANCED, MORE UNBALANCED, and VERY UNBALANCED—is plausible. And the actual unbalanced rate will matter a great deal to future urban performance in the Third World.

The contrasting results in Figures 6.5 and 6.6 suggest an obvious moral. Urban economists believe that "the income elasticity of demand for goods provide clues as to why cities and economic growth invariably seem to accompany each other" (Mohan, 1979, pp. 6–7). As an economy grows, the proportion spent on food does indeed decline, increasing the relative demand for urban-produced non-food products. Presumably, the faster the growth, the more rapid the demand shift toward urban-based activities. While the argument certainly makes qualitative sense, the results in Figures 6.5 and 6.6 suggest that it isn't so much the overall rate of productivity growth—helping drive per capita income improvement—that counts, but rather the *unbalanced* character of that growth is the driving force behind urban change.

4. SUMMARY

Demographers have long noted a typical pattern of spatial development associated with the transition from agrarian poverty to modern industrial affluence. They call it the "urban transition," where the population share in urban areas rises from low to high levels along a non-linear path of first high and then low rates of urbanization. The key demographic component of the urban transition is rural-urban migration, and this experience tends to be non-linear as well. The rate of city in-migration tends to rise to high levels in early stages of modern economic growth, while subsequently falling through time in later stages of growth. Rogers (1977) and Zelinsky (1971) suggest we call this the "mobility transition," a term to be added to "demographic transition," as another central demographic feature of modern economic growth requiring explanation.

Certainly the mobility transition needs an explicit economic explanation. The Kelley–Williamson model of Third World urbanization and economic growth is one such framework which offers an endogenous explanation of the mobility transition. It conforms with the stylized facts, and economic forces are doing the work in driving that transition. But the model also shows how changes in the underlying demographic, technological, and price environment of modern economic growth can change the pace and character of the transition. Unique historical variants to the stylized "mobility transition" are not only possible, but likely. This chapter has shown which of those demographic, technological, and price environments is likely to matter most in contributing to historical variety across nations.

From this perspective we can now see that the city growth problems of the 1960s and 1970s *were* unusually severe, and that, on average, the Third World has passed its high watermark. They would have been severe even if external conditions had not been especially favorable to city growth up to the mid-1970s. They were especially severe, however, since these conditions *were* especially pro-urban. The 1980s and the 1990s are likely to be different. The endogenous forces of "mobility transition" would have guaranteed that result, but the less pro-urban demographic, technological, and price environment up to the year 2000 is likely to ease city growth problems even more.

CHAPTER SEVEN

Summing Up

1. MODELING CITY GROWTH

Can the complex social process that produces urbanization and city growth be modeled? This book has shown that it is indeed possible, and, more important, the model developed in Chapter 2 appears to replicate much of recent Third World urban history. We have shown that our dynamic, eight-sector general equilibrium model accounts for the aggregate growth, industrialization, accumulation, inequality, *and* city growth trends during the 1960s and early 1970s prior to the OPEC price shocks. Moreover, many of the "problems" of Third World city growth seem to be reproduced by the model: the "urban transition" drives the bell-shaped pattern of city growth rates; excess demand for urban housing and social overhead is generated in early stages of growth, especially among the urban poor who flock to the "squatter settlements" on the fringe of the booming cities; urban land values surge at rates far exceeding output and employment growth in the cities; and rising density, congestion, and rents tend to increase the relative cost of city life.

Such tests of the model's ability to replicate recent Third World history are crucial, for how else can economic/demographic models of city growth gain credibility? We think our model passes the test, warranting its use to answer the question "what drives Third World city growth?"

2. WHAT HAVE WE LEARNED?

The Urban Transition

In the absence of any changes in the exogenous economic/demographic environment facing the Third World over the next two decades, the model predicts that the vast majority of the urban transition will be completed by the year 2000. The equilibrium share of the population living in urban areas is, according to the model, about 85 percent, a figure that would be reached at the end of the century 1960–2060. By the year 2000, however, it appears that the RDC economy will have passed through almost nine-tenths of the complete urban transition. And by that date, the model predicts that the Third World will have passed through a historical time-path following the conventional logistic curve, with rising and then falling city growth and in-migration rates. Based on these predictions, many urban problems associated with high *growth* rates will be far less severe by the end of the century, fewer complaints will be heard from the urban planners, and reports of urban environmental decay will lose some of their popular interest. By the year 2000, the Third World will simply find it easier to cope with the far lower city growth rates. On the hand, whether the social and political problems associated with urban agglomerations will have become more manageable is yet another matter, and one about which our model is silent.

Over-urbanization

This books offers little evidence in support of the over-urbanization view adopted by the pessimists. One version of this view is that urbanization tends to outpace industrialization in the Third World. In contrast, we find abundant evidence supporting the opposite view: industrialization (and manufacturing employment growth) has been the "engine of urbanization" in the past and will continue to be so in the future.

Economics versus Demography

The advantage of the approach taken in this book lies with its endogenous treatment of city in-migration rates, an approach that emphasizes the critical role of macro economic events on the individual migration decision. This is not true of the demographic models, where rural-urban migration rates are treated as exogenous. We find the demographers' approach unattractive since it is not well equipped to explore the impact of various nationwide events (including policy) on city in-migration and city growth. Furthermore, the demographers' assumption of exogeneity implies an understatement of future city growth as well as the speed of the urban transition. When the predictions of our general equilibrium model are compared with those of the demographer, we find the predicted urban transition far more rapid: city growth rates accelerate more sharply in early stages of development, peak rates of city growth are higher, and the retardation from that peak is more dramatic. This difference can be explained largely by our endogenous treatment of migration, coupled with the forces of economywide growth and structural change. As it turns out, Third World economic development embodies forces that are far more favorable to city in-migration than the demographic models would suggest. Since the endogenous forces of economic development tend to generate increasing city "pull" in the early stages of growth, the demographic models fail to capture fully the very forces that drive the mobility transition.

Exogenous Shocks and Departures from Smooth Urban Transitions

What happens when the Third World is shocked by changes in its exogenous economic/demographic environment? The "urban transition" can be and has been sharply retarded, halted, or accelerated by such changes in the past, and most Third World countries have little or no control over such shocks.

Conditions prior to the 1973–74 OPEC price shocks were unusually favorable to rapid Third World city growth. While city in-migration and city growth would have been high and rising in the absence of these favorable conditions, they were even higher due to their presence. Furthermore, the modest city growth slowdown in the Third World during the remainder of the 1970s was initiated *entirely* by the appearance of unfavorable exogenous conditions. Had the favorable pre-OPEC conditions prevailed after 1973, city growth rates would have risen still further, making Third World urban problems more severe than they were. Which of these two sets of conditions will prevail over the next two decades? The answer will have important implications for Third World city growth up to the year 2000, although the main dimensions of the long-run urban transition will be apparent in both cases.

Which Exogenous Shocks Matter Most?

Apart from policy, this book has explored the impact of six "shocks" which comprise the macroeconomic/demographic environment of the Third World economies in our model: population pressure and demographic transition; unbalanced productivity advance; the terms of trade between primary products and manufactures; the relative scarcity of imported fuels and raw materials; the increasing scarcity of arable land; and the relative austerity of international capital markets and the availability of foreign capital. Some of these have a predictable impact on city growth. Others offer surprises. In any case, our motivation from the start has been to sort out the influence of each of these forces in the past as well as their likely influence in the future.

It is commonly believed that agricultural land scarcity has played an important role in pushing labor into Third World cities. While the qualitative argument is certainly correct, has rural land scarcity been an important *quantitative* ingredient of Third World city growth? The answer is unambiguously "no." First, Chapter 4 showed that even under the best of circumstances land is a relatively insignificant determinant of city growth. Second, Chapter 5 showed that trends in arable land stock growth should have tended to *raise* the rate of city growth in the 1970s, above that of the 1960s. In fact, city growth slowdown was typical of the 1970s. Third, Chapter 5 also showed that Third World city growth rates in the pre-OPEC period would have been only slightly higher had the arable land stock failed to grow at all over the period. Thus, trends in land stock growth cannot account for trends in city growth. So much for agricultural land scarcity as a significant source of "push" to the cities.

Given the relative capital-intensity of the cities, W. Arthur Lewis (1977) has suggested that urban growth breeds foreign capital dependence and that the relative abundance of foreign capital must therefore be a significant determinant of city growth. This hypothesis encourages the view that foreign capital inflows to the Third World must have played a critical role in accounting for the rapid city growth up to 1973–74. After all, the Third World was a heavy recipient of foreign capital during the 1960s and 1970s, reaching an average 3 percent of GDP for the forty countries underlying our analysis. Yet Chapter 4 has shown the comparative static impact of foreign capital on urbanization to be small. More to the point, Chapter 5 showed that city growth rates between 1960 and 1973 would have been pretty much the saame had there been *no* net foreign capital inflows into the Third World. Chapter 6 reaches a similar conclusion regarding the next two decades: conditions in foreign capital markets will simply not matter much for long-run city growth up to the year 2000.

The remaining four forces appear to be far more crucial to Third World city growth, past, present, and future. But even here we have some surprises: the unbalanced character of productivity advance across sectors is far more important than the overall economywide rate; the terms of trade between primary products and manufactures is far more important than is the relative scarcity of imported fuels and raw materials; and the Malthusian "bomb" plays a smaller role than conventional wisdom would suggest. Consider each of these assertions in more detail.

Popular accounts of Third World city growth and urbanization suggest that high rates of population growth lie at the core of the "problem." Indeed, a World Bank team recently told us that "the increase in population growth of the twentieth century is the single most important factor distinguishing present and past urbanization" (Beier et al., 1976, p. 365). Similar comments can be found elsewhere in the literature. The argument certainly seems plausible, yet the impact multipliers in Chapter 4 suggest that conventional wisdom requires significant modification, the extent depending on which aspect of urbanization and city growth is of interest. As far as urbanization is concerned—here defined as the percentage of total population urban—population growth does *not* offer an explanation for Third World experience since it has precisely the opposite effect. As far as in-migration and city growth are concerned, Chapter 4 reports the more conventional result—rapid population growth does foster rapid in-migration and city growth. Yet, even here the impact multipliers are smaller than might be expected. In any case, Chapter 5 shows that, contrary to conventional wisdom, "the increase in population growth in the twentieth century" is *not* "the single most important factor." Had the Third World undergone American nineteenth-century population growth or even twentieth century European population growth, the rate of in-migration and city growth would have still been unusually high. In short, it appears that the role of population pressure has been overdrawn as a source of Third World urbanization in the recent past. Furthermore, the forces of demographic transition over the next two decades are unlikely to have a significant impact on future city growth.

What about world markets, domestic price policy, natural resource scarcity, and the cost of imported fuel? Here we appear to have found one of the key determinants of Third World city growth. Not only does Chapter 4 confirm that the model is sensitive to the terms of trade between primary products and manufactures as well as to the relative price of imported raw materials and fuels, but it appears that past, present, and future trends in these prices will matter a great deal. Much of the city growth slowdown after 1973 can be attributed to price trends, and the unusually favorable city growth conditions in the 1960s and early 1970s are largely due to unusually favorable price trends. Future price trends will matter a great deal to Third World urbanization experience over the next two decades. Chapter 6 showed that if post-OPEC price trends in the 1970s were to prevail in the future, the rate of urbanization would slow down sharply during the 1980s, stopping entirely by the year 1990!

But *which* relative price trends matter most? Here we have a surprise. The terms of trade between urban-based manufactures and rural-based primary products have been and will be a far more important determinant of Third World city growth performance than the relative price of imported fuels and natural resources, in spite of the fact that urban-based activities are more fuel- and natural-resource-intensive than rural-based primary product activities.

Finally, what about the pace and character of technological progress? The conventional wisdom has it that "the income elasticity of demand for goods provide[s] clues as to why cities and economic growth invariably seem to accompany each other" (Mohan, 1979, pp. 6–7). As an economy grows, the proportion spent on food does indeed decline, increasing the relative demand for urban-based nonfood products. Presumably, the faster the growth—induced by rapid rates of economywide total-factor productivity advance—the more rapid the demand shift toward urban-based activities. While this conventional argument certainly makes sense, Chapters 5 and 6 suggest that it is not so much the overall rate of productivity advance—helping drive per capita income improvement—that counts, but rather the *unbalanced* character of that growth that has done and will do most of the work.

By unbalanced total-factor productivity advance we simply mean that technical change is usually more rapid in the modern, urban-based manufacturing sectors than in the traditional, rural-based primary products sectors. Traditional service sectors, of course, also tend to lag behind. The size of the bias and the magnitude of the unbalancedness varies across nations, but it has been a technological fact of life since Britain's first Industrial Revolution, and in spite of past agricultural revolutions and contemporary Green Revolutions. Chapter 5 argues that the unbalanced rate of technological progress in the Third World was the key favorable condition that accounted for the unusually rapid rates of city growth in the 1960s and 1970s. It follows that if the productivity slowdown currently characterizing the industrialized nations spills over into the industrializing Third World over the next two decades, Third World city growth rates will retard as well. Finally, this book has shown that among the eight sectors in the model, it is the unbalancedness between two of them, agriculture versus manufacturing, that matters most to city growth.

Housing, Social Overhead, and the Service Sectors

There are five service sectors in our general equilibrium model, three of which deal with housing needs for various socioeconomic classes. What role do they play in understanding city growth?

Among the many issues the book confronts, two will suffice to illustrate the importance of service sector activities to the city growth process.

First, what role does the alleged trade-off between housing-cum-social overhead investment and conventional investment in plant capacity play (Coale and Hoover, 1958)? While both of these investment activities have short-run employment-generating effects, they have quite different long-run job-creating effects. Investment in urban housing, for example, generates a demand for labor to create the housing stock, but it has little or no employment-generating effects after the housing stock is in place. In contrast, investment in manufacturing plant creates urban jobs in the future. The contrast is less striking in the case of social overhead, but even here while investment in plant and equipment has a *direct* impact on employment, investment in urban social overhead has only an *indirect* impact by improving the relative profitability of urban-based production. One would have thought, therefore, that housing-cum-social overhead investment would retard urban job creation and thus reduce the rate of city in-migration and city growth. According to the model, however, it appears that this job creation effect is offset by cost-of-living effects. That is, our model views the migration decision as being driven by *real* earnings differentials between city and countryside. The relative scarcity of housing, high rents, and thus the rural-urban cost-of-living differential is important to the analysis of city in-migration experience. Thus, a shift in policy favoring urban housing may well *increase* the long-run rate of city in-migration and city growth, rather than retard it. If intensive city-building investment is forgone in the hopes of accelerating the creation of future urban jobs by industrial investment, city growth may well decline.

Second, what role does the "informal" service sector play? Rapid city growth in the Third World has been accompanied by an impressive expansion of traditional or informal service sector employment. Until recently, many economists thought that this sector was low-productivity employment, and most viewed it simply as a residual sector, dominated by an underemployed reserve army. This view encouraged Michael Todaro (1969) and others to develop a simple search model of spatial migration where employment expectations in the formal or modern sectors were central. This well-known model was popular since it explained the puzzling contradiction of continued city in-migration in the face of (apparent) urban unemployment. The model was especially attractive since it could link "usually rapid" Third World city growth to poor policy. That is, under the reasonable stylized production function facts listed in

Chapter 4, Todaro could show that any urban wage policy that increased the institutionally-fixed wage in the modern sectors would serve to *raise* the city growth rate and urbanization levels.

Unfortunately, Todaro's prediction—increasing urban wages fostering an increase in the urban labor force—is inconsistent with the labor economist's conventional wisdom. In contrast, Chapter 4 shows that our model makes precisely the opposite prediction: a rise in the wage gap between the urban informal and formal sectors serves to *lower* city in-migration rates, to *lower* city growth rates, and to *lower* the share of the labor force in urban areas.

The source of the difference between the predictions of these two models lies with their treatment of the urban informal service sector. For Todaro, the informal service sector passively accepts all workers who wish to wait there for employment selection by the modern sectors. Wages do not fall in response to this labor glut. Nor are labor demand conditions in the traditional urban service sector of any importance since any urban worker failing to secure employment in the modern sectors can always find a place in the informal service sector at a fixed wage (zero). In short, labor absorption problems in the residual informal sector are assumed away by Todaro. We reject this view. Instead, we have adopted the position that traditional urban service employment is determined by supply-and-demand forces, just as in any other labor market that escapes government and union restrictions.

In summary, our model reveals that a policy that pegs modern sector wages above market levels will serve to choke off city growth: the opposite is true of the Todaro model. The difference is explained by alternative interpretations of the wage flexibility and absorptive capacity of the informal sector. Todaro's model was motivated by the apparent inconsistency between rising (under)employment in informal urban services and continued in-migration to the city. His explanation was based on the assumption of expectations of modern sector job selection—the higher pegged wage in the modern sector inducing in-migration by workers who hoped to be selected from the informal sector queue. Informal service sector employment expands as a result. Our model offers a different explanation of the same events. The higher pegged wage in the modern sectors displaces workers there, swelling the ranks of those employed in informal urban services, depressing wages there and elsewhere in the economy.

When one adopts this view, the *active* role of the urban informal sector as a source of urban jobs is clarified, especially as an important city-building and facilitating service activity geared toward the needs of the urban poor themselves.

3. WHERE DO WE GO FROM HERE?

These conclusions are all conditional upon the assumptions of the dynamic general equilibrium model used throughout this book. That is true of any analytical effort. The conclusions may also be specific to the group of countries underlying our data base. That is true of any empirical effort. So it is that the conclusions of this book must be viewed as working hypotheses only. They must be tested against new data—in particular, tested by the accumulation of country studies. And they must be tested against new models— especially models that introduce more of the institutional realities of the Third World than are present in our simple general equilibrium approach.

This, then, is only the start.

Mathematical Statement of the Core Economic Model

SUBSCRIPTS

Sector Subscripts (Production)

A: agriculture

H, KS: urban luxury housing; housing stock originally constructed in KS sector

H, RS: rural housing; housing stock originally constructed in RS sector

H, US: urban "slum" housing; housing stock originally constructed in US sector

KS: capital-intensive services (electricity, gas, water, transportation and communications, defense, construction of urban "luxury" housing stock, education)

M: manufacturing (manufacturing and mining)

RS: rural labor-intensive services (domestics, personal services, construction of rural housing stock)

US: urban labor-intensive services (domestics, personal services, construction of "slum" housing stock)

Factor Subscripts (Production)

K: capital

L: unskilled labor

R: land

S: skilled labor

Z: imported raw materials, including fuel

Location Subscripts

R: rural

U: urban

Commodity Subscripts (Demand)

A: food (A sector)

H: rent (H sector)

M: clothing durables, and other manufactures (M sector)

S: labor-intensive personal services (RS or US sector)

T: transportation and communications (KS sector)

Household Subscripts (Demand)

C: capitalists and landlords

KS: urban "favored" unskilled employed in KS sector

M: urban "favored" unskilled employed in M sector

R: rural unskilled from A and RS sectors

S: skilled from M and KS sectors

US: urban unskilled employed in US sector

PARAMETERS

$a_{H,RS}$: coefficient for translating housing stock into "rental units" for rural housing

$\alpha_{A,j}$: output elasticity (and cost share) of jth primary input in A sector, $j = K, L, R$

α_G: intercept in the government saving function

$\alpha_{i,F}$: output elasticity (and cost share) of composite of primary inputs in the ith sector, $i = M, KS$ (a value-added share in gross output)

$\alpha_{i,Z}$: output elasticity (and cost share) of Z in the ith sector, $i = A, M, KS$

$\alpha_{i,j}$: output elasticity (and cost share) of jth intermediate input in the ith sector, $i \neq j = A, M, KS$

α_i: returns to scale parameter in the informal service sectors, $i = US, RS$

$\alpha_{H,j}$: output elasticity (and cost share) of housing structures in urban housing production functions, $j = US, KS$

$\alpha_{R,j}$: output elasticity (and cost share) of urban land in urban housing production function, $j = US, KS$

β_G: marginal propensity to save out of government revenue (taxes and foreign "aid")

$\beta_{i,j}$: marginal propensity to consume the ith commodity out of supernumerary income, by the jth household type

c_k: marginal cost of training skilled workers of the kth (formal) educational attainment

γ_G: coefficient measuring the impact of increased urban population on government saving

$\gamma_{i,j}$: subsistence bundle, ith commodity, jth household type

$\delta_{H,j}$: depreciation rate on residential (housing) structures, $j = US, RS, KS$

δ_i: depreciation rate for physical ("productive") capital, $i = A, M, KS$

ε_H: elasticity parameter in the net housing investment functions

$\theta_{H,j}$: multiplicative parameter in the net housing investment function, $j = US, RS, KS$

κ: fixed "wage-gap" between unskilled labor in M and KS relative to US

$l_{i,j,k}$: labor force participation rate, $i =$ age, $j =$ sex, $k =$ location

$\lambda_{H,j}$: rate of total-factor productivity growth in the jth housing sector attributable to neutral, disembodied, sector-specific technological change, $j - US, RS, KS$

λ_i: rate of total-factor productivity growth in the ith sector attributable to neutral, disembodied, sector-specific technological change, $i = M, KS, A$

λ_K: rate of augmentation of physical capital through technological change

λ_L: rate of augmentation of unskilled labor through technological change

λ_S: rate of augmentation of skilled labor through technological change

ξ_i: distribution parameter in the ith sector value-added CES production function ($Q_{i,F}$), $i = M, KS$

ξ_i': distribution parameter in the ith sector composite capital function (ϕ_i), $i = M, KS$

ρ: rate of land growth

σ_i: elasticity of substitution between "composite capital" ϕ_i and unskilled labor in the ith sector value-added production function ($Q_{i,F}$), $i = M, KS$

σ_i': elasticity of substitution between capital and skilled labor in the ith sector composite capital function (ϕ_i), $i = M, KS$

τ_M: sales-tax rate on consumption of M sector goods

$\tau_{A,M}$: tax (or subsidy) rate on agricultural intermediate inputs purchased from manufacturing

$\tau_{\Pi,KS}$: proportional "corporate" profit tax rate in KS "mixed-enterprise" sector

$\tau_{\Pi,M}$: proportional "corporate" profit tax rate in M sector

$\tau_{H,j}$: urban property tax rate imposed on current value according to jth type of residential housing, $j = US, KS$

τ_Y: proportional income tax rate on property income and skilled earnings

ϕ_C: share of capitalists and landlords in the total population

ψ_i: after tax, "corporate" pay-out rate, $i = M, KS$

c_M: nominal cost of migration

Exogenous Variables

$A_{H,j}$: intercept in the jth housing production function, $j = US, KS$

A_i: intercept in the ith sector's production function, $i = A, M, US, RS, KS$

C: number of capitalists and landlords

$\bar{F}$: nominal value of "foreign aid" and private capital inflow

L: total unskilled labor stock

m_S: net mortality (and retirement) rate of urban skilled workers

N: population

$N_{i,j,k}$: population, $i = $ age, $j = $ sex, $k = $ location

$\bar{P}_A$: domestic market price received by producers of A goods

$\bar{P}'_A$: per unit domestic value-added price of A goods

$\bar{P}_M$: domestic market price received by producers of M goods

$\bar{P}'_M$: per unit domestic value-added price of M goods

$\bar{P}_Z$: price per unit of imported raw materials

R_A: land stock in agriculture

R_U: urban land stock

T_M: tariff and custom duty revenues (nominal values)

T_X: export tax revenues (nominal values)

x: augmentation level of physical capital through technological change

y: augmentation level of skilled labor through technological change

z: augmentation level of unskilled labor through technological change

ENDOGENOUS VARIABLES

c: marginal cost of training per skilled worker

c_j: nominal consumption, jth household

COL_j: cost-of-living in the jth household

d_A: nominal rent per hectare of farmland

d_U: nominal rent per hectare of urban land

$d_{U,j}$: nominal rent per hectare of urban land containing jth type structure, $j = US, KS$

D_A: total private consumption demand for A goods

$D_{H,j}$: total rental demand for jth type housing, $j = US, RS, KS$

D_{KS}: total private consumption demand for KS goods

D_M: total private consumption demand for M goods

D_{RS}: total private consumption demand for RS goods

D_{US}: total private consumption demand for US goods

G_{KS}: government current expenditures, net of investment in training (education) or "productive" capital

G_S: government saving available for training or "productive" capital accumulation

H_j: jth type housing stock, $j = US, RS, KS$

HOUSING: total gross investment in housing

i: economy-wide discount rate

$I_{H,j}$: gross housing investment, jth type housing, $j = US, RS, KS$

$I_{H,j}^N$: net housing investment in jth type housing, $j = US, RS, KS$

$I_{i,M}$: gross sectoral investment, "productive" physical capital, $i = A, M, KS$

I_M: total gross investment, "productive" physical capital

$I_{S,KS}$: KS outputs purchased for skills investment

K_i: physical (productive) capital in the ith sector, $i = A, M, KS$

L_i: unskilled labor in the ith sector, $i = A, M, US, RS, KS$

L_R: unskilled labor in rural area

L_U: unskilled labor in urban area

$L_{U,k}$: potential stock of unskilled urban "trainables" of the kth (formal) educational attainment

M_M: net imports of M goods

$P_{H,j}$: nominal rental cost per unit of jth type of housing

$P_{H,j}^S$: net rent on urban housing units received by owner after property tax, $j = US, KS$

$P_{i,j}$:   price of ith commodity paid by jth household

P_{KS}:   per unit price of KS output

P'_{KS}:   per unit value-added price of KS output

P_{RS}:   per unit price of RS output

P_{US}:   per unit price of US output

ϕ_i: "composite capital" in the ith sector, $i = M, KS$

$\phi_{S,j}$:   anticipated gain in profits due to investment in skilled workers, $j = M, KS$

$Q_{H,j}$:   "rental units" produced by the jth type housing stock, $j = US, RS, KS$

Q_i: output of the ith sector, $i = A, M, KS, US, RS$

$Q_{i,F}$:   composite of primary inputs in the ith sector, $i = M, KS$

$Q_{i,j}$:   intermediate input of jth good into the ith sector

$\hat{r}_{H,j}$:   profitability index on the jth type of housing, $j = US, RS, KS$

$r_{H,j}$:   structure rents on the jth type of housing, $j = US, RS, KS$

$\tilde{r}_i$:   pre-tax returns to efficiency capital in ith sector, $i = A, M, KS$

$\tilde{r}_i^*$:   quasi-rents per unit of efficiency capital in ith sector, $i = A, M, KS$

r_i: pre-tax returns to physical capital in ith sector, $i = A, M, KS$

$\hat{r}_{S,j}$:   profitability index on skills investment in the jth industry, $j = M, KS$

$R_{U,j}$:   urban land stock for the jth type housing, $j = US, KS$

R_A: land in farms

s_j: nominal saving, jth household

SAVINGS: total economy-wide savings

S: total skilled labor stock

S_i: skilled labor in the ith sector, $i = M, KS$

$\dot{S}$:   total skilled workers trained

$\dot{S}_j$:   skilled workers trained in the jth sector

T: total government tax revenue

TRAINING COSTS: total costs of training skilled workers

V_A: value of farmland, per hectare

$V_{H,j}$:   value of urban residential property per dwelling

$v_{i,j}$:   nominal expenditures by jth households on ith commodity

$\tilde{w}_{i,L}$:   efficiency wage, unskilled labor in ith sector

$w_{i,L}$: annual earnings, unskilled labor in ith sector

$\tilde{w}_{i,S}$: efficiency wage, skilled labor in ith sector

$w_{i,S}$: annual earnings, skilled labor in ith sector

$\tilde{w}_U$: expected urban unskilled earnings facing potential out-migrant

X_A: net exports of A goods

y_j^*: disposable income, jth households

Z_i: raw material (imported) inputs used in the ith sector, $i = A, M, KS$

PRODUCTION

$$Q_i = A_i Q_{i,F}^{\alpha_{i,F}} Z_i^{\alpha_{i,z}} \prod_{j=A,M,KS} Q_{i,j}^{\alpha_{i,j}}, \qquad i = M, KS \neq j$$

$$Q_{i,F} = \{\xi_i \phi_i^{(\sigma_i-1)/\sigma_i} + (1-\xi_i)[zL_i]^{(\sigma_i-1)/\sigma_i}\}^{\sigma_i/(\sigma_i-1)},$$
$$i = M, KS$$

$$\phi_i = \{\xi_i'[xK_i]^{(\sigma_i-1)/\sigma_i} + (1-\xi_i')[yS_i]^{(\sigma_i-1)/\sigma_i}\}^{\sigma_i/(\sigma_i-1)},$$
$$i = M, KS$$

$$\sum \alpha_{i,j} = 1, \qquad i = M, KS \neq j = F, Z, A, M, KS$$

(1), (2)

$$Q_A = A_A[xK_A]^{\alpha_{A,K}}[zL_A]^{\alpha_{A,L}} R_A^{\alpha_{A,R}} Z_A^{\alpha_{A,z}} \prod_{j=M,KS} Q_{A,j}^{\alpha_{A,j}}$$

$$\sum \alpha_{A,j} = 1, \qquad j = K, L, R, M, KS, Z$$

(3)

$$Q_i = A_i[zL_i]^{\alpha_i}, \qquad 0 < \alpha_i < 1, \qquad i = US, RS \tag{4), (5}$$

$$Q_{H,j} = A_{H,j} H_j^{\alpha_{H,j}} R_{U,j}^{\alpha_{R,j}}, \; \alpha_{H,j} + \alpha_{R,j} = 1, \qquad j = US, KS \tag{6), (7}$$

$$Q_{H,RS} = H_{RS}/a_{H,RS} \tag{8}$$

COMMODITY, SERVICE, AND LAND PRICE RELATIONSHIPS

$$\bar{P}_M' = \bar{P}_M - \bar{P}_Z \frac{Z_M}{Q_M} - \bar{P}_A \frac{Q_{M,A}}{Q_M} - P_{KS} \frac{Q_{M,KS}}{Q_M} \equiv \alpha_{M,F} \bar{P}_M \tag{9}$$

$$\bar{P}_A' = \bar{P}_A - \bar{P}_Z \frac{Z_A}{Q_A} - \bar{P}_M(1 + \tau_{A,M}) \frac{Q_{A,M}}{Q_A} - P_{KS} \frac{Q_{A,KS}}{Q_A}$$

$$\equiv (\alpha_{A,K} + \alpha_{A,L} + \alpha_{A,R})\bar{P}_A \tag{10}$$

$$P_{KS}' = P_{KS} - \bar{P}_Z \frac{Z_{KS}}{Q_{KS}} - \bar{P}_M \frac{Q_{KS,M}}{Q_{KS}} - \bar{P}_A \frac{Q_{KS,A}}{Q_{KS}} \tag{11}$$

$$V_A = \frac{d_A}{i} \tag{12}$$

$$V_{H,j} = \frac{P_{H,j}}{(i + \tau_{H,j})}, \qquad j = US, KS \tag{13), (14}$$

$$P_{H,j}^S = \left[\frac{i}{(i + \tau_{H,j})}\right] P_{H,j}, \qquad j = US, KS \tag{15), (16}$$

Primary Factor Markets

Labor Markets

$$\tilde{w}_{i,L} = P_i' \frac{Q_i}{Q_{i,F}} (1 - \xi_i) \left[\frac{Q_{i,F}}{zL_i}\right]^{1/\sigma_i} = \frac{w_{i,L}}{z}, \tag{17), (18}$$

$$i = M, KS, \text{ and where } P_M' = \bar{P}_M'$$

$$\tilde{w}_{A,L} = \bar{P}_A \alpha_{A,L} \left[\frac{Q_A}{zL_A}\right] = \frac{w_{A,L}}{z} \tag{19}$$

$$\tilde{w}_{i,L} = \frac{P_i Q_i}{zL_i} = \frac{w_{i,L}}{z}, \qquad i = US, RS \tag{20), (21}$$

$$\tilde{w}_{i,S} = P_i' \frac{Q_i}{Q_{i,F}} \xi_i (1 - \xi_i') \left[\frac{Q_{i,F}}{\phi_i}\right]^{1/\sigma_i} \left[\frac{\phi_i}{yS_i}\right]^{1/\sigma_i'} = \frac{w_{i,S}}{y}, \tag{22), (23}$$

$$i = M, KS, \text{ and where } P_M' = \bar{P}_M'$$

Labor Migration

$$w_{A,L} = w_{RS,L} \tag{24}$$

$$w_{M,S} = w_{KS,S} \tag{25}$$

$$w_{M,L} = w_{KS,L} = \kappa w_{US,L}, \qquad \kappa > 1 \tag{26}$$

$$\frac{w_{A,L}}{COL_R} = \frac{w_U - c_M}{COL_{US}} \tag{27}$$

$$w_U = \left[(1 - \tau_y)w_{M,S}\right]\left[\frac{\dot{S}(-1)}{L_U(-1)}\right] + \left[1 - \frac{\dot{S}(-1)}{L_U(-1)}\right]$$

$$\times \left[w_{M,L}\frac{L_M(-1)}{L_U(-1)} + w_{KS,L}\frac{L_{KS}(-1)}{L_U(-1)} + w_{US,L}\frac{L_{US}(-1)}{L_U(-1)}\right] \tag{28}$$

Capital Markets

$$\tilde{r}_i = P_i' \frac{Q_i}{Q_{i,F}} \zeta_i' \zeta_i \left[\frac{Q_{i,F}}{\phi_i} \right]^{1/\sigma_i} \left[\frac{\phi_i}{xK_i} \right]^{1/\sigma_i} = \frac{r_i}{x}, \qquad (29), (30)$$

$$i = M, KS, \text{ and where } P_M' = \bar{P}_M'$$

$$\tilde{r}_A = \bar{P}_A \alpha_{A,K} \left[\frac{Q_A}{xK_A} \right] = \frac{r_A}{x} \qquad (31)$$

Investment Allocation

$$
\underset{I_{i,M}}{\text{MINIMIZE}}
\left[
\begin{array}{l}
\text{RETURN DIFFERENTIALS} \\
= \left| \left[\tilde{r}_A^* - \tilde{r}_M^* (1 - \tau_{\Pi,M}) \right] \right| \\
\quad + \left| \left[\tilde{r}_A^* - \tilde{r}_{KS}^* (1 - \tau_{\Pi,KS}) \right] \right| \\
\quad + \left| \left[\tilde{r}_M^* (1 - \tau_{\Pi,M}) - \tilde{r}_{KS}^* (1 - \tau_{\Pi,KS}) \right] \right|
\end{array}
\right]
$$

such that

$$I_M = \sum_i I_{i,M}, \qquad i = A, M, KS \qquad (32)$$

where

$$\tilde{r}_i^* = \left\{ \tilde{r}_i + \frac{\partial r_i}{\partial K_i} (-1) \Big|_{K_i} \left[I_{i,M} - \delta_i K_i \right] \right\} - \delta_i \bar{P}_M,$$

$$i = A, M, KS$$

$$i = \left[\sum_i (1 - \tau_{\Pi,i}) x K_i(\tilde{r}_i^*) \right] \left[\bar{P}_M \sum_i K_i \right]^{-1}, \qquad (33)$$

$$i = A, M, KS$$

Intermediate Input Markets

$$\bar{P}_Z = \bar{P}_i \alpha_{i,Z} \frac{Q_i}{Z_i}, \qquad i = A, M \qquad (34), (35)$$

$$\bar{P}_Z = P_{KS} \alpha_{KS,Z} \frac{Q_{KS}}{Z_{KS}} \qquad (36)$$

$$P_{KS} = \bar{P}_i \alpha_{i,KS} \frac{Q_i}{Q_{i,KS}}, \qquad i = A, M \qquad (37), (38)$$

$$\bar{P}_M = P_{KS} \alpha_{KS,M} \frac{Q_{KS}}{Q_{KS,M}} \qquad (39)$$

$$\bar{P}_M(1 + \tau_{A,M}) = \bar{P}_A \alpha_{A,M} \frac{Q_A}{Q_{A,M}} \qquad (40)$$

$$\bar{P}_A = \bar{P}_M \alpha_{M,A} \frac{Q_M}{Q_{M,A}} \qquad (41)$$

$$\bar{P}_A = P_{KS} \alpha_{KS,A} \frac{Q_{KS}}{Q_{KS,A}} \qquad (42)$$

Land Markets (With Land Segmentation)

$$d_A = \bar{P}_A \alpha_{A,R} \frac{Q_A}{R_A} \qquad (43)$$

$$d_{U,j} = P_{H,j}^S \alpha_{R,j} \frac{Q_{H,j}}{R_{U,j}}, \qquad j = US, KS \qquad (44), (45)$$

$$d_{U,KS} = d_{U,US} \qquad (46)$$

Factor Employment

$$L_U = L_M + L_{KS} + L_{US} \qquad (47)$$

$$L_R = L_A + L_{RS} \qquad (48)$$

$$L = L_U + L_R \qquad (49)$$

$$S = S_M + S_{KS} \qquad (50)$$

$$R_U = R_{U,US} + R_{U,KS} \qquad (51)$$

FOREIGN TRADE SECTOR

$$[\bar{P}_M M_M - T_M + \bar{P}_Z(Z_{KS} + Z_M + Z_A)] - [\bar{P}_A X_A + T_X + \bar{F}] = 0 \qquad (52)$$

GOVERNMENT SECTOR

Government Taxes

$$\begin{aligned}
T = \tau_M[\bar{P}_M D_M] &+ \tau_{H,US} V_{H,US} Q_{H,US} + \tau_{H,KS} V_{H,KS} Q_{H,KS} \\
&+ \tau_{A,M}[\bar{P}_M Q_{A,M}] + \tau_Y[\psi_M(1 - \tau_{\Pi,M})(r_M - \delta_M \bar{P}_M)K_M \\
&+ \psi_{KS}(1 - \tau_{\Pi,KS})(r_{KS} - \delta_{KS}\bar{P}_M)K_{KS} + r_A K_A + d_A R_A \\
&+ (w_{M,S} S_M + w_{KS,S} S_{KS})] + \tau_{\Pi,M}(r_M - \delta_M \bar{P}_M)K_M \\
&+ \tau_{\Pi,KS}(r_{KS} - \delta_{KS}\bar{P}_M)K_{KS} + T_M + T_X
\end{aligned} \qquad (53)$$

Government Spending and Saving

$$G_S = \alpha_G + \beta_G[T + \bar{F}] + \gamma_G[\dot{N}_U(-1)] \qquad (54)$$

$$G_{KS} = [T + \bar{F}] - G_S \qquad (55)$$

Household Demand, Saving, And Income

$$v_{i,j} = P_{i,j}\gamma_{i,j} + \beta_{i,j}\left\{y_j^* - \sum_k P_{k,j}\gamma_{k,j}\right\}, \qquad k = A, M, T, S, H$$

$$c_j = \sum_i v_{i,j} \qquad\qquad\qquad\qquad\qquad\qquad\qquad\qquad (56)$$

$$s_j = y_j^* - c_j$$

$$COL_j = \sum_i P_{i,j}\frac{v_{i,j}}{c_j} \qquad (57)$$

where the *commodity index* is:

$i = A \equiv$ food (A sector)

$\quad M \equiv$ clothing, durables and other manufactures (M sector)

$\quad T \equiv$ transportation and communications (KS sector)

$\quad S \equiv$ labor-intensive personal services (RS or US sector)

$\quad H \equiv$ rent (imputed to housing sectors)

and the *household index* is:

$j = R \equiv$ rural (L_A and L_{RS}) households

$\quad US \equiv$ urban unskilled (L_{US}) households

$\quad M \equiv$ urban favored unskilled (L_M) households

$\quad KS \equiv$ urban favored unskilled (L_{KS}) households

$\quad S \equiv$ skilled (S_M and S_{KS}) households

$\quad C \equiv$ capitalist and landlord households

and where *household incomes* are: $\qquad\qquad\qquad\qquad (58)$

$$y_R^* = w_{RS,L} + \frac{P_{H,R}Q_{H,RS}}{L_R}$$

$$= w_{A,L} + \frac{P_{H,R}Q_{H,RS}}{L_R}$$

and where

$$y_{US}^* = w_{US,L} + \frac{P_{H,US}^S Q_{H,US}}{L_U}$$

$$y_M^* = w_{M,L} + \frac{P_{H,US}^S Q_{H,US}}{L_U}$$

$$y_{KS}^* = w_{KS,L} + \frac{P_{H,US}^S Q_{H,US}}{L_U}$$

$$y_S^* = (1 - \tau_Y)w_{M,S} + \frac{P_{H,KS}^S Q_{H,KS}}{C + S}$$

$$= (1 - \tau_Y)w_{KS,S} + \frac{P_{H,KS}^S Q_{H,KS}}{C + S}$$

$$y_C^* = (1 - \tau_Y)\left\{ \frac{\psi_M[(1 - \tau_{\Pi,M})(r_M - \delta_M \bar{P}_M)K_M]}{C} \right.$$

$$+ \left. \frac{\psi_{KS}(1 - \tau_{\Pi,KS})(r_{KS} - \delta_{KS}\bar{P}_M)K_{KS} + r_A K_A + d_A R_A}{C} \right\}$$

$$+ \frac{P_{H,KS}^S Q_{H,KS}}{C + S}$$

and *households face the following prices:* (59)

$$P_{A,j} = \bar{P}_A \qquad \text{for all } j$$

$$P_{M,j} = \bar{P}_M(1 + \tau_M) \qquad \text{for all } j$$

$$P_{T,j} = P_{KS} \qquad \text{for all } j$$

$$P_{S,R} = P_{RS}$$

$$P_{S,j} = P_{US} \qquad \text{for } j = US, M, KS, S, C$$

$$P_{H,j} = P_{H,KS} \qquad \text{for } j = S, C$$

$$P_{H,j} = P_{H,US} \qquad \text{for } j = US, M, KS$$

$$P_{H,R} = P_{H,RS}$$

PRIVATE CONSUMPTION DEMAND

$$\bar{P}_A D_A = v_{A,R}L_R + v_{A,US}L_{US} + v_{A,M}L_M + v_{A,KS}L_{KS}$$
$$+ v_{A,S}S + v_{A,C}C \qquad (60)$$

$$(1 + \tau_M)\bar{P}_M D_M = v_{M,R}L_R + v_{M,US}L_{US} + v_{M,M}L_M + v_{M,KS}L_{KS}$$
$$+ v_{M,S}S + v_{M,C}C \tag{61}$$

$$P_{KS}D_{KS} = v_{T,R}L_R + v_{T,US}L_{US} + v_{T,M}L_M + v_{T,KS}L_{KS}$$
$$+ v_{T,S}S + v_{T,C}C \tag{62}$$

$$P_{US}D_{US} = v_{S,US}L_{US} + v_{S,M}L_M + v_{S,KS}L_{KS} + v_{S,S}S + v_{S,C}C \tag{63}$$

$$P_{RS}D_{RS} = v_{S,R}L_R \tag{64}$$

$$P_{H,RS}D_{H,RS} = v_{H,R}L_R \tag{65}$$

$$P_{H,US}D_{H,US} = v_{H,US}L_{US} + v_{H,M}L_M + v_{H,KS}L_{KS} \tag{66}$$

$$P_{H,KS}D_{H,KS} = v_{H,S}S + v_{H,C}C \tag{67}$$

INVESTMENT AND SAVINGS

Housing Investment

$$\left.\begin{array}{l} I_{H,RS} = \text{Min}\{s_R L_R P_{RS}^{-1}, I_{H,RS}^N + \delta_{H,RS}H_{RS}\} \\ I_{H,RS} = \text{Max}\{0, I_{H,RS}\} \\ I_{H,RS}^N = \theta_{H,RS}[\hat{r}_{H,RS}^{\varepsilon_H} - 1] \end{array}\right\} \tag{68}$$

$$\left.\begin{array}{l} I_{H,US} = \text{Min}\{[s_{US}L_{US} + s_M L_M + s_{KS}L_{KS}]P_{US}^{-1}, \\ \qquad\qquad I_{H,US}^N + \delta_{H,US}H_{HS}\} \\ I_{H,US} = \text{Max}\{0, I_{H,US}\} \\ I_{H,US}^N = \theta_{H,US}[\hat{r}_{H,US}^{\varepsilon_H} - 1] \end{array}\right\} \tag{69}$$

$$\left.\begin{array}{l} I_{H,KS} = \text{Min}\{[s_S S + s_C C]P_{KS}^{-1}, I_{H,KS}^N + \delta_{H,KS}H_{KS}\} \\ I_{H,KS} = \text{Max}\{0, I_{H,KS}\} \\ I_{H,KS}^N = \theta_{H,KS}[\hat{r}_{H,KS}^{\varepsilon_H} - 1] \end{array}\right\} \tag{70}$$

$$\hat{r}_{H,j} = \frac{r_{H,j} - \delta_{H,j}P_j}{iP_j}, \qquad j = US, KS, RS \tag{71)–(73}$$

$$r_{H,j} = \left\{\frac{A_{H,j}P_{H,j}^S \alpha_{H,j}^{\alpha_{H,j}} \alpha_{R,j}^{\alpha_{R,j}}}{d_{U,j}^{\alpha_{R,j}}}\right\}^{1/\alpha_{H,j}}, \tag{74), (75}$$
$$j = US, KS$$

$$r_{H,RS} = \frac{P_{H,RS}}{a_{H,RS}} \tag{76}$$

$$\text{HOUSING} = P_{RS}I_{H,RS} + P_{US}I_{H,US} + P_{KS}I_{H,KS} \tag{77}$$

Training and Skills Investment

$$\phi_{S,j} = K_j[1-\tau_{\Pi,j}]\frac{\partial r_j}{\partial S_j}\Big|_{S_j + \dot{S}_j}, \qquad j = M, KS \tag{78}, (79)$$

$$\hat{r}_{S,j} = \frac{\phi_{S,j}}{i}, \qquad j = M, KS \tag{80}, (81)$$

$$c = \begin{cases} c_0 w_{M,L}(-1), & 0 \leq \dot{S} \leq L_{U,0}, k = 0, \; Ed > n \text{ years} \\ c_1 w_{M,L}(-1), & L_{U,0} < \dot{S} \leq L_{U,1}, k = 1, n-1 < Ed \leq n \\ \vdots & \vdots \\ c_n w_{M,L}(-1), & L_{U,n-1} < \dot{S} \leq L_{U,n}, k = n, \quad Ed = 0 \end{cases} \tag{82}$$

$$\hat{r}_{S,j} = c, \qquad j = M, KS \tag{83}, (84)$$

$$\dot{S} = \sum_j \dot{S}_j \leq L_U, \qquad j = M, KS \tag{85}$$

where l = optimal class trained satisfying (83) and (84), we can define

$$\text{TRAINING COSTS} = w_{M,L}(-1)\left\{\sum_k c_k L_{U,k} + c_l\left[\dot{S} - \sum_k L_{U,k}\right]\right\}, \tag{86}$$
$$k = 0, \ldots, l-1$$

$$\text{TRAINING COSTS} = P_{KS} I_{S,KS} \tag{87}$$

Aggregate Savings

$$\begin{aligned} \text{SAVINGS} = {}& (1-\psi_M)[(1-\tau_{\Pi,M})(r_M - \delta_M \bar{P}_M)K_M] + \delta_M \bar{P}_M K_M \\ & + (1-\psi_{KS})[(1-\tau_{\Pi,KS})(r_{KS} - \delta_{KS}\bar{P}_M)K_{KS}] \\ & + \delta_{KS}\bar{P}_M K_{KS} + s_{US}L_{US} + s_M L_M + s_{KS}L_{KS} + s_R L_R \\ & + s_C C + s_S S + G_S \end{aligned} \tag{88}$$

$$\bar{P}_M I_M = \text{SAVINGS} - \text{HOUSING} - \text{TRAINING COSTS} \tag{89}$$

MARKET CLEARING

$$Q_M + M_M = D_M + I_M + Q_{A,M} + Q_{KS,M} \tag{90}$$

$$Q_A = D_A + X_A + Q_{M,A} + Q_{KS,A} \tag{91}$$

$$Q_{KS} = D_{KS} + \frac{G_{KS}}{P_{KS}} + I_{H,KS} + Q_{M,KS} + Q_{A,KS} + I_{S,KS} \tag{92}$$

$$Q_{US} = D_{US} + I_{H,US} \tag{93}$$

$$Q_{RS} = D_{RS} + I_{H,RS} \tag{94}$$

$$Q_{H,US} = D_{H,US} \tag{95}$$

$$Q_{H,RS} = D_{H,RS} \tag{96}$$

$$Q_{H,KS} = D_{H,KS} \tag{97}$$

$$GDP = \bar{P}'_M Q_M + P'_{KS} Q_{KS} + \bar{P}'_A Q_A + P_{US} Q_{US} + P_{RS} Q_{RS}$$
$$+ \sum_j P_{H,j} Q_{H,j}, + \tau_M (\bar{P}_M D_M) + T_X + T_M,$$
$$j = KS, US, RS \tag{98}$$

DYNAMIC EQUATIONS

Accumulation of Capital and Residential Structures

$$K_i = (1 - \delta_i) K_i(-1) + I_{i,M}(-1), \qquad i = A, M, KS \tag{99--101}$$

$$H_j = (1 - \delta_{H,j}) H_j(-1) + I_{H,j}(-1), \qquad j = US, RS, KS \tag{102--104}$$

Land Growth and Technological Progress

$$x = x(-1) e^{\lambda_K} \tag{105}$$

$$y = y(-1) e^{\lambda_S} \tag{106}$$

$$z = z(-1) e^{\lambda_L} \tag{107}$$

$$A_i = A_i(-1) e^{\lambda_i}, \qquad i = M, KS, A \tag{108--110}$$

$$A_{H,j} = A_{H,j}(-1) e^{\lambda_{H,j}} \qquad j = US, KS \tag{111, 112}$$

$$R_A = (1 + \rho) R_A(-1) \tag{113}$$

$$R_U = (1 + \rho) R_U(-1) \tag{114}$$

Labor Force Growth and Skill Accumulation

$$C = \dot{C} + C(-1) \tag{115}$$

$$\dot{C} = \phi_C \dot{N} \tag{116}$$

$$S = \dot{S} + (1 - m_S) S(-1) \tag{117}$$

$$L_U = \dot{L}_U + L_U(-1) \tag{118}$$

$$\dot{L}_U = \sum_i \sum_j l_{i,j,U} \, \dot{N}_{i,j,U} - [\dot{S} - m_S S(-1)] - \dot{C},$$
$$i = 1, \ldots, n \text{ age classes}$$
$$j = 1, 2 \text{ sex classes}$$
$$\tag{119}$$

$$L_R = \dot{L}_R + L_R(-1) \tag{120}$$

$$\dot{L}_R = \sum_i \sum_j l_{i,j,R} \dot{N}_{i,j,R}, \qquad i = 1, \ldots, n \text{ age classes}$$
$$j = 1, 2 \text{ sex classes}$$
$$\tag{121}$$

The Representative LDC in 1960

B.1 THE CONCEPT OF THE REPRESENTATIVE DEVELOPING COUNTRY (RDC)

Since our "prototype" approach is defended in Chapter 3 at length, it should suffice here simply to repeat that the RDC is constructed in three steps. First, a group of developing countries must be drawn to generate the data base; second, this experience must somehow be summarized; and third, some relevant starting point in the post-World War II period must be selected. The criteria employed in selecting the developing countries is taken up in Section B.2. The early 1960s is taken as the starting point in the analysis, as close to 1960 as possible. This date represents the earliest year for which a fairly complete data set is available, and one that still provides a period long enough (fifteen–twenty years) to identify and evaluate long-run trends. Finally, the record of these developing countries is summarized by computing unweighted averages for each variable of interest.

B.2 SELECTING THE RDC GROUP

Beginning with the list of 101 developing countries provided in the *World Tables, 1976*, 24 countries were eliminated since they failed to supply two or more major categories of industrial production data for 1960. Since the analysis of patterns of production over time is central to the modeling effort, such data deficiencies were considered sufficient to exclude a country from the group.[1] The *World Tables, 1976* does not offer a clear definition of "developing country," but a figure of $500 per capita income in 1960 appears to represent a reasonable threshold beyond which a country would have been considered "developed." This criterion eliminates Argentina, Finland, Greece, Israel, and Spain, further reducing the group to 72.

[1] Countries excluded by the criterion include Afghanistan, Burma, Burundi, Fiji, Guinea, Iceland, Ireland, Kuwait, Laos, Lesotho, Liberia, Libyan Arab Republic, Madagascar, Nepal, Oman, Papua, Qatar, Saudi Arabia, Sierra Leone, Somalia, Tanzania, Tunisia, Upper Volta, and Venezuela.

Three additional criteria have been imposed. Countries are excluded with:

—a share of mineral exports in 1960 gross domestic product exceeding 20 percent;

—a net deficit in the foreign trade account in the period 1960–1965 exceeding 10 percent of gross domestic product; and

—per capita income growth during the 1960s falling short of 1 percent per annum.

The model does not possess a detailed trade specification. It was designed to examine those nations whose exports in 1960 were primarily agricultural goods, and whose imports were composed largely of industrial products and raw materials. However, a significant group of developing countries were and are heavily committed to mineral exports, oil-producers included. In the 1970s, the latter were also "price-setters," behavior at variance with the model's small country "price-taker" specification. Thus, we have excluded those nations that have been significantly dependent on mineral exports. Furthermore, we have excluded those countries that have been heavily dependent on foreign capital.[2]

Finally, the RDC model is designed to analyze a country undergoing successful and sustained economic development. It does not confront issues of prolonged stagnation, retardation, or politically and militarily induced instability. Thus, those countries that experienced either negative or relatively poor growth in per capita income (less that 1 percent per annum) over the 1960s are excluded from the RDC group.

Table B.1 lists the thirty-two developing countries with sufficient documentation but eliminated from the RDC group for the reason(s) given. The most prevalent excluding factor was poor growth performance (fourteen). This was followed by high dependence on capital inflows (eight), and heavy reliance on mineral exports (seven).

A total of forty nations remain to form the Representative Developing Country group (Table B.2). Of this total twenty-five provide data on output shares at factor costs; the remaining fifteen provide comparable data at market prices. The difference in these values is indirect taxes. Could the incidence of these taxes be sufficient to distort the underlying output structure in the initial period? An examination reveals that the output distributions are quite similar between the two sets of countries, and that we can reject the hy-

---

[2] The dependence on foreign capital inflows was measured by the net trade deficit of goods and services and non-factor services as a share of gross domestic product over the period 1960–1965. Those countries with deficits exceeding 10 percent of GDP were excluded.

TABLE B.1
Developing Countries with Sufficient Documentation but Excluded from the RDC Group and Reason for Exclusion

Reason for Exclusion	Countries
Foreign Capital Dependence	Barbados, Botswana, Malta, Congo, Cyprus, Jordan, Lebanon, Malawi
Mineral Export Dependence	Bolivia, Gabon, Iran, Iraq, Jamaica, Mauritania, Zaire
Negative Per Capita Income Growth	Central African Republic, Chad, Niger, Rwanda, Senegal, Sudan, Trinidad
Per Capita Income Growth, <1%	Benin, Cambodia, Ghana, Mali, Mauritius, Rhodesia, Uruguay
Combination of above	Guyana, South Vietnam, Zambia

TABLE B.2
The Forty-Country RDC Sample

Algeria	El Salvador	Malaysia	Portugal
Bangladesh	Ethiopia	Mexico	Sri Lanka
Brazil	Gambia	Morocco	Swaziland
Cameroon	Guatemala	Nicaragua	Syria
Chile	Honduras	Nigeria	Taiwan
Colombia	India	Pakistan	Thailand
Costa Rica	Indonesia	Panama	Togo
Dominican Republic	Ivory Coast	Paraguay	Turkey
Ecuador	Kenya	Peru	Uganda
Egypt	Korea	Philippines	Yugoslavia

pothesis that the subsets are drawn from a different country population. We have thus lumped together these countries in the RDC group.

To obtain some perspective on the representativeness of our RDC group, it might be helpful to compare key attributes of the RDC group with the larger group analyzed by Chenery and Syrquin in their *Patterns of Development* (1975). The comparison is confined to three attributes: population size (small = population less than 15 million; large otherwise); location (Asia, Africa, Latin America); and the Chenery and Syrquin international trade classification (small primary; small balanced; small industry; large). To provide comparability, we have examined only those non-European developing countries which Chenery and Syrquin (1975, Table 12) included in their analysis of trade patterns. Table B.3 displays the results.

It can be seen in Table B.3 that there is considerable correspondence between the two groups, although the RDC group is slightly larger in population size, a bit more Latin American, and has a

TABLE B.3

Comparison of Key Attributes in the RDC and
Chenery–Syrquin Groups

	% Distribution within Attribute	
Attribute	Chenery–Syrquin	RDC
Size		
Large	25.0	36.8
Small	75.0	63.2
Location		
Asia	35.0	28.9
Africa	36.6	34.2
Latin America	28.4	36.0
Trade Orientation		
Small, Primary	38.3	31.3
Small, Balanced	21.7	25.0
Small, Industry	15.0	6.3
Large	25.0	37.4

trade orientation geared toward larger countries. Moreover, the small industrial country is underrepresented in the RDC group. Nevertheless, the RDC group has considerable diversity in overall economic structure.

Finally, and perhaps most important, the RDC forty-country group contains *all* of the eleven largest developing countries outside of China. Given that one exception, eleven of our RDC countries account for 71 percent of the population among the ninety-one less developed countries equal to or greater than one million in size (Keyfitz, 1980, pp. 18–19): India, Indonesia, Brazil, Bangladesh, Pakistan, Nigeria, Mexico, the Philippines, Thailand, Turkey, and Egypt. In short, the RDC group covers more than 80 percent of the developing countries' population outside China, and includes all of the eleven largest.

B.3 INDUSTRIAL STRUCTURE, AGGREGATE DEMAND MIX, AND EMPLOYMENT DISTRIBUTION

Industrial Structure

All data documenting sectoral output shares are taken from the *World Tables, 1976*, with the background computer tapes providing further detail. Whenever possible, these sectoral output shares are taken as a percentage in GDP at factor cost, although a few countries supply these shares only at market prices.

The empirical counterparts to the model's sectors are as follows:

UN ISIC Definition	Model's Sector
Agriculture, livestock, forestry, fishing, hunting	*A*
Manufacturing; Mining and quarrying	*M*
Construction; Electricity, gas and water; Transportation; Banking and real estate; Public administration and defense	*KS*
Commerce and trade	*KS, RS, US*
Ownership of dwellings	*H*
Services; Other; Statistical discrepancy	*RS, US, H*

We confronted two major difficulties in making the national accounts correspond to the model's sectoral definitions: estimating the service flow on rental and owner-occupied housing stocks, and allocating some portion of commerce and trade to the *KS* sector. Once these two difficulties have been resolved, the informal service sector share will appear as a residual. The allocation of informal-sector output between *US* and *RS* is then guided by Preston's labor force distribution (discussed below) and by the innocuous assumption of roughly equal average labor productivities in the two informal service sectors.

The second difficulty can be quickly dispatched. In the absence of concrete evidence, we apply an arbitrary fraction of the commerce and trade total to the *KS* sector. After some experimentation with equilibrium solutions to the comparative static model, that fraction is set so that approximately 76 percent of service output is delivered by *KS*, with the remainder delivered by the two informal service sectors combined.

The share of rental service flows from housing stocks requires more discussion. The national income accounts do not report a total house rental component, and when rents do appear they are limited to rents on owner-occupied housing ("ownership of dwellings"). Rental streams from the "ownership of dwellings" is reported in the *World Tables, 1976*, and for the RDC group the share averages 5.4 percent (mean 5.425, standard deviation 2.325). This figure is too low since it excludes rented dwellings, the latter buried in "banking, insurance, and real estate or services and statistical discrepancy," but never reported separately. The UN's *Habitat* (1976, Table 4.2, p. 141), however, supplies sufficient information to estimate that about 60 percent of all LDC housing was owner-occupied in the

TABLE B.4
1960 GDP Output Shares in the RDC Group

Sector Name	Notation	% Share
Agriculture	*A*	36.6
Manufacturing and Mining	*M*	15.9
Modern Capital-Intensive Services	*KS*	29.6
Urban Informal Labor-Intensive Services	*US*	6.2
Rural Informal Labor-Intensive Services	*RS*	3.2
Housing, All Sectors	*H*	8.5
TOTAL	GDP	100.0

early 1960s. This suggests that the total share of rental service flows from housing stocks in GDP was in the neighborhood of 8.5 percent, and we shall use this estimate in all that follows.[3]

Table B.4 displays the GDP share estimates for six of the model's sectors—*A*, *M*, *KS*, *US*, *RS*, and *H*. While computed standard deviations indicate considerable variance around the "typical" RDC pattern, these average GDP shares will be taken as the RDC's initial conditions in 1960.

Aggregate Demand Mix

Going from the industrial output mix to the structure of aggregate demand is a relatively simple task once input-output flows have been estimated—an exercise that appears below in section B.5, and indirect taxes have been documented—an exercise that appears below in section B.6. With few exceptions, the remaining data requirements are satisfied by the national accounts reported for our RDC group in the *World Tables* for 1960. The RDC national accounts estimated for 1960 are summarized in Table 3.2. Here we simply highlight some key attributes of the RDC group: the investment share in GDP (at market prices) was 15.6 percent in 1960, about one-fifth of which was housing investment; government current expenditures were already almost 14 percent of GDP; the

[3] This estimate is close to that implied by household budget studies. Lluch, Powell, and Williams (1977), for example, report the housing expenditure share in household disposable income for Korea, Jamaica, the Philippines, Panama, and Thailand as 13.3 percent. This figure includes non-rent housing costs and is based on disposable income rather than GDP. When these two adjustments are made, the derived GDP share estimate is slightly below 8 percent, close to the 8.5 percent figure derived in the text for the far larger RDC group.

trade balance deficit was 3 percent of GDP; household final demand comprised 71 percent of GDP; and of household aggregate expenditures, 41 percent was devoted to foodstuffs, 12 percent to housing (including imputed owner-occupied rents and property taxes), 24 percent to manufactures (inflated by sales taxes), and the remainder to services of all kinds.

Sectoral Employment Distribution

Table B.5 reports labor force distribution between A, M, and the remainder of the economy. These data are derived from ILO *Yearbooks* (Table 2a, "Structure of the Economically Active Population," various issues). The ILO figures for the early 1960s are based

TABLE B.5
Labor Force Distribution (%)

		Sectors		
RDC Country	*Year*	*A*	*M*	*Residual*
Brazil	1960	51.6	11.4	37.0
Chile	1960	29.5	23.2	47.3
Taiwan	1956	55.9	13.9	30.2
Colombia	1964	48.9	14.9	36.2
Dominican Republic	1960	65.9	9.1	25.0
Ecuador	1962	57.4	15.3	27.3
Egypt	1960	58.3	9.7	32.0
El Salvador	1961	60.9	13.0	26.1
Guatemala	1964	65.8	11.6	22.6
Honduras	1961	70.0	8.5	22.5
India	1961	73.8	10.1	16.1
Indonesia	1961	73.3	6.1	20.6
Korea	1960	65.9	7.6	26.5
Mexico	1960	54.6	15.1	30.3
Nicaragua	1963	59.9	12.5	27.6
Pakistan	1961	75.6	8.3	16.1
Paraguay	1962	55.9	15.4	28.7
Peru	1961	51.8	16.0	32.2
Philippines	1960	65.9	11.0	23.1
Portugal	1960	43.7	21.8	34.5
Sri Lanka	1963	60.0	10.6	29.4
Syrian Arab Republic	1960	54.1	12.9	33.0
Thailand	1960	84.0	3.7	12.3
AVERAGE	1956–64	60.1	12.2	27.7

on labor force surveys, but these are available for only twenty-three of the RDC group. While these surveys were taken at various times, they tend to cluster around 1960, the initial starting point in the simulations. One adjustment has been made to the ILO data. The *Yearbooks* report three miscellaneous categories ("activities not adequately described," "persons seeking work for the first time," and "unemployed"). These categories, which rarely account for more than 2 or 3 percent of the labor force, have been distributed proportionately over the sectoral classifications.

What remains is the allocation of "residual employment" in Table B.5 among the three service sectors, *KS*, *US*, and *RS*. Preston's recent book, *Patterns of Urban and Rural Population Growth* (1979, Table 5.3), offers useful data to guide this allocation. While Preston does not classify labor by sector, he does supply occupational distributions. Furthermore, he develops a strong case for the high correlation between results using the alternative approaches. Preston's service employment figures are divided between the UN definitions of urban and rural, on the one hand, and between professional and administrative, clerical and sales, and traditional, on the other. We have assumed the following in deriving the summary statistics in Table B.6:

—all professionals and administrative employees are allocated to *KS*;
—half of the clerical and sales employees in urban areas are allocated to *KS* and the remaining to *US*;
—all rural clerical and sales employees are allocated to *RS*; and
—urban and rural traditional employment can be allocated to *US* and *RS*, respectively.

As Table B.6 indicates, these assumptions yield a share of urban to total labor in 1960 equal to 32.6 percent. In spite of all the problems associated with definitions of "urban," this 32.6 percent figure is quite close to the urbanization share implied by the *World Tables, 1976*; there, the 1960 figures averaged over the forty-country RDC group is 29.6 percent.

All that remains is to estimate the skilled component of the labor force and distribute it between *KS* and *M*, the only sectors that use such labor in our model. The production function parameters estimated in the literature and discussed in section B.5 are based on skilled labor inputs defined by those with eight or more years of education. While we would like to use the same criteria here, the *Demographic Yearbooks* supply such information only for those with seven or more years of education. Based on the *Demographic*

TABLE B.6
*Labor Force Distribution by Skill and Sector
Estimated for the RDC Group (%)*

Sector	Unskilled (L)	Skilled (S)	Total (L + S)
A	60.1	—	60.1
RS	7.3	—	7.3
Total Rural	67.4	—	67.4
M	9.7	2.5	12.2
KS	2.9	7.5	10.4
US	10.0	—	10.0
Total Urban	22.6	10.0	32.6
TOTAL	90.0	10.0	100.0

Yearbooks, the RDC group yields for 1968 (the year closest to 1960 for which such data exists) an average of 12.9 percent "skilled." This must be viewed as an overstatement for two reasons already noted: it is based on a year later than 1960, and it includes those with seven or more years of education, rather than eight or more. To accommodate this overstatement we have adjusted the percent of the labor force "skilled" downwards to 10 percent.

These 1960 estimated RDC labor force distributions are summarized in Table B.6.

B.4 CAPITAL AND LAND STOCKS

While there is little or no information on capital stocks and their distribution in the developing countries, especially during the 1960s, we can be guided by some stylized facts and by data on sectoral incremental capital-output ratios (ICORs).

To begin with, GDP (at market prices) is set arbitrarily at 100 in the base year. The RDC national accounts imply from this that GDP at factor cost is 88.48 (see Table 3.2). The next step is to assume an economywide capital-output ratio (ACOR) which, when including housing, we take to be 2.5 in the base period. The 2.5 figure is close to values assumed in various Third World macro-modeling exercises, for example, the 2.3 ACOR assumed by de Melo and Robinson (1978, Table 1, p. 12) for Colombia. The estimate also falls well within the range, 2.4 to 2.8, of long-period ICORs that have been documented (Higgins, 1968, Table 18-5, p. 393). It is, however, somewhat lower that the figures implied by the *World Tables*. The *World Tables* report data for twenty-two of the RDC group which make it possible to compute ICORs between 1961 and 1964, the average of which is 2.9.

Given GDP at factor cost and given the assumed ACOR of 2.5, the total value of the capital stock implied (including housing) is 221.3. The final step is to distribute this capital stock between sectors, implying sectoral ACORs.

While few would deny a rank order of ACORs reading down from housing, to modern services, to manufacturing, and finally to agriculture, establishing 1960 quantitative values is another matter. Consistent with the comparative static solutions of the model, and guided by the sectoral estimates by Gianaris (1970), we have assumed that agriculture's ACOR was about half of the economywide figure, that manufacturing was about three-quarters, and that the *KS* sector was a bit more than one-and-one-half times the economy-wide rate, while housing was almost three times the average. This implies the capital stock distributions in Table B.7. Table B.7 also displays some evidence drawn from the UN world model which supports the RDC assumptions. Leontief et al. (1977) supply estimates for 1970 which imply ACOR sectoral rankings that are quite close to the implied 1960 RDC rankings.

TABLE B.7
Capital Stock and Its Distribution Assumed in the RDC Model

Sector	(1) Value of Capital Stock (1960 Prices)	(2) GDP at Factor Cost (1960 Prices)	(3) ACOR (1) ÷ (2)	(4) ACOR Rankings 1960 RDC Model	(5) (ACOR$_M$ = 100) 1970 UN World Model
Manufacturing and Mining (M)	25.81	14.07	1.83	100	100
"Modern" Services (KS)	104.44	26.19	3.99	218	226
Agriculture (A)	36.75	32.38	1.13	62	52
Housing (H)	54.30	7.52	7.22	395	n.a.
Informal Services (US + RS)	—	8.32	—	—	n.a.
TOTAL	221.30	88.48	2.50	137	n.a.

NOTES AND SOURCES: Col. (2) is from Table 3.2, Col. (3) is estimated in the text, Col. (1) is simply Cols. (2) × (3), and Col. (4) converts Col. (3) into ACOR$_M$ = 100. Col. (5) is based on the UN world model (Leontief et al. [1977]), conveniently reproduced in Stern and Lewis (1980, Table 8.3). We have used the 1960 RDC output weights to aggregate the UN world model's sectors to the RDC sectors, and the figures reported here are averages for the $750 and $1,550 group used by Stern and Lewis (1970 prices).

As far as the land stock is concerned, the initial distribution is quite arbitrary, but it is guided in part by the UN *Habitat*'s figures on residential housing densities by housing type.

B.5 TECHNOLOGICAL PARAMETERS

Input/Output Relations

Input/output tables for the early 1960s are available for ten of the countries in the RDC sample.[4] We require data in a form whereby the gross value of a given sector's output can be first diminished by the value of its own input use, and the remainder can then be distributed between the supplying sources: primary inputs, imported intermediate (non-competitive) inputs, and domestic intermediate inputs purchased from the other two sectors. Table B.8 aggregates this data to conform with the RDC sector definitions. While there is considerable variation for any given cell across the country matrices, the intermediate input resource utilization patterns represented by the averages in Table B.8 appear to be reflected in most individual country statistics.

Production Parameters: M, KS, and H Sectors

P. R. Fallon and P.R.G. Layard (1975) have developed parameter estimates for the nested, three factor CES production function, using international cross-section data for the period 1961–1963, and applying definitions of unskilled and skilled labor (eight or more years of education) corresponding to the classifications employed in the present study. Their estimation sample comprises twenty-three developed and developing nations, half of which are included in our RDC sample. The latter countries include Brazil, Chile, Colombia, India, Kenya, Mexico, the Philippines, Korea, Turkey, Thailand, and Uganda.

[4] The ten countries (and year of estimation) are:

Bangladesh (1963)	Khan and MacEwan (1967)
Ecuador (1963)	Yotopoulos and Nugent (1976, pp. 58–59)
Korea (1966)	Song (1975)
Malaya (1960)	UN, *Economic Bulletin* (1965)
Mexico (1960)	Goreux and Manne (1973)
Morocco (1964)	Sheira (1968)
Pakistan (1963)	Khan and MacEwan (1967)
The Philippines (1961)	*The 1961 Interindustry Accounts of the Philippines* (see Palanca, 1974)
Sri Lanka (1963)	Perera (1967)
Taiwan (1961)	UN, *Economic Bulletin* (1965)

TABLE B.8
Input-Output Relationships for the RDC Model

Sector of Origin	Sector of Destination		
	A	M	KS
A	0	.159	.007
M	.065	0	.153
KS	.077	.122	0
Z	.040	.225	.029
Value Added (F)	.818	.494	.811
Gross Output	1.000	1.000	1.000

Fallon and Layard's sectoral classification is confined to mining, manufacturing, construction, and electricity-gas-water (EGW). While their manufacturing conforms to our M sector, their construction and EGW sectors comprise only a portion of our KS sector. We have elected to use their estimates for construction and EGW, combining these parameters using weights corresponding to the relative importance of these sectors in the RDC sample. The resulting elasticity of substitution estimates are $\sigma_M = 1.11$, $\sigma_{KS} = .93$, $\sigma'_M = .85$, $\sigma'_{KS} = .73$. With the exception of σ_M, these estimates conform to our a priori expectation that substitution possibilities in M and KS are more limited than in agriculture, and that physical capital and skills are (relative) factor complements. These results are also consistent with other estimates in a large and expanding literature, and conform with case study applications to developing countries (Bowles, 1970; Edmonston, Sanderson, and Sapoznikow, 1976; Lysy and Taylor, 1977; Adelman and Robinson, 1978).

Empirical studies of housing production functions are scarce. We will draw upon Muth's (1971) work which finds output elasticities of land and structures in housing production to be around .1 and .9, respectively.

Production Parameters: A Sector

Production parameter estimates for LDC agriculture in the early 1960s are surprisingly abundant, although they are available largely in case-study form for individual countries and regions, and display wide diversity in terms of factor definitions and production coverage. No single source is ideal from the perspective of the present study, but some "stylized facts" can be pieced together from several sources, empirical characterizations that few agricultural specialists would find objectionable.

First, recall the information on total value-added and intermediate input shares in A provided above. These data represent the average experience of those ten RDCs that possess input-output tables for this period. The following are provided in Table B.8: $\alpha_{A,M} = .065$, $\alpha_{A,KS} = .077$, $\alpha_{A,Z} = .040$, and $\alpha_{A,F} = .818$.

Next it is necessary to decompose value-added into the component factor shares for land, labor, and capital. The most comprehensive study providing such information is by Yujiro Hayami and Vernon Ruttan (1971). They have fitted an intercountry cross-section production function (Cobb-Douglas) for agriculture for 1960 (1957–1962 averages) based on the experience of some thirty-eight countries. While many of these countries are developed, eleven are included in the RDC sample: Brazil, Chile, Colombia, India, Mexico, Peru, the Philippines, Sri Lanka, Syria, Taiwan, Turkey, and Egypt.

Of the many regressions they estimate, we have selected the one with the best fit (Table 5-1, p. 93, col. Q2-IV). This regression provides estimates for output elasticities on land, labor, capital, and livestock inputs. However, our model does not explicitly consider livestock as factor input, and, as a result, the remaining factor share estimates provided by Hayami and Ruttan are in a sense underestimated by reference to our model specifications. We have therefore elected to use the relative factor share information they provide for land, labor, and capital, and to decompose the total value-added share of .818 accordingly. This yields the following estimates: $\alpha_{A,L} = .581$, $\alpha_{A,R} = .128$, and $\alpha_{A,K} = .109$.

B.6 Government Expenditures, Saving, and Tax Sources

Tax Sources

We need tax revenue sources for two purposes: to establish 1960 RDC initial conditions, and to derive the tax parameters (τ_i) which yield the total tax revenues (T). The 1960 share of total tax revenue (excluding foreign aid, F, but including operating surpluses of government enterprises) in GDP at market prices was 15.1 percent. This estimate is taken from the *World Tables*, averaged over the twenty-four countries in the RDC group for which tax distribution data were available. The same source reports that these governments saved (allocated to capital expenditures) 24.6 percent of total income sources ($T + F$). All that remains is to identify the 1960 sources of tax revenues and for this we relied on Chelliah's (1971) excellent survey.

TABLE B.9

The Sources of Tax Revenues Estimated for the RDC Model

Tax Source	Model Notation	1960 Share in Total Tax Revenue (%)
Sales Taxes	$\tau_M[\bar{P}_M D_M]$	36.9
Property Taxes	$\sum_j \tau_{H,j}[V_{H,j} Q_{H,j}], j = US, KS$	6.7
Import Duties	T_M	25.3
Export Taxes	T_X	7.4
Income Taxes	τ_Y [taxable income]	10.6
Profits Taxes	$\sum_j \tau_{\pi,j}(r_j - \delta_j \bar{P}_M) K_j, j = M, KS$	13.1
Tax Share in GDP	T	15.1

NOTE: "Taxable income" is defined as the sum of corporate profits distributed to households, rents and returns to capital in agriculture, and all wage income accruing to skilled workers. See Appendix A, equation (54).

Chelliah offers a breakdown of total tax revenues into sources for the same twenty-four RDCs mentioned above, and these sources can be easily forced to conform to the model's needs. The results are summarized in Table B.9, and they reflect the usual "stylized facts" of fiscal underdevelopment; that is, direct income taxes are a small share of the total in 1960 (23.7 percent), property taxes were even a more modest source (6.7 percent), while sales taxes (36.9 percent) and customs duties (32.7 percent) dominated the revenue stream.

The Government Savings Function

The government sector's expenditure and savings behavior is summarized in the model by the following two equations:

$$G_S = \alpha_G + \beta_G(T + \bar{F}) + \gamma_G \dot{N}_U(-1)$$

$$G_{KS} = (T + \bar{F}) - G_S.$$

Given total sources $(T + \bar{F})$[5] and savings generated by an estimated *GS* function, then government current expenditures *GKS* are determined residually. This section will describe the estimation of α_G, β_G, and γ_G in the G_S function. Note, however, that while the estimated β_G can be used directly in the RDC model, the values of α_G and γ_G

---

[5] The model takes $F = \bar{F}$ as exogenously given.

must be derived in terms of the RDC's units. γ_G will be derived as part of the initial conditions solution from an elasticity calculated at the sample means on the basis of the estimated γ_G. α_G will be derived residually since the values of government savings and revenue as well as urban growth are all known for the initial period.

Data

The *World Tables* provide the following data for general government (all levels) for 1960:

TR/GDP: total current revenue (excluding foreign aid but including the operating surplus of government enterprises) as % of GDP.

G_{KS}/GDP: total current expenditure as % of GDP.

S_G/TR: general government saving as % of total revenue (excluding foreign transfers).

S_G/G_S: general government saving as % of public investment. While "public investment" is taken to be government savings (G_S) is the RDC model, there is not a perfect correspondence between the two. Public investment is defined to be the total expenditure on gross domestic fixed capital (excluding that for defense) by general government and public corporations. There is, therefore, a certain amount of unavoidable overlap with capital investment by the KS sector.

G/GDP can be derived from these variables.

The *World Tables* also provide the following data necessary for the estimation: .

Annual GDP in constant US dollars (average 1967–1969). These data are used to obtain government savings and total revenues from GDP share data.

Annual population figures, and 1960 and 1970 figures for urban population as a percent of total population. These data are used to compile estimates of urban population growth. From the present urban and total population, urban population is determined for mid-year 1960 and 1970. Once the exponential rate of growth is calculated, we can solve for NU in any year. $\dot{N}U$ follows readily.

To maximize the data input for the analysis of government savings, the country-specific data for the years 1960, 1965, and 1970 have been pooled. This provides a total of eighty-one observations. For these three years, the number of RDC's is eighteen, twenty-nine, and thirty-four respectively. The estimated linear equation for government saving is as follows:

$$G_S = -11.65 + .34(T + \bar{F}) - .11\dot{N}_U(-1) \qquad r^2 = .79$$
$$\quad\;\; (-.65) \qquad (11.37) \qquad\quad (-1.09)$$

where the t-statistics are in parentheses.[6]

The high marginal savings rate accords broadly with expectations, as does the sign on the urban growth parameter, although the latter is not statistically significant. This is likely to be attributable to collinearity between the two independent variables, their simple correlation being .90. If interaction between these variables is not present, or if it is relatively small in magnitude, then the estimated parameter is still largely unbiased. We will use this estimate in the RDC model to capture the effects of urban growth on government savings.

B.7 HOUSEHOLD DEMAND AND ECONOMYWIDE SAVING

Household Demand and Saving Behavior

The model provides the capacity for differentiating per capita demand parameters for six commodity classes and six household types. All in all, seventy-two household demand parameters (thirty-six $\beta_{i,j}$ and thirty-six $\gamma_{i,j}$) should be estimated for the model's extended linear expenditure system. However, even a quick review of the LDC literature reveals a surprising lack of hard evidence concerning household demand and saving parameters by occupation, source of income, and location. It seems clear, therefore, that some household and commodity aggregation must be performed to make any progress at all. Thus, a series of assumptions have been made to reduce the number of demand parameters to manageable proportions. First, we assume the same marginal propensities to consume across all households; i.e.,

$$\beta_i = \beta_{i,j}, \text{ for all } i,j.$$

Second, we assume the same minimum subsistence parameter, $\gamma_{i,j}$, across all household types and for each commodity. While there is

---

[6] As in most studies of savings, heteroskedasticity was found in the error structure. The parameter estimates have been corrected for heteroskedasticity by dividing each term in the equation by (Total Revenue)$^{v/2}$, thus reducing the variance of the error term from σ^2 (Total Revenue)^v to σ^2. v was estimated to be .634 by running the regression $\log|e| = v \log(\text{Total Revenue})$.

reason to believe that subsistence *expenditure-shares* of disposable income vary by household type, there is less reason to maintain this condition for subsistence *quantities*. Thus,

$\gamma_{A,j} = \gamma_{A,k}$ for all $j \neq k$ households

$\gamma_{KS,j} = \gamma_{KS,k}$ for all $j \neq k$ households

$\gamma_{US,j} = \gamma_{US,k}$ for all $j \neq k$ *urban* households (*RS* otherwise)

$\gamma_{M,j} = \gamma_{M,k}$ for all $j \neq k$ households

$\gamma_{H,j} = \gamma_{H,k}$ for all $j \neq k = US, M, KS$ *urban* households

$\gamma_{H,j} = \gamma_{H,k}$ for all remaining $j \neq k = C, S$ *urban* households (*H, RS* otherwise)

Note that the subsistence parameter is allowed to vary between rural and urban households for labor-intensive (*US, RS*) and housing (*H*) requirements since, of course, these services are location-specific.

With these simplications, we have been able to estimate the $\beta_{i,j}$, the implied expenditure elasticities, and the marginal propensity to save. They are all reported in Table B.10. These estimates are guided by Houthakker's (1957) expenditure elasticity estimates from fifteen developing regions, by Musgrove's (1978) evidence drawn primarily from Latin American cities, and most of all by Lluch, Powell, and Williams in *Patterns in Household Demand and Saving* (1977), where the ELES system is estimated for a number of developing regions, Korea, Thailand and Taiwan among them. The 1960 average household saving rate of .08 is taken from the same sources.

TABLE B.10
Household Demand in the RDC Model

Expenditure Type (i)	MPC out of Supernumerary Disposable Income (β_i)	Expenditure Elasticity (η_i)	1960 Share in Total Expenditures	1960 Share in Disposable Income
A	0.231	0.608	41.29%	37.99%
M	0.314	1.404	24.30	22.36
KS	0.149	1.190	13.61	12.52
UR, RS	0.065	0.797	8.87	8.16
H	0.103	0.939	11.93	10.97
TOTAL	0.816		100.00	92.00

NOTE: All statistics relate to the average household.

Sources and Uses of Economywide Saving

The previous pages in this appendix have confronted at various points both the sources and uses of saving. This information is presented in Table 3.4. While the underlying data is taken from the RDC group documented in the *World Tables*, this 1960 snapshot has also been twisted a bit to conform to the model's structure. Nonetheless, the key stylized facts of Third World accumulation and its finance is revealed in Table 3.4. Households finance all of housing investment, and few have sufficient surplus remaining to finance accumulation in other sectors. Thus, only the high-income skilled worker, capitalist, and landlord households allocate a significant portion of their savings to finance accumulation elsewhere in the economy (80 percent). "Productive" investment is, therefore, financed mainly by corporate reinvestment (39 percent) and government sources (35 percent, including foreign capital), with households accounting for the remaining 27 percent. The average saving rates for households (8 percent), the government (24.6 percent), and the economy as a whole (15.6 percent without training and 17.9 percent with) are all based on the *World Tables* and other evidence discussed in previous sections of this appendix. The corporate reinvestment rate from after-tax profits and the average saving rates across household types (4.2, 6.5, and 12.0 percent for rural, unskilled urban, and skilled-capitalist households, respectively) are in large part necessary values to satisfy the accounting discipline of the general equilibrium model. Nevertheless, they appear to replicate the stylized facts of the RDC group in the early 1960s.

B.8 COMPLETE STATEMENT OF COMPARATIVE STATIC PARAMETERS

Derivation of a Consistent Set of Initial Conditions for the RDC[7]

One of the major challenges of general equilibrium modeling is to obtain a solution that replicates some initial benchmark date. There are a large number of parameters and exogenous variables in the model. Although reliable estimates can be and have been made for many of the parameters, there still remains a subset whose values are either specific to units of measurement or for which reliable information is not readily available. Examples of the former would include all parameters that serve as intercepts in demand and supply schedules and thus that are conditional on the numeraire adopted

---

[7] The following section draws heavily on Schmidt (1981), Appendix F. The reader interested in technical details on estimating and solving the model is encouraged to consult Schmidt, where these details are exposed at length.

for the RDC model in 1960. Included in this group are the $A_i \geq 0$, intercepts in the sectoral production functions; α_G, the intercept in the government saving function; $\theta_{H,j}$, the intercept in the three housing investment demand functions; and ξ_i, the capital-intensity parameter in the CES production functions. Fortunately, examples of the latter—parameters for which reliable quantitative information is not available—are less numerous. Furthermore, we have fair qualitative information even on these. For example, while we know little about the $\gamma_{i,j}$, commodity subsistence expenditure in the household demand system (discussed in Section B.7), we do know that it must lie within the range

$$0 \leq P_{i,j}\gamma_{i,j} \leq y_j^*$$

(i.e., non-negative but not exceeding household disposable income), and

$$\sum_i P_{i,j}\gamma_{i,j} \leq y_j^*$$

(i.e., aggregate subsistence expenditures cannot exceed disposable income). In addition, we have hunches that the ratio $P_{i,j}\gamma_{i,j}/y_i$ is higher for some commodities (like food and housing) than others (like manufactures). Apart from these restrictions, and some notions regarding the relative importance of subsistence expenditure commitments in total household expenditures on some given commodity j, the values of $\gamma_{i,j}$ are unknown. In contrast, some parameters escape our intuition even in qualitative values: for example, we have little knowledge regarding $\varepsilon_H \geq 0$, the elasticity parameter in the net housing investment functions, or regarding $\eta_i < 1$ ($i = US, RS$), the returns to scale parameter in the informal service sectors.

Complicating matters still further is the desire for a solution that simultaneously satisfies the equations of the comparative static model and replicates initial conditions observed for the base year (1960). Fortunately, the theoretical framework underlying the general equilibrium model makes it possible to derive a full set of parameter values that are consistent with these initial conditions. This is accomplished by imposing additional constraints (e.g., sectoral production shares and sectoral labor force distributions) on the first-period solution. In a sense, the comparative static model is transformed into what we call an initial condition (IC) model. The IC model simply rewrites the comparative static system in Appendix A so that known parameters and known 1960 initial conditions become exogenous variables, while unknown parameters and unknown initial conditions become endogenous variables. This process began as a simple "counting-up" exercise of unknown parameters and exogenous variables, as well as endogenous variables for which 1960 values had been estimated. Subtraction of the latter figure from the former indicated the number of additional equations (constraints) that were necessary to complete the IC model. A certain number of these constraints, reflecting structural characteristics of the economy, were readily imposed. For example, the 1960 sectoral output shares and labor force distributions documented in section B.3 must be reproduced by the initial solution. However, other constraints only become apparent after the model's decomposition and reformulation was begun. Most of these are reported in the tables that follow, but some are not, the most important of which involve factor markets. These should be stated explicitly before proceeding to the tables themselves:

1) Land markets are assumed *initially* to be in long-run equilibrium. That is, 1960 shadow and market rents are assumed to be equated among all urban and rural uses. Disequilibrium may, of course, become an attribute of the economy over time and a diverse structure of land rents is likely to emerge given segmented land markets and unbalanced growth in derived demands over time.

2) Capital markets are assumed *initially* to be in long-run equilibrium. That is, 1960 post-tax rates of return to capital A, M, and KS are assumed to be equated. Disequilibrium may, of course, become an attribute of the economy over time and sectoral rate of return differentials may emerge given a finite national savings pool and unbalanced growth in derived sectoral capital requirements over time.

3) An initial structure of nominal labor earnings is imposed on the 1960 RDC, guided by the "stylized facts" as suggested for India by Deepak Lal (1974, 1979), and for Latin America by J. S. Carillo (n.d.), T. Paul Schultz (1979), and others. Taking farm labor as a base, we assume for 1960:[8]

---

[8] Manipulating T. Paul Schultz's Colombian data (1979, Tables A-6, A-8, and A-10), for example, yields:

Agricultural sector earnings (ISC 1)	1.00
Informal rural services earnings (assumed ISC 1)	1.00
Informal urban services earnings (split out from ISC 38)	1.25
M and KS unskilled earnings (ISC 5 = 37)	1.84

Schultz's M and KS unskilled earnings exceed informal urban services by 47 percent, somewhat higher than the 28 percent suggested by the Peruvian data, reported by Dipak Mazumdar (1976, Table 7, formal blue-collar relative to informal employees). Our initial conditions lean on the lower figure.

Agricultural labor earnings	1.00
Informal rural services earnings	1.00
Informal urban services earnings	1.45
M and KS unskilled earnings	1.82
M and KS skilled earnings	3.63

Over time, the endogenous wage structure may, of course, evolve towards greater earnings inequality, dispersion, and "wage-stretching."

TABLE B.11
List of the Comparative Static Model's Parameter Values, Cited in Appendix B Text

Parameter	Estimate	Source
$\alpha_{M,A}$	0.159	Appendix B.5
$\alpha_{M,KS}$	0.122	Appendix B.5
$\alpha_{M,Z}$	0.225	Appendix B.5
$\alpha_{M,F}$	0.494	Appendix B.5
$\alpha_{KS,A}$	0.007	Appendix B.5
$\alpha_{KS,M}$	0.153	Appendix B.5
$\alpha_{KS,Z}$	0.029	Appendix B.5
$\alpha_{KS,F}$	0.811	Appendix B.5
$\alpha_{A,M}$	0.065	Appendix B.5
$\alpha_{A,KS}$	0.077	Appendix B.5
$\alpha_{A,Z}$	0.040	Appendix B.5
$\alpha_{A,F}$	0.818	Appendix B.5
σ_M	1.11	Appendix B.5
σ_{KS}	0.93	Appendix B.5
σ'_M	0.85	Appendix B.5
σ'_{KS}	0.73	Appendix B.5
$\alpha_{H,KS}$	0.90	Appendix B.5
$\alpha_{H,US}$	0.90	Appendix B.5
$\alpha_{R,KS}$	0.10	Appendix B.5
$\alpha_{R,US}$	0.10	Appendix B.5
$\alpha_{A,L}$	0.581	Appendix B.5
$\alpha_{A,R}$	0.122	Appendix B.5
$\alpha_{A,K}$	0.109	Appendix B.5
β_G	0.344	Appendix B.6
$\beta_{A,j}$ for all jth households	0.231	Appendix B.7
$\beta_{M,j}$ for all jth households	0.314	Appendix B.7
$\beta_{KS,j}$ for all jth households	0.149	Appendix B.7
$\left.\begin{matrix} \beta_{US,j} \\ \beta_{RS,j} \end{matrix}\right\}$ for all jth households	0.065	Appendix B.7
$\beta_{H,j}$ for all jth households	0.103	Appendix B.7

RDC Comparative Static Parameter Listing

With these preliminaries dispatched, the reader may now turn to Tables B.11, B.12, and B.13 where the comparative static parameters are displayed for the 1960 RDC.

TABLE B.12
List of Comparative Static Model's Parameter Values, Not Cited in Appendix B Text

Parameter	Estimate	Source and Comments
$\alpha_{H,RS}$	7.96373	Solved in IC model
α_G	-1.43714	Solved in IC model, given 1960 G_s
α_{US}	0.95	Assumed
α_{RS}	0.95	Assumed
C_k, for all k	3.43972	Solved in IC model, given 1960 $\dot{S}/S = .067$
γ_G	-0.09756	Derived from $\hat{\gamma}_G = -0.11$, estimated in Appendix B.6, and given $\dot{N}u/Nu = .046$ in the early 1960s for the RDC group
$\delta_{H,US}$	0.050 ⎫	Assumed given housing stock distribution (based on house value per occupant ratios across RS, KS, and US), and given 1960 share of "consumption of fixed capital" in GDP for 21 RDCs reported in the UN *Yearbook of National Accounts Statistics* (1974).
$\delta_{H,RS}$	0.025 ⎪	
$\delta_{H,KS}$	0.020 ⎪	
δ_M	0.027 ⎬	
δ_{KS}	0.027 ⎪	
δ_A	0.027 ⎭	
ε_H	3.0	Assumed
$\theta_{H,KS}$	3.07787 ⎫	Solved in IC model, assuming $\theta_{H,j} = \theta_{H,k}$ all $j = k = KS$, US, RS
$\theta_{H,US}$	3.07787 ⎬	
$\theta_{H,RS}$	3.07787 ⎭	
κ	1.25	Assumed, discussed in text to Appendix B.8
$l_{i,j,k}$, for all i, j, k	0.35	Estimate for 1960s, taken from ILO *Yearbook*, 21 RDCs, average of 1960 and 1970
ξ_M	0.52388 ⎫	Solved in IC model, given 1960 outputs of and inputs of M and KS, plus parameters in Table B.11 above
ξ_{KS}	0.93693 ⎪	
ξ'_M	0.63156 ⎬	
ζ'_{KS}	0.77963 ⎭	
ρ	0.01	Estimate for 1960s, taken from Simon (1980)
τ_M	0.47268	Solved in IC model, given T_M estimated for 1960 in Table B.9 and structure of demand in Table 3.2

able B.12   (continued)

arameter	Estimate	Source and Comments
$,M$	0	Assumed
$,KS$	0.11332⎫	Solved in IC model, given T_π estimated
$,M$	0.22664⎭	for 1960 in Table B.10, assuming $\tau_{\pi,M} = 2\tau_{\pi,KS}$
$,KS$	0.01830⎫	Solved in IC model, given T_H estimated
$,US$	0.01830⎭	for 1960 in Table B.10, assuming $\tau_{H,KS} = \tau_{H,US}$
	0.05045	Solved in IC model, given T_Y estimated for 1960 in Table B.9
	0	Assumed
$\,$	0.0291	Derived from Appendix B.3
M	0.69669⎫	Solved in IC model, given SAVINGS/
KS	0.69669⎭	GDP = 0.156 estimated for 1960 in Appendix B.3
$,US$	0.22783⎫	Solved in IC model, given 1960 estimate for rental flows, housing stock and land
$,KS$	0.18653⎭	use, plus parameters in Table B.11, above
$\,$	1.15117⎫	
M	3.66055⎪	Solved in IC model, given 1960 estimates
US	0.61972⎬	of sectoral outputs and inputs in Appendix B.3 and B.4, plus parameters in
RS	0.42270⎪	Table B.11 above
KS	1.31291⎭	
$,j$ for all jth households	0.18611⎫	
s,j for all jth households	0.02984⎪	
s,j for all jth urban households	0.06035⎪	Solved in IC model, given 1960 household
s,j for $j = RS$	0.01935⎪	expenditure mix in Table B.10 and the
$,j$ for all jth households	0.02198⎬	constraints discussed above in Section
$,j$ for $j = US, M, KS$	0.07827⎪	B.8
$,j$ for $j = C, S$	0.03406⎪	
$,j$ for $j = RS$	0.02559⎭	

TABLE B.13
*Initial Values of Dynamic Parameters, Not Cited in
Appendix B Text*

Parameter	1960 Initial Value	Source and Comments
P_Z	1.0 ⎫	Appendix C.2 for dynamic
P_A	1.0 ⎬	values, 1960 value set
P_M	1.0 ⎭	arbitrarily at 1.0
P_{KS}	1.0 ⎫	
P_{RS}	1.0	
P_{US}	1.0	Endogenous variable, 1960
$P_{H,KS}$	1.0 ⎬	value normalized arbitrarily
$P_{H,US}$	1.0	at 1.0
$P_{H,RS}$	1.0 ⎭	
$\bar{F}$	3.0	Initial value based on RDC 1960 group average of $\bar{F}/\text{GDP}$ ratio $= 3\%$ (Table B.5), $\bar{F}(t) = .03\ \text{GDP}(t)$ in dynamics
x	1.0 ⎫	Appendix C.1 for dynamic
y	1.0 ⎬	values, 1960 value set
z	1.0 ⎭	arbitrarily at 1.0
R_A	90.00 ⎫	Dynamic values determined
R_U	8.71	by ρ in Table B.12 above,
$R_{U,KS}$	4.96 ⎬	1960 values derived from
$R_{U,US}$	3.75 ⎭	IC model
		Dynamic values determined
T_X	1.11740 ⎫	from *World Tables*, 1960
T_M	3.82030 ⎭	values derived from Table B.9

Dynamic Parameters

C.1 TECHNOLOGICAL CHANGE, 1960–1979

Introduction

Our goal is to secure estimates of sectoral total-factor productivity growth ($\text{TFPG}_i = \overset{*}{T}_i$) for our RDC group. The sectors requiring documentation are those corresponding to the RDC model: agriculture (A), manufacturing and mining (M), the modern service sector (KS), the three housing sectors combined (H), and the two traditional service sectors combined (LS).

In spite of extensive empirical attention to total-factor productivity performance in developed economies since Solow (1957) and Abramovitz (1956) first directed our attention to it, there has been surprisingly little work done on the developing economies in the Third World. Even less has been done on the pre-OPEC period. We are hardly the first to note the deficiency. In a recent paper by Krueger and Tuncer (1980, p. 2), the authors state that:

> Failure to analyze TFPG has been so all-pervasive that there has been little attention paid to it, either analytically or empirically, anywhere in the development literature. [This state of affairs is especially surprising since] ... all evidence, from both developed and developing countries, strongly suggests that increased quantities of inputs per head of factors of production cannot explain differences in output per head ... between countries, and especially between the North and the South.

It is not difficult to find confirmation of this view in the literature. For example:

> The measurement of productivity change has been predominantly a developed country enterprise. ... Yet, there is a pressing need for undertaking productivity measurement in the developing economies. [Evenson, 1976, p. 326]

> Technical change, capital accumulation and investment in education are considered to be the most important factors affecting economic growth, but their effects have not been quantified for many LDC's. [Levy, 1978, p.1]

Furthermore, what is true of economywide rates of total-factor productivity growth is even more true of sectoral rates, an astonishing state of affairs given the importance of unbalanced productivity advance to structural change. Yet, in spite of this dismal assessment, there *is* enough evidence to guide our "guesstimates" of sectoral total-factor productivity growth, at least for the pre-OPEC RDC simulation.

To summarize what follows, we have been able to construct estimates for Latin America, the Middle East, Southern Europe, and Asia, as well as for all three regions combined. The Latin American estimates are based on seven observations, the Asian on six, and the Middle Eastern/Southern European on three: ten of these countries are members of our RDC sample (Brazil, Chile, Colombia, India, Korea, Mexico, Peru, the Philippines, Taiwan, and Turkey) while six are not (Argentina, Greece, Hong Kong, Iraq, Singapore, and Venezuela). The Asian data turns out to be the most complete and reliable, and many of the attributes of unbalanced sectoral TFPG uncovered there are assumed to prevail in the other two regions which are not so well documented. We were not able to find any estimates for the housing sector. Of the remaining sectors, A and M are by far the best documented, KS less so, and LS is almost nonexistent. Given the estimates of economywide TFPG, the trick is to devise a method whereby the service sectors can be estimated residually.

*Aggregation Rules and Interindustry Total-Factor
Productivity Growth*

If TFPG in the service sectors is to be estimated residually, it must be done with care since economywide TFPG is composed of two parts, both of which must be included in the estimation: *interindustry* TFPG ($\overset{*}{T}_{RA}$) resulting from improved resource allocation between sectors, a source of growth of which much has been made in the development literature; and *intraindustry* TFPG, resulting from productivity improvements within sectors, due both to pure technological change and the changes in efficiency by which known technology is applied (Jorgenson and Nishimizu, 1978, 1979; Nishimizu and Page, 1981). The intra-industry estimates are needed for the RDC model, but attention to interindustry TFPG is also necessary to estimate those intraindustry rates from historical time series.

The following expression must hold:

$$\overset{*}{T} = \sum_i v_i \overset{*}{T}_i + \overset{*}{T}_{RA} = \sum_i v_i \overset{*}{T}_i + z\overset{*}{T}$$

or

$$\overset{*}{T} = (1 - z)^{-1} [v_A \overset{*}{T}_A + v_M \overset{*}{T}_M + v_{KS} \overset{*}{T}_{KS} + v_{LS} \overset{*}{T}_{LS}]$$

where the parameter z expresses interindustry TFPG as a share of economywide TFPG, and v_i denotes the sectoral value added share where $\sum_i v_i = 1$.

What do we know about z? Clearly, it is a function of initial factor market disequilibria: the size of the initial discrepancies between sectoral marginal factor productivities will influence the magnitude of the potential gains from improved resource allocation. It is also a function of the equilibrating adjustment: the speed of resource reallocation associated with structural adjustment will also influence measured intraindustry TFPG gains. Certainly the first of these influences implies that z must be considerably larger in the Third World than in Western Europe or North America. The only estimates of z for advanced economies of which we are aware come from Edward F. Denison. Table C.1 offers some comparative data

TABLE C.1

The Relative Importance of Interindustry Total-Factor Productivity Growth in Eleven Nations

Country or Region	Time Period	Source	Estimate of z
United States	1950–52	Denison, 1974, p. 344	.20
	1929–67	Denison, 1974, p. 344	.22
Northwestern Europe	1950–62	Denison, 1967, p. 300	.22
United Kingdom	1950–62	Denison, 1967, p. 314	.10
Netherlands	1950–62	Denison, 1967, p. 310	.22
Germany	1950–62	Denison, 1967, p. 308	.22
Belgium	1950–62	Denison, 1967, p. 302	.25
France	1950–62	Denison, 1967, p. 306	.25
Italy	1950–62	Denison, 1967, p. 316	.33
Denmark	1950–62	Denison, 1967, p. 304	.34
Norway	1950–62	Denison, 1967, p. 312	.38
Japan	1953–71	Denison and Chung, 1976, p. 38	.19
	1953–61	Denison and Chung, 1976, p. 38	.23
Canada	1950–67	Denison and Chung, 1976, p. 42 based on Walters, 1970	.32

NOTE: z is calculated as the ratio of total-factor productivity attributable to "improved resource allocation" to the growth in total "output per unit of total input."

computed as the ratio of gains from "improved resource allocation" to TFPG.[1]

While we would certainly expect the rapidly growing LDC to exhibit values of z in the high range of Table C.1, securing precise information is more difficult. The qualitative literature suggests that z is at least as large in the LDCs, but we were able to find hard estimates only in the fine study of the Philippines by Mitsuo Ezaki. Ezaki (1975, Table 9, p. 429), offers two estimates for the late 1960s, and we have adopted the estimate $z = .31$, a figure that lies at the top of the range reported for advanced countries in Table C.1.

With this estimate of z in hand, we shall now proceed under the assumption that it applies to the other LDCs in our sample. As we shall see, this assumption seems to hold up well, at least for Latin America.

Estimates from Asia

Table C.2 presents sectoral and total-factor productivity growth rate estimates for six countries, four of which were very fast growers (Hong Kong, Singapore, Korea, and Taiwan), and two of which were relatively slow growers (India and the Philippines). Typically, the TFPG rates are available for agriculture, manufacturing, and economywide only, so the service sector must be inferred. Two critial assumptions are made in constructing the estimates in Table C.2. First, to repeat, we have assumed the Philippine experience with interindustry TFPG, as a share in economywide TFPG, is similar in the remaining five Asian countries. Second, we have assumed that the KS and LS sectors share the same rate of TFPG. This second assumption may appear extreme since utilities and transportation, for example, might be expected to exhibit quite dynamic productivity performance. Yet, public administration, finance, and other business services are also part of the KS sector and they are likely to exhibit very low rates of TFPG. Precisely this kind of diversity can be seen in the Philippine performance as estimated by Ezaki (1975, Tables 7 and 8, pp. 421 and 426) for the late 1960s.

The next step is to aggregate the experience of these six nations into estimates for Asia as a whole. Table C.3 supplies four such aggregations, weighted and unweighted, including and excluding India. The weights across sectors are the sectoral value added figures

---

[1] The range for z in Table C.1 is large, from .10 to .38, but it corresponds very closely to Simon Kuznets's (1957, Table 24) estimate of the share of per capita income growth explained by intrasectoral labor force shifts for the first half of the twentieth century, from .11 to .32 (excluding Australia and New Zealand).

Table C.2

Sectoral Total Factor Productivity Growth Estimates: Six Asian Nations

Country	Period	$\overset{*}{T}$	$\overset{*}{T}_A$	$\overset{*}{T}_M$	$\overset{*}{T}_{KS}$	$\overset{*}{T}_{LS}$	Source
Hong Kong	1960–70	4.29	—	2.29	2.46	2.46	Chen, 1977
Singapore	1957–70	3.62	—	3.75	1.61	1.61	Chen, 1977
South Korea	1960–70	4.48	4.77	3.47	1.20	1.20	Chen, 1977
Taiwan	1960–70	4.33	2.10	3.59	1.86	1.86	Chen, 1977
Philippines	1965–69	1.63	1.44	1.87	0.39	0.39	Ezaki, 1975
India	1960–70	(0.60)	0.60	(0.60)	0.06	0.06	Evenson and Jha, 1973

NOTES: The figures for India in parentheses are estimates based on the assumption that TFPG was equated between A, M, and economywide. We were able to find estimates for Indian manufacturing only for the 1950s. See Sakong and Narasimham (1974). The first three columns are directly estimated in the sources listed except for India. The last two columns are derived using the expression

$$\overset{*}{T} = (1 - z)^{-1}[v_A\overset{*}{T}_A + v_M\overset{*}{T}_M + v_{KS}\overset{*}{T}_{KS} + v_{LS}\overset{*}{T}_{LS}], \quad \overset{*}{T}_{KS} = \overset{*}{T}_{LS}$$

where the v_i are taken from UN, *Yearbook of National Accounts Statistics, 1977* except for Taiwan which comes from the 1970 *Yearbook*. The weights are midpoint simple averages of 1960 and 1970, except for Taiwan, where 1969 data replaces 1970, and Hong Kong, where only 1970 data is used. The calculation assumes $\overset{*}{T}_{KS} = \overset{*}{T}_{LS}$ and takes $z = .31$. The Indian estimates for agriculture are given in Evenson and Jha by states. We have applied state food grain production indices as weights to get the all India figure.

In constructing the value added share weights of (v_i) the following conventions were used:

Sector Description	Model's Notation
Mining and Quarrying	M
Manufacturing	M
Agriculture, Forestry, Fishing	A
Electricity, Gas and Water	KS
Construction	KS
Transport, Storage, Communication	KS
Finance, Insurance, Real Estate, Business Services (Other)	KS
Public Administration, Defense	KS
Wholesale and Retail Trade, Restaurants, Hotels	LS
Finance, etc. (Owner-Occupied Buildings)	LS
Community, Social and Personal Services	LS
Domestic Services of Households	LS

Import duties and/or statistical discrepanices were excluded.

TABLE C.3

Sectoral Total-Factor Productivity Growth: Asia, the 1960s

	Unweighted				Weighted			
	(A) Including India		(B) Excluding India		(C) Including India		(D) Excluding India	
Sector								
Economywide	3.67%	(1.23)	3.67%	(1.23)	1.52%	(1.01)	3.46%	(1.25)
A	2.23	(0.75)	2.77	(0.93)	1.04	(0.69)	3.02	(1.09)
M	2.99	(1.00)	2.99	(1.00)	1.51	(1.00)	2.77	(1.00)
KS	1.81	(0.61)	1.53	(0.51)	0.59	(0.39)	1.34	(0.48)
LS	1.81	(0.61)	1.53	(0.51)	0.59	(0.39)	1.34	(0.48)

NOTES: See text for aggregation procedure. The country data is taken from Table C.2. Figures in parentheses are relative, with manufacturing TFPG taken as the base.

in domestic currency units (*UN Yearbook of National Accounts Statistics*), converted to dollars by average annual exchange rates reported in the IBRD *World Tables, 1976*. Similarly, for the economy-wide figures GDP weights are used, calculated as midpoints in the decade of the 1960s. Our preferred estimate is Case A, "unweighted, including India." The weighted figures place too great stress on Indian performance while the unweighted averages, including India, seem to come closest to our notion of the RDC.

Using the Case A estimates, the reader will note the unbalanced character of TFPG during the 1960s: the highest rates were obtained in manufacturing; agriculture exhibited lower, but still very high, rates; services had the lowest rates, but still quite impressive; and the economywide rate far exceeds that of any sector since interindustry TFPG was quite pronounced. To the extent that the reader finds the experience of Hong Kong, Singapore, Korea, and Taiwan unusually rapid, he may prefer the weighted figures, including India (Case C)—a procedure that places far heavier weight on the slow growers. In this case, the ranking of sectoral rates of TFPG were exactly the same but the degree of unbalancedness is more pronounced and the levels, of course, are lower.

Estimates from Latin America

Sectoral estimates for Latin America are almost non-existent. Only Mexico supplied some figures (Barraza–Allende, 1968) but even these estimates are dubious. The economywide estimates in Table C.4 are taken from Elias (1978), while the sectoral rates are

TABLE C.4

Sectoral Total-Factor Productivity Growth Estimates: Seven Latin American Nations, the 1960s

Country	Case	$\overset{\bullet}{T}$	$\overset{\bullet}{T}_A$	$\overset{\bullet}{T}_M$	$\overset{\bullet}{T}_{KS}$	$\overset{\bullet}{T}_{LS}$
Argentina	A	0.59%	0.36%	0.48%	0.29%	0.29%
	B	0.59	0.45	0.48	0.24	0.24
	C	0.59	0.40	0.58	0.23	0.23
	D	0.59	0.51	0.47	0.23	0.23
Brazil	A	1.34	0.82	1.09	0.66	0.66
	B	1.34	1.01	1.09	0.56	0.56
	C	1.34	0.92	1.33	0.52	0.52
	D	1.34	1.17	1.07	0.51	0.51
Chile	A	1.55	0.95	1.26	0.77	0.77
	B	1.55	1.17	1.26	0.64	0.64
	C	1.55	1.06	1.53	0.60	0.60
	D	1.55	1.35	1.24	0.60	0.60
Colombia	A	1.65	1.01	1.34	0.82	0.82
	B	1.65	1.25	1.34	0.68	0.68
	C	1.65	1.12	1.63	0.64	0.64
	D	1.65	1.44	1.32	0.63	0.63
Mexico	A	1.90	1.16	1.54	0.94	0.94
	B	1.90	1.43	1.54	0.79	0.79
	C	1.90	1.30	1.88	0.73	0.73
	D	1.90	1.66	1.52	0.73	0.73
Peru	A	1.45	0.89	1.18	0.72	0.72
	B	1.45	1.10	1.18	0.60	0.60
	C	1.45	0.99	1.44	0.56	0.56
	D	1.45	1.26	1.16	0.56	0.56
Venezuela	A	1.22	0.74	0.99	0.60	0.60
	B	1.22	0.92	0.99	0.50	0.50
	C	1.22	0.83	1.21	0.47	0.47
	D	1.22	1.07	0.98	0.47	0.47

NOTES: The economywide rates of TFPG are taken from Elias (1978). The sectoral rates are derived under Cases A–D reported in parentheses in Table C.3. Thus, *levels* of TFPG are based on Elias's Latin American economywide TFPG rates, but the *sectoral relatives* are assumed to have the same attributes of those estimated for Asia. These figures imply an interindustry rate of TFPG which need not be equal to the $z = .31$ estimate found for the Philippines and applied to the Asian LDCs in our sample. We have not reported the interindustry TFPG estimate, but it can easily be calculated from sectoral value added data reported in the UN *Yearbooks*.

We are aware that Elias's estimates for Mexico differ from those offered by Reynolds (1979) as well as those implied by Barraza–Allende (1968), but we prefer the estimating procedures used by Elias.

TABLE C.5

Sectoral Total-Factor Productivity Growth: Latin America, the 1960s

	Case A		Case B	
Sector	Weighted	Unweighted	Weighted	Unweighted
Economywide	1.37%	1.39%	1.37%	1.39%
A	0.86	0.85	1.06	1.05
M	1.09	1.13	1.09	1.13
KS	0.64	0.69	0.54	0.57
LS	0.71	0.69	0.60	0.57

NOTES: See text for aggregation procedure. Country data from Table C.4 and the source of the weights are the same as those used in Table C.2.

derived from assumptions that the Table C.3 relatives apply to Latin America as well.[2]

Table C.5 aggregates these country estimates under various weighting schemes,[3] but it seems clear that Latin America TFPG during the 1960s was considerably below that of most Asian countries for which we have documentation.

Estimates from the Middle East/Southern Europe

The Middle Eastern/Southern European sample includes Greece, Iraq, and Turkey. Exactly the same procedure has been applied in Tables C.6 and C.7 as in the Latin American case except that here we have TFPG estimates for manufacturing and none for any other sector.

Third World Summary

Table C.8 reports summary statistics for all sixteen countries for which we have estimated sectoral total-factor productivity growth rates. The aggregation is based on the country data in Tables C.2, C.4, and C.6. The unweighted averages supply two estimates, where the Asian country data is first combined with Case A for Latin America and the Middle East/Southern Europe, and then combined with Case B data from the two regions. The weighted averages also

[2] While this assumption may appear extreme, we note that Colosio's (1979) and Reynolds's (1979) application of "shift share" analysis to Mexico in the 1960s implies a value of $z = 0.28$, quite close to the assumed estimate of $z = 0.31$ discussed above.

[3] The country weights used in deriving weighted averages are shares of regional value added by sector in total Latin American value added by sector.

Case C		Case D	
Weighted	*Unweighted*	*Weighted*	*Unweighted*
1.37%	1.39%	1.37%	1.39%
0.96	0.95	1.22	1.21
1.30	1.37	1.07	1.11
0.50	0.54	0.50	0.53
0.55	0.54	0.55	0.53

TABLE C.6
*Sectoral Total-Factor Productivity Growth Estimates:
Three Middle Eastern/Southern European Nations*

Country	Case	$\overset{\cdot}{T}$	$\overset{\cdot}{T}_A$	$\overset{\cdot}{T}_M$	$\overset{\cdot}{T}_{KS}$	$\overset{\cdot}{T}_{LS}$
Iraq	A	4.92%	3.00%	4.00%	2.44%	2.44%
	B	4.92	3.72	4.00	2.04	2.04
	C	4.04	2.76	4.00	1.56	1.56
	D	5.00	4.36	4.00	1.92	1.92
Greece	A	2.58	1.58	2.10	1.28	1.28
	B	2.58	1.95	2.10	1.07	1.07
	C	2.12	1.45	2.10	0.82	0.82
	D	2.63	2.29	2.10	1.01	1.01
Turkey	A	3.69	2.25	3.00	1.83	1.83
	B	3.69	2.79	3.00	1.53	1.53
	C	3.03	2.07	3.00	1.17	1.17
	D	3.75	3.27	3.00	1.44	1.44

NOTES: All three countries have estimates available for manufacturing only (Levy, 1978; Lianos, 1976; and Krueger and Tuncer, 1980). The remaining figures are derived under Cases A–D reported in parentheses in Table C.3. See notes to Table C.4. The figures for Iraq relate to the period 1960–1972, Greece for 1958–1968, and Turkey for 1963–1976.

supply two estimates, one based on the Case C data from Latin America and the Middle East/Southern Europe and the other based on Case D. Sectoral value added weights were applied throughout.

While the range of estimates reported in Table C.8 may seem large, it should be noted that the *relative* pattern of sectoral TFPG

TABLE C.7
*Sectoral Total-Factor Productivity Growth: Middle East/Southern Europe,
the 1960s*

	Case A		Case B	
Sector	Weighted	Unweighted	Weighted	Unweighted
Economywide	3.25%	3.37%	3.25%	3.73%
A	2.05	2.28	2.54	2.28
M	2.68	3.03	2.68	3.03
KS	1.61	1.85	1.34	1.55
LS	1.55	1.85	1.29	1.55

NOTES: See text for aggregation procedure. Country data from Table C.6 and the
source of the weights are the same as those used in Table C.2.

TABLE C.8
*Sectoral Total-Factor Productivity Growth: Sixteen
LDCs in the 1960s*

	Unweighted		Weighted	
Sector	Case A	Case B	Case C	Case D
Economywide	2.49%	2.49%	1.53%	1.58%
A	1.54	1.76	1.08	1.27
M	2.03	2.03	1.46	1.29
KS	1.12	1.01	0.56	0.58
LS	1.12	1.01	0.61	0.62

NOTE: See text for aggregation procedure

seems to be quite invariant to the aggregation rules used. In any
case, our preferred estimates are Cases A and B.

*An Algorithm for Deriving Consistent Technological
Change Parameters*

As Chapter 2 points out, factor-augmenting and disembodied
technical progress are both present in our model. Recall the following definitions:

Factor	Exogenous Efficiency Levels	Factor-Augmenting Rates
K	x	λ_K
S	y	λ_S
L	z	λ_L

Case C		Case D	
Weighted	*Unweighted*	*Weighted*	*Unweighted*
2.67%	3.06%	3.31%	3.79%
1.89	2.09	2.98	3.31
2.68	3.03	2.68	3.03
1.03	1.18	1.26	1.46
0.99	1.18	1.22	1.46

Sector	Exogenous Efficiency Levels	Disembodied Rates
M	A_M	λ_M
KS	A_{KS}	λ_{KS}
A	A_A	λ_A
H, US	$A_{H,US}$	$\lambda_{H,US}$
H, KS	$A_{H,KS}$	$\lambda_{H,KS}$
H, RS	$A_{H,RS} = a_{H,RS}^{-1}$	$\lambda_{H,RS}$
US	A_{US}	λ_{US}
RS	A_{RS}	λ_{RS}

What additional assumptions must we make to estimate these eleven λ's given information on $\overset{*}{T}_i$ contained in Table C.8? A system of eight equations states our problem (with time subscripts suppressed for clarity):

$$\overset{*}{T}_A = \lambda_A + \alpha_{AK}\lambda_K + \alpha_{AL}\lambda_L$$

$$\overset{*}{T}_M = \lambda_M + \alpha_{MK}\lambda_K + \alpha_{ML}\lambda_L + \alpha_{MS}\lambda_S$$

$$\overset{*}{T}_{KS} = \lambda_{KS} + \alpha_{KSK}\lambda_K + \alpha_{KSL}\lambda_L + \alpha_{KSS}\lambda_S$$

$$\overset{*}{T}_{RS} = \lambda_{RS} + \alpha_{RS}\lambda_L$$

$$\overset{*}{T}_{US} = \lambda_{US} + \alpha_{US}\lambda_L$$

$$\overset{*}{T}_{H,KS} = \lambda_{H,KS}$$

$$\overset{*}{T}_{H,US} = \lambda_{H,US}$$

$$\overset{*}{T}_{H,RS} = \lambda_{H,RS}$$

Since this system is underdetermined, the following restrictions are imposed: first, we assume no productivity advance in the supply of housing from fixed housing stocks (in contrast with *construction*),

$$\lambda_{H,KS} = \lambda_{H,US} = \lambda_{H,RS} = 0;$$

second, we assume that the informal service sectors only undergo labor-augmenting productivity advance,

$$\lambda_{RS} = \lambda_{US} = 0;$$

third, we assume that unskilled and skilled labor exhibit the same factor-augmenting rates,

$$\lambda_L = \lambda_S;$$

fourth, we assume that productivity advance tends to be relatively labor-augmenting over time,

$$\lambda_L = \hat{\beta}\lambda_K, \qquad \hat{\beta} > 1;$$

and finally, we assume that the degree of unbalancedness is stable over time,

$$\overset{*}{T}_A = \hat{\beta}_A \overset{*}{T}_M, \qquad \hat{\beta}_A < 1,$$

$$\overset{*}{T}_{KS} = \hat{\beta}_{KS} \overset{*}{T}_M, \qquad \hat{\beta}_{KS} < 1,$$

$$\overset{*}{T}_{US} = \overset{*}{T}_{RS} = \hat{\beta}_{RS} \overset{*}{T}_M, \qquad \hat{\beta}_{RS} < 1, \text{ since } \alpha_{RS} = \alpha_{US} \text{ (Appendix B.8)}.$$

These assumptions—common in the literature and consistent with qualitative stylized facts in the Third World—imply the following system:

$$\lambda_K = (\hat{\beta}_{RS}/\alpha_{RS} \cdot \hat{\beta}) \overset{*}{T}_M$$

$$\lambda_A = [\hat{\beta}_A - (\hat{\beta}_{RS}/\alpha_{RS} \cdot \hat{\beta})(\alpha_{AK} + \hat{\beta}\alpha_{AL})] \overset{*}{T}_M$$

$$\lambda_M = [1 - (\hat{\beta}_{RS}/\alpha_{RS} \cdot \hat{\beta})(\alpha_{MK} + \hat{\beta}[\alpha_{ML} + \alpha_{MS}])] \overset{*}{T}_M$$

$$\lambda_{KS} = [\hat{\beta}_{KS} - (\hat{\beta}_{RS}/\alpha_{RS} \cdot \hat{\beta})(\alpha_{KSK} + \hat{\beta}[\alpha_{KSL} + \alpha_{KSS}])] \overset{*}{T}_M$$

Given the α_{ij} from the IC model in Appendix B.8 (following the new conventions of productivity accounting by using gross output shares as in Gollop, 1979), the $\hat{\beta}_i$ implied by Table C.8 above, $\overset{*}{T}_M = 2$ percent per annum suggested by Cases A or B in Table C.8, and an economywide *intraindustry* rate of total-factor productivity growth around 1.8 percent per annum (or a total rate, intraindustry plus interindustry, around 2.5 percent per annum as in Cases A or B in Table C.8), then $\hat{\beta} = 3.836$.

All this implies the following pre-OPEC technological change parameter estimates:

Parameter	RDC Assumed Value
λ_K	.00207
λ_S	.00794
λ_L	.00794
λ_M	.00786
λ_{KS}	.00362
λ_A	.00826
$\lambda_{H,US}$	0
$\lambda_{H,KS}$	0
$\lambda_{H,RS}$	0
λ_{US}	0
λ_{RS}	0

In the absence of evidence, Chapter 5 will assume these pre-OPEC technological conditions to have prevailed in 1973–1979 as well.

C.2 PRICES, 1960–1979

Overview

There are three prices exogenous to the model whose historic time series must be documented: P_A, the domestic market price of A-goods received by primary sector producers, a net exporting sector at least in the early 1960s; P_M, the domestic market price of M-goods received by home manufacturers, a net importing sector at least in the 1960s; and P_Z, the price per unit of imported raw materials and fuels paid by domestic users. Since our model is not equipped to confront problems of inflation in the general price level, and since only relative prices matter in clearing the model's markets, one of these three prices can be established as the numeraire. We have selected the exportable A-good to play that role, so the historical data we require are time series on the prices of the importables, Z and M, relative to A.

Construction of these time series is fraught with problems, and they can be organized around two issues: first, the imperfect correspondence between the model and reality; and second, the inherent problems associated with time-series analysis of prices (Kravis and Lipsey, 1981). The first issue will become apparent as this section unfolds. The second has always lurked behind the "deteriorating terms of trade in the Third World" debate since Raul Prebisch (see the survey in Kravis and Lipsey, 1981) raised the issue thirty years ago. The problems are well known. For example, while world market prices are relatively easy to document, f.o.b. export prices will most certainly diverge from c.i.f. import prices. Furthermore, both diverge from domestic selling prices, and it is the latter that drive economic agents in our model. To complicate matters further, prices are extremely unstable in the short run, especially for the raw materials and foodstuffs which dominate the A-good bundle in the Third World; thus, choice of benchmark dates matters a great deal to the long-run price trends documented. In addition, traded commodities are usually quoted in terms of unit value rather than quality-adjusted prices, and the difference may matter in the computation of relative price trends over long periods. Furthermore, the selection of commodity weights will matter in the construction of aggregate price indices, and these weights vary across countries over time. The list of computational problems is almost endless.

The Relative Price of Manufactures

In a recent paper, Kravis and Lipsey (1981) have developed time-series estimates of P_A/P_M which include quality adjustments to the M-goods category. However, Kravis and Lipsey were able to make their adjustments only through 1977. We have extended their series by using UN "unit value" data for 1978 and 1979—linked with Kravis and Lipsey at 1977, and by assuming a linear projection of their adjustment factor over 1977–1979. The results of this exercise are presented in Table C.9.

The OPEC watershed is certainly apparent in Table C.9. Taking three-year averages so as to minimize the influence of short-run instability, the relative price of P_M (quality-adjusted) declines at 1 percent per annum over the period 1960/62–1971/73. (The figure is -0.6 percent per annum in the unadjusted series.) The rising pro-industry policy bias of the 1960s, however, drove a larger and larger wedge between domestic and foreign manufacturer's prices over the decade. To reflect these influences we set $\overset{*}{P}_M = -0.7$ percent per annum in the model for the pre-OPEC period, 1960–1973. For the more recent post-OPEC period, the decline in the relative price of P_M has been even faster, -1.6 percent per annum in the quality-adjusted series 1971/73–1978/79. Thus, we have set $\overset{*}{P}_M = -1.6$ percent per annum for the post-OPEC period, 1973–1979.

The Relative Price of Imported Fuels and Raw Materials

Since quality-adjustment is not a serious factor in the case of Z (or A) goods, Kravis and Lipsey (1981) make no effort to report the

TABLE C.9
The Terms of Trade, P_A/P_M, 1960–1979

Year	(1) P_A	(2) P_M	(3) Quality- Adjustment Factor	(4) P_A/P_M	(5) $P_A/P_M \div$ (3)
1960	98	99.9	1.011	.981	.970
1961	93	100.5	1.009	.925	.917
1962	92	100.0	1.007	.920	.914
1963	100	100.0	1.000	1.000	1.000
1964	102	101.5	.996	1.005	1.009
1965	96	103.0	.992	.932	.940
1966	97	104.8	.986	.926	.940
1967	95	105.6	.979	.900	.920
1968	93	104.7	.970	.888	.916
1969	100	107.6	.970	.929	.958
1970	103	113.8	.965	.905	.938
1971	100	120.7	.963	.829	.860
1972	118	129.4	.959	.912	.951
1973	184	145.1	.961	1.268	1.320
1974	240	171.4	.957	1.400	1.463
1975	198	189.2	.952	1.047	1.099
1976	225	193.3	.947	1.164	1.229
1977	280	208.6	(.942)	1.342	1.425
1978	291	249.4	(.937)	1.167	1.245
1979	317	275.3	(.932)	1.151	1.235

SOURCES AND NOTES: For the period 1960–1977: Col. (1) from Kravis and Lipsey (1981), Table 4, col. (3); Col. (2) from Kravis and Lipsey (1981), Table 1, col. (1); and Col. (3) from Kravis and Lipsey (1981), Table 3, cols. (2) ÷ (1). For the period 1977–1978:

$$P_A = \sum_j \omega_{jx}^{77} P_j^x$$

where j = food and raw materials (excluding fuels), and 1977 export (x) value weights from the UN *Yearbook* (1979) are applied to the two export prices, also taken from the UN *Yearbook* (1979), Special Table C, "unit value" index for developing market economies' exports to market economies;

$$P_M = \sum_j \omega_{jM}^{77} P_j^M$$

where j = machinery and other manufactures, and 1977 import (M) value weights from the UN *Yearbook* (1979) are applied to the two import prices, the prices also taken from the UN *Yearbook* (1979), Special Table C, "unit value" index for market economies' exports to developing market economies. Identical calculations were used for the 1978–1979 period, although the price data were taken from UN (1981), Special Table E. The quality-adjustment factor in Col. (3) for 1977–1979 is based on a linear projection.

relative price of Z (fuels, raw materials, and chemicals). For that purpose, we have relied on UN unit value series, where

$$P_Z = \sum_j \omega_{jZ}^t P_j^Z$$

and where j = fuels, raw materials, and chemicals. The weight applied to these three import prices are import values, 1960–1969 using 1960 weights, 1970–1974 using 1970 weights, and 1975–1979 using 1977 weights.

The results appear in Table C.10 where the OPEC watershed is evident. Since there is no evidence of trend in P_Z/P_A up to the early 1970s, the model assumes $\overset{*}{P}_Z = 0$ for the pre-OPEC period, 1960–1973. Between 1970/72 and 1977/79, however, the relative price of P_Z grew at a very fast rate, 5.2 percent per annum. Thus, we have set $\overset{*}{P}_Z = 5.2$ percent per annum for the more recent post-OPEC period, 1973–1979.

TABLE C.10
The Relative Price of Imported Fuels and Raw Materials, P_Z/P_A, 1960–1979

	(1)	(2)	(3)
Year	P_A	P_Z	P_Z/P_A
1960	98	107.1	1.093
1961	93	103.5	1.113
1962	92	100.6	1.093
1963	100	99.6	.996
1964	102	100.5	.985
1965	96	102.4	1.067
1966	97	101.6	1.047
1967	95	99.3	1.045
1968	93	94.5	1.016
1969	100	96.7	.967
1970	103	100.0	.971
1971	100	110.1	1.101
1972	118	114.9	.974
1973	184	151.7	.824
1974	240	318.0	1.325
1975	198	335.1	1.692
1976	225	350.1	1.556
1977	280	376.7	1.345
1978	291	385.4	1.324
1979	317	507.5	1.601

SOURCES AND NOTES: See text and Table C.9

Table C.11

Trends in $\bar{P}_A$, $\bar{P}_M$, and $\bar{P}_Z$ Assumed for the RDC Model, 1960–1979

Year	$\bar{P}_A$	$\bar{P}_M$	$\bar{P}_Z$
1960	1.00	1.00	1.00
1961	1.00	.99	1.00
1962	1.00	.99	1.00
1963	1.00	.98	1.00
1964	1.00	.97	1.00
1965	1.00	.97	1.00
1966	1.00	.96	1.00
1967	1.00	.95	1.00
1968	1.00	.95	1.00
1969	1.00	.94	1.00
1970	1.00	.93	1.00
1971	1.00	.93	1.00
1972	1.00	.92	1.00
1973	1.00	.91	1.00
1974	1.00	.90	1.05
1975	1.00	.88	1.11
1976	1.00	.87	1.16
1977	1.00	.86	1.22
1978	1.00	.84	1.29
1979	1.00	.83	1.39

NOTE: All entries under $\bar{P}_M$ and $\bar{P}_Z$ are rounded

RDC Price Trends Assumed in the Simulation, 1960–1979

This relative price information is summarized in Table C.11 where assumptions about RDC trends in the three exogenous prices are made explicit for the pre-OPEC and post-OPEC periods.

C.3 POPULATION GROWTH, LAND EXPANSION, AND FOREIGN CAPITAL INFLOWS, 1960–1979

Population Growth

The 1976 *World Tables* supplies population estimates for our RDC group across the 1960s, implying a population growth rate of 2.54 percent per annum. In the absence of good employment data, we have used this figure for the model's employment (and population) growth over the pre-OPEC period, 1960–1973. The 1980 *World Tables* supplies population estimates for our RDC groups for 1970–1977. These imply growth rates of 2.68 percent per annum, rates that are assumed for the model's post-OPEC period, 1973–1979.

Land Expansion

Here we stand on less stable ground, but a recent survey by Julian Simon (1980) offers estimates of land stock growth in Third World countries. Guided by his estimates, the pre-OPEC simulations adopt a land stock growth rate figure which is fairly high, 1 percent per annum from 1960 to 1973. Since there is considerable evidence that the Third World is rapidly exhausting its ability to extend the margin of cultivation, the rate of growth of R_A is set at 0.5 per annum 1973–1980, finally falling to zero growth 1980–2000. In contrast, we assume urban land endowments to continue their pre-OPEC growth, so that R_U grows at 1 percent per annum 1960–2000.

Foreign Capital Inflows

Whatever concept one chooses to measure "foreign capital inflows," the *World Tables* (1980) and the *World Development Report* (1981) both document considerable instability across the 1960s and early 1970s. Since there is little evidence of trends in the share of foreign capital inflow in gross domestic product ($F/$GDP), and given an average share documented for oil-importing developing countries in the 1981 *World Development Report* equal to about 3 percent, we have in fact assumed $F/$GDP to have remained stable at this 3 percent level throughout. The issue is discussed in section C.4 at greater length, but we thought it inappropriate to introduce annual variations in $F/$GDP for simulations generated by a long-run equilibrium system which ignores balance of payments adjustment problems.

C.4 Dynamic Parameters Assumed in
The Projections, 1980–2000

Population and Labor Force Projections

In *Labor Force Estimates and Projections, 1950–2000* (1977, vols. 1–6), the ILO reports total labor force estimates to the year 2000, by country, under "high," "low," and "middle" projections. For our RDC group, the following unweighted labor force growth averages have been computed:

| | Per Annum Growth | |
	1980–1990	1990–2000
High	2.83%	3.02%
Middle = BASELINE	2.79	2.84
Low	2.73	2.65

The BASELINE (or middle) projection has been used throughout in Chapter 6.

Land Expansion

As we pointed out in Section C.3, we have only qualititative evidence to guide us here. The BASELINE in Chapter 6 assumes that the trend toward exhaustion of the extensive margin observed across the 1960s and 1970s warrants a zero rate of growth in agricultural land 1980–2000. The BASELINE assumes urban land to grow at the constant rate of 1 percent per annum.

Foreign Capital Inflows

The 1981 *World Development Report* (pp. 12–19 and 49–63) devoted considerable space to capital flow projections, especially for the oil-importing developing countries, the group most relevant for us. Projections are most hazardous, as the abundant qualifications in the *Report* point out. Nevertheless, the *Report* (1981, Table 5.3, p. 62) offers estimates for three "foreign capital inflow" concepts. The most relevant concept for our purposes is the "resource gap," which equals imports of goods and nonfactor services minus exports of goods and nonfactor services (or, gross domestic investment minus domestic savings). As a share in GNP, the resource gap is estimated in the *Report* as:

| | | | 1985 | | 1990 | |
	1970	1980	High	Low	High	Low
Resource Gap/GNP	2.5%	4.6%	2.7%	2.3%	2.5%	2.0%

Since 1980 (and 1974/1975) were years of unusually high capital inflows (associated with short-run fuel price shocks), an average F/GDP for the 1970s might be taken to have been around 3 percent.

TABLE C.12
World Bank Price Projections, 1980–1990

Price	1980	1981	1982	1985	1990
Petroleum	100	112.2	111.4	152.0	234.3
A-goods (P_A)	100	94.3	91.6	127.9	181.8
M-goods (P_M)	100	95.5	102.9	127.9	171.1
Non-foods	100	87.2	92.1	143.9	200.6
Timber	100	75.2	93.2	129.7	178.2
Metals & Minerals	100	91.6	100.7	144.8	207.4
Raw Materials	100	88.7	97.4	143.2	202.4
Z-goods (P_Z)	100	94.5	100.9	145.4	210.3

Using the Report's projection to guide us, we assume in Chapter 6.
the following values of F/GDP:

Case	1980	1990	2000
High	3.0%	3.0%	3.0%
Middle = BASELINE	3.0	2.7	2.4
Low	3.0	2.4	1.8

The BASELINE (or middle) projection has been used throughout
in Chapter 6, where linear interpolation is applied to intervening
years.

Relative Prices

The Economic Analysis and Projections Department of the
World Bank recently has produced some estimates of commodity
prices to 1990. The aggregates of greatest interest to us are reproduced in Table C.12. These estimates imply that the relative price
of fuels and raw materials facing our forty-country group of oil-
importing developing countries is likely to grow at 1.5 percent per
annum (the growth in P_Z/P_A is $\overset{*}{P}_Z$); the relative price of manufactures, on the other hand, is likely to decline at 0.6 percent per annum

Source and Notes
IBRD/EPDCE (1982, Table 3)
IBRD/EPDCE (1982, Table 3). Thirty-three primary products (excluding petroleum) weighted by 1974–76 developing countries' export values
IBRD/EPDCE (1982, Table 4). Industrialized countries' cif index of manufactured exports to developing countries
IBRD/EPDCE (1982, Table 3). Component of A-goods, containing cotton, jute, rubber, and tobacco
IBRD/EPDCE (1982, Table 3). Component of A-goods, containing logs
IBRD/EPDCE (1982, Table 3). Component of A-goods containing copper, iron ore, nickel, bauxite, aluminium, lead, zinc, etc.
Weighted average of non-food (15.0), timber (4.4) and metals plus minerals (29.4), using 1974–76 developing countries' import values as weights
Weighted average of petroleum (18) and raw materials (82), using 1977 developing countries' import values as weights

(the growth in P_M/P_A is P_M). This BASELINE projection, used throughout in Chapter 6, can be compared with four alternatives:

	1980–2000	
	$\overset{*}{P}_Z$	$\overset{*}{P}_M$
BASELINE	+1.5%	−0.6%
Stable Price Relatives	0	0
Pre-OPEC Historical (1960–73)	0	−0.7
Post-OPEC Historical (1973–79)	+5.2	−1.6
Average Historical (1969–79)	+1.7	−1.0

References

Abramovitz, Moses A. 1956. Resource and output trends in the United States since 1870. *American Economic Review* (May) 46:2–23.

Adelman, I., and S. Robinson. 1978. *Income distribution policy in developing countries: a case study of Korea.* Stanford: Stanford U. Pr.

Ahmed, F. 1974. Migration and employment in a multi-sector model—an application to Bangladesh. Ph.D. diss., Princeton University.

Alonso, W. 1964. *Location and land use: toward a general theory of land rent.* Cambridge: Harvard U. Pr.

Arnott, R. J., and F. D. Lewis. 1977. The transition of land to urban use. Queen's University at Kingston, Ontario. Mimeo.

Artle, Roland. 1972. Urbanization and economic growth in Venezuela. *Papers and Proceedings of the Regional Science Association* 27:63–93.

Atkinson, A. B. 1970. On the measurement of inequality. *Journal of Economic Theory* 2:244–263.

Barlow, R. 1967. The economic effects of malaria eradication. *American Economic Review* 57:130–157.

———, and Gordon W. Davies. 1974. Policy analysis with a disaggregated economic-demographic model. *Journal of Public Economics* 3(1):43–70.

Barraza–Allende, L. 1968. A three-sectoral model of growth for Mexico. Ph.D. diss., University of Wisconsin, Madison.

Baumol, W. 1967. Macroeconomics of unbalanced growth: the anatomy of urban crises. *American Economic Review* 57(3):415–426.

Beals, R. E.; M. B. Levy; and L. N. Moses. 1967. Rationality and migration in Ghana. *Review of Economics and Statistics* 49(4):480–486.

Beier, George J. 1976. Can third world cities cope? *Population Bulletin* 31(4):1–32.

———; A. Churchill; M. Cohen; and B. Renaud. 1976. The task ahead for the cities of the developing countries. *World Development* 4(5):363–409.

Bellante, D. 1979. The north-south differential and the migration of heterogeneous labor. *American Economic Review* 69:166–175.

Bergman, L. 1978. *Energy policy in a small open economy: the case of Sweden.* Laxenburg, Austria: International Institute for Applied Systems Analysis (RR-78-16).

Berndt, E., and D. Wood. 1975. Technology, prices and the derived demand for energy. *Review of Economics and Statistics* 57:259–268.

Betancourt, R. R. 1980. The analysis of the patterns of consumption in less developed countries. In *Consumption and income distribution in Latin America,* ed. R. Ferber. Washington, D.C.: Organization of American States.

Bhagwati, J., and P. Grinols. 1975. Foreign capital, dependence, destabilization and feasibility of transition to socialism. *Journal of Development Economics* 2:85–98.

Bhalla, Surjit S. 1980. The measurement of permanent income and its application to savings behavior. *Journal of Political Economy* 88:722–44.

Binswanger, H. P. 1974. The measurement of technical change biases with many factors of production. *American Economic Review* 64(6):964–976.

Bird, R. M. 1976. Assessing tax performance in developing countries: a critical review of the literature. *Finanzarchiv* 34(2):244–265.

Blitzer, C. R.; P. B. Clark; and L. Taylor, eds. 1975. *Economy-wide models and development planning.* Oxford: Oxford U. Pr.

Bolnick, B. R. 1978. Tax effort measures in developing countries: what do regression measures really measure? In *Taxation and development,* ed. John Toye. London: Frank Cass.

Bowles, S. 1970. The aggregation of labor in the study of growth and planning: experiments with a two-level CES function. *Journal of Political Economy* 78:68–80.

Brown, A., and A. Deaton. 1972. Surveys in applied economics: models of consumer behavior. *Economic Journal* 82:1145–1236.

Bruno, Michael. 1982. Raw materials, profits, and the productivity slowdown. Working Paper No. 660R. National Bureau of Economic Research.

Carillo, J. S. n.d. The structure of wages in Latin American manufacturing. ECIEL. Mimeo.

Chelliah, R. J. 1971. Trends in taxation in developing countries. *Staff Papers* 18(2). Washington, D.C.: International Monetary Fund.

————; H. Bass; and M. Kelley. 1975. Tax ratios and tax efforts in developing countries. *Staff Papers* 22(1). Washington, D.C.: International Monetary Fund.

Chen, E.K.Y. 1977. Factor inputs, total factor productivity, and economic growth: the Asian case. *The Developing Economies* 15(2): 121–143.

Chenery, H. B. 1960. Patterns of industrial growth. *American Economic Review* 50: 624–654.

———. 1979. *Structural change and development policy.* New York: Oxford U. Pr.

———, and W. J. Raduchel. 1971. Substitution in planning models. In *Studies in development planning,* ed. H.B. Chenery. Cambridge: Harvard U. Pr.

———, and A. M. Strout. 1966. Foreign assistance and economic development. *American Economic Review* 56: 679–733.

———, and M. Syrquin. 1975. *Patterns of development, 1950–1970.* London: Oxford U. Pr.

Chiswick, B. R. 1974. *Income inequality.* New York: Columbia U. Pr.

Christensen, L. R., and D. Cummings. 1974. Real product, real factor input, and total factor productivity in Korea, 1960–1973. Workshop Series Paper 7505. Madison, Wis.: Social Science Research Institute, University of Wisconsin.

Clark, C. 1957. *Conditions of economic progress.* 3rd ed. New York: Macmillan.

Cline, W. R. 1975. Distribution and development: a survey article. *Journal of Development Economics* 2: 359–400.

Coale, A. J. 1969. *Population and economic development.* Office of Population Research, Princeton University. Also in *The population dilemma,* ed. P. M. Hauser. 2nd ed. Englewood Cliffs, N.J.: Prentice-Hall.

———, and E. M. Hoover, 1958. *Population growth and economic development in low-income countries.* Princeton: Princeton U. Pr.

Colosio, Donaldo. 1979. Urbanization and economic development in Mexico. International Institute for Applied Systems Analysis, Laxenburg, Austria (WP-79-19). Mimeo.

Cooper, Russel J., and Keith R. McLaren. 1981. Specification and estimation of ELES. *Economic Record* 57(156): 74–79.

Corden, W., and R. Findlay. 1975. Urban unemployment, intersectoral capital mobility and development policy. *Economica* 42: 59–78.

David, P. A., and T. Van de Klundert. 1965. Biased efficiency growth in the U.S. *American Economic Review* 60(3): 357–394.

Davis, Kingsley, 1975. Asia's cities: problems and options. *Population and Development Review* 1: 71–86.

de Bever, L. 1976. The role of the state in early Japanese growth. Ph.D. diss. University of Wisconsin, Madison.

de Melo, J. 1976. The effects of distortions in the factor market: some general equilibrium estimates. Discussion Paper No. 34. Washington, D.C.: Department of State, Agency for International Development.

———. 1977. Distortions in the factor market: some general equilibrium estimates. *Review of Economics and Statistics* 59:398–405.

———. 1978. A simulation of development strategies in an economywide policy model. Washington, D.C.: World Bank (IBRD). Mimeo.

———, and S. Robinson. 1978. Trade policy and income distribution in a small, open, developing economy. Washington, D.C.: World Bank. Mimeo.

———. 1980. The impact of trade policies on income distribution in a planning model for Colombia. *Journal of Policy Modeling* 2:81–100.

———. 1982. Trade adjustment policies and income distribution in three archetype developing economies. *Journal of Development Economics* 10(1):67–92.

Denison, Edward F. 1967. *Why growth rates differ*. Washington, D.C.: The Brookings Institution.

———. 1974. *Accounting for the United States economic growth, 1929–1969*. Washington, D.C.: The Brookings Institution.

———, and William K. Chung. 1976. *How Japan's economy grew so fast*. Washington, D.C.: The Brookings Institution.

Denton, F., and B. Spencer. 1976. Household and population effects on aggregate consumption. *Review of Economic Studies* 58:86–95.

Dervis, K.; J. de Melo; and S. Robinson. 1982. *General equilibrium models for development policy*. Cambridge: Cambridge U. Pr.

———, and S. Robinson. 1978. The foreign exchange gap, growth and industrial strategy in Turkey: 1973–1983. Working Paper No. 36. Washington, D.C.: World Bank (IBRD).

Dixit, Avinash. 1973. Models of dual economics. In *Models of economic growth*, ed. James A. Mirrlees and Nicholas H. Stern. New York: Wiley.

Eckaus, R. S. 1955. The factor proportions problem in underdeveloped areas. *American Economic Review* 45:539–565.

Edmonston, B.; W. C. Sanderson; and J. Sapoznikow. 1976. Welfare consequences of population changes in Colombia: an economic-demographic analysis. Memorandum No. 27. Center for Research in Economic Growth, Stanford University. Mimeo.

Elias, V. J. 1978. Sources of economic growth in Latin American countries. *Review of Economics and Statistics* 60:362–370.

Enke, S. 1971. Description of the economic-demographic model. Santa Barbara, Cal.: Tempo Center for Advanced Studies, General Electric Company.

Evenson, Robert. 1976. Productivity measurement in the developing countries: the Indian case. In *On the measurement of factor productivities,* ed. Franz–Lothar Altmann. Göttingen: Vandenhoeck and Ruprecht.

———, and Dayanatha Jha. 1973. The contribution of agricultural research system to agricultural production in India. *Indian Journal of Agricultural Economics* 28:212–230.

Ezaki, Mitsuo. 1975. Growth accounting of the Philippines. *The Philippine Economic Journal* 14:399–435.

Fallon, P. R., and P.R.G. Layard. 1975. Capital-skill complementarity, income distribution, and output accounting. *Journal of Political Economy* 83(2):279–301.

Fei, J.C.H., and A. C. Chiang. 1966. Maximum-speed development through austerity. In *The theory and design of economic development,* ed. I. Adelman and E. Thorbecke. Baltimore: Johns Hopkins U. Pr.

———, and G. Ranis. 1961. A theory of economic development. *American Economic Review* 51:533–565.

———. 1964. *Development of the labour surplus economy: theory and policy.* Homewood, Ill.: Richard D. Irwin.

Fields, Gary. 1982. Place-to-place migration in Colombia. *Economic Development and Cultural Change* 30(3):539–558.

Fishlow, A. 1972. Brazilian size distribution of income. *American Economic Review* 62(2):391–402.

Fogel, R. W. 1964. *Railroads and American economic growth: essays in econometric history.* Baltimore: Johns Hopkins U. Pr.

———. 1967. The specification problem in economic history. *Journal of Economic History* 27:283–308.

Frisch, R. 1959. A complete scheme for computing all direct and cross price elasticities in a model with many sectors. *Econometrica* 27:177–196.

Gandhi, V. P. 1971. Wagner's law of public expenditures: do recent cross-section studies confirm it? *Public Finance* 26(1):44–56.

Gianaris, Nicholas V. 1970. International differences in capital-output ratios. *American Economic Review* 60:465–477.

Goldberger, A. S. 1967. Functional form and utility: a review of consumer demand theory. SFM 6703. Madison, Wis.: Social Systems Research Institute, University of Wisconsin, Mimeo.

Gollop, Frank M. 1979. Accounting for intermediate aggregate measures of productivity. In *Measurement and interpretation of productivity*. Washington, D.C.: National Academy of Sciences.

Gordon, R. A. 1961. Differential changes in the prices of consumers' and capital goods. *American Economic Review* 51:937–957.

Goreux, Louis, and Alan S. Manne, eds. 1973. *Multi-level planning: case studies in Mexico*. Amsterdam: North-Holland.

Griffin, K. B., and J. L. Enos. 1970. Foreign assistance: objectives and consequences. *Economic Development and Cultural Change* 18(3):313–337.

Grilliches, Z. 1969. Capital-skill complementarity. *Review of Economics and Statistics* 51:456–468.

Grinols, E., and J. Bhagwati. 1976. Foreign capital, savings and dependence. *Review of Economics and Statistics* 58(4):416–424.

Gurley, J. G., and E. S. Shaw. 1955. Financial aspects of economic development. *American Economic Review* 45:515–538.

———. 1956. Financial intermediaries and the saving-investment process. *Journal of Finance* 2:257–276.

———. 1967. Financial structure and economic development. *Economic Development and Cultural Change* 15:257–268.

Hamermesh, D., and J. Grant. 1979. Econometric studies of labor—labor substitution and their implications for policy. *Journal of Human Resources* 14:518–542.

Harris, J. R., and M. Todaro. 1970. Migration, unemployment and development: a two-sector analysis. *American Economic Review* 60(1):126–142.

Hayami, Y., and V. W. Ruttan. 1971. *Agricultural development: an international perspective*. Baltimore: Johns Hopkins U. Pr.

Heller, P. S. 1975. A model of public fiscal behavior in developing economies. *American Economic Review* 65(3):429–445.

Henderson, J. V. 1977. *Economic theory and the cities*. New York: Academic Pr.

Henley, J. S., and W. J. House. 1978. The changing fortunes of an aristocracy: determinants of wages and conditions of employment in Kenya. *World Development* 6:83–95.

Higgins, Benjamin. 1968. *Economic development: principles, problems and policies*. Revised ed. New York: W. W. Norton.

Hoffmann, K. C., and D. W. Jorgenson. 1977. Economic and technological models for evaluation of energy policy. *The Bell Journal of Economics* 8:444–466.

Hopkins, M.J.D., and O.D.K. Norbye. 1978. Meeting basic human needs: some global estimates. Working paper. Geneva: World Employment Program Research, International Labour Office. Mimeo.

Hoselitz, Bert. F. 1955. Generative and parasitic cities. *Economic Development and Cultural Change* 3:278–294.

———. 1957. Urbanization and economic growth in Asia. *Economic Development and Cultural Change* 5:42–54.

House, W. J., and H. Rempel. 1978. Labor market pressures and wage determination in less developed economies: the case of Kenya. *Economic Development and Cultural Change* 26(3):609–619.

Houthakker, H. S. 1957. An international comparison of household expenditure patterns, commemorating the centenary of Engel's Law. *Econometrica* 25:532–551.

———. 1960. Additive preferences. *Econometrica* 28:244–257.

Howe, H. J. 1975. Development of the extended linear expenditure system from simple saving assumptions. *European Economic Review* 6:305–310.

Hulten, C. R., and M. Nishimizu. 1982. The Japanese productivity slowdown. Working Paper No. 1476. Washington, D.C.: The Urban Institute.

Hymer, S., and S. Resnick. 1969. A model of an agrarian economy with non-agricultural activities. *American Economic Review* 59:493–501.

Ingram, G. K. 1977. *Residential location and urban housing markets.* Cambridge, Mass.: Ballinger.

———, and A. Carroll. 1978. The spatial structure of Latin American cities. Paper read at the Annual Meeting of the American Economic Association, 26–28 December, Chicago, Ill.

IBRD/EPDCE. 1982. Commodity price projections: update. Office memorandum, 4 January 1982, H. Bothwell.

International Bank for Reconstruction and Development (IBRD). 1976. *World tables, 1976.* Baltimore: Johns Hopkins U. Pr.

———. 1980. *World tables, 1980.* Baltimore: Johns Hopkins U. Pr.

———. 1981. *World development report 1981.* Washington, D.C.: The World Bank. International Labour Office (ILO). 1977. *Labour force estimates and projections, 1950–2000.* 2nd ed. Geneva: ILO.

———. *Yearbook of labour statistics.* Selected years. Geneva: ILO.

Isard, P. 1976. How far can we push the law of one price? International Discussion Papers No. 84. Washington, D.C.: Federal Reserve Board.

Johansen, L. 1959. *A multisectoral study of economic growth.* Amsterdam: North-Holland.

Johnson, G. E., and W. E. Whitelaw. 1974. Urban-rural transfers in Kenya: an estimated remittances function. *Economic Development and Cultural Change* 22:473–479.

Johnston, B. F., and P. Kilby. 1975. *Agriculture and structural transformation.* New York: Oxford U. Pr.

————, and S. T. Nielson. 1966. Agriculture and structural transformation in a developing economy. *Economic Development and Cultural Change* 14:279–301.

Jorgenson, D. W. 1961. The development of a dual economy. *The Economic Journal* 71:309–334.

————. 1967. Surplus agricultural labor and the development of a dual economy. *The Economic Journal* 19:288–312.

————, and M. Nishimizu. 1978. U.S. and Japanese economic growth, 1952–1974: an international comparison. *The Economic Journal* 88:707–726.

————. 1979. Sectoral differences in levels of technology. Paper presented at the Econometric Society Summer meetings, 29 August–3 September, Montreal, Canada.

Kamerschen, D. R. 1969. Further analysis of over-urbanization. *Economic Development and Cultural Change* 17:235–253.

Kelley, A. C. 1969. Demand patterns, demographic change and economic growth. *Quarterly Journal of Economics* 83(1):110–126.

————. 1973. Population growth, the dependency rate, and the pace of economic development. *Population Studies* 27:406–420.

————. 1976a. Demographic change and the size of the government sector. *Southern Economic Journal* 43(2):1056–1066.

————. 1976b. Savings, demographic change and economic development. *Economic Development and Cultural Change* 24(4):683–693.

————; W. C. Sanderson; and J. G. Williamson. 1983. *Modeling growing economies in equilibrium and disequilibrium.* Durham, N.C.: Duke Pr. Policy Studies.

————, and J. G. Williamson. 1968. Household saving behavior in the developing economies: the Indonesian case. *Economic Development and Cultural Change* 16:385–403.

————. 1974. *Lessons from Japanese development: an analytical economic history.* Chicago: U. of Chicago Pr.

————. 1980. *Modeling urbanization and economic growth.* Laxenburg, Austria: International Institute for Applied Systems Analysis (RR-80-22).

————. 1982. The limits to urban growth: suggestions for macro-modelling Third World economies. *Economic Development and Cultural Change* 20(3):595–623.

————; J. G. Williamson; and R. J. Cheetham. 1972. *Dualistic economic development: theory and history.* Chicago: U of Chicago Pr.

Kemper, Robert V. 1977. *Migration and adaptation: Tzintzuntzan peasants in Mexico City.* Beverly Hills, Cal.: Sage Publications.

Kendrick, J W 1961 *Productivity trends in the United States.* New York: National Bureau of Economic Research.

———. 1973. *Postwar productivity trends in the United States, 1948–1969.* New York: National Bureau of Economic Research.

Kesselman, J. R.; S. H. Williamson; and E. R. Berndt. 1977. Tax credits for employment rather than investment. *American Economic Review* 67(3):330–349.

Keyfitz, N. 1980. Do cities grow by natural increase or by migration? *Geographical Analysis* 12(2):142–156.

Khan, A. R., and Arthur MacEwan. 1967. Regional current input-output tables for the East and West Pakistan economies, 1962–1963. Research Report No. 63. Pakistan Institute of Development Economics.

Kravis, I. B., and R. E. Lipsey. 1977. Export prices and the transmission of inflation. *American Economic Review* 67:155–163.

———. 1981. Prices and terms of trade for developed-country exports of manufactured goods. Working Paper No. 774. National Bureau of Economic Research.

Krueger, Anne O., and Baran Tuncer. 1980. Estimating total factor productivity growth in a developing country. Staff Working Paper No. 422. The World Bank.

Kuznets, Simon. 1957. Quantitative aspects of the economic growth of nations, II: industrial distribution of national product and labor force. *Economic Development and Cultural Change*, Supplement to 5(4):3–111.

———. 1966. *Modern economic growth: rate, structure, and spread.* New Haven: Yale U. Pr.

Lal, Deepak. 1974. The structure of earnings in India. Technical Working Paper No. 8. PAD, Planning Commission, New Delhi.

———. 1979. Theories of industrial wage structures: a review. *Indian Journal of Industrial Relations* 15(2):167–195.

Ledent, J. 1980. *Comparative dynamics of three demographic models of urbanization.* Laxenburg, Austria: International Institute of Applied Systems Analysis. (RR-80-1).

———. 1982. Rural-urban migration, urbanization, and economic development. *Economic Development and Cultural Change* 30(3):507–538.

———, and A. Rogers. 1979. Migration and urbanization in the Asian Pacific. Laxenburg, Austria: International Institute of Applied Systems Analysis (WP-79-51).

Leontief, Wassily et al. 1977. *The future of the world economy*. New York: Oxford U. Pr.

Levy, Victor. 1978. *Total factor productivity, nonneutral technical change and economic growth*. The Committee of Public Policy Studies, University of Chicago.

Lewis, W. A. 1954. Development with unlimited supplies of labor. *Manchester School of Economics and Social Studies* 20:139–192.

———. 1977. The evolution of the international economic order. Discussion Paper No. 74. Woodrow Wilson School, Research Program in Development Studies, Princeton University.

Lianos, T. P. 1976. Factor augmentation in Greek manufacturing, 1958–1969. *European Economic Review* 8(1):15–31.

Linn, J. 1979. Policies for efficient and equitable growth of cities in developing countries. Staff Working Paper No. 342. World Bank.

Lipton, Michael. 1976. *Why poor people stay poor: urban bias in world development*. Cambridge: Harvard U. Pr.

Lluch, Constantino. 1973. The extended linear expenditure system. *European Economic Review* 4:21–32.

———. 1974. Development in segmented economies. Washington, D.C.: The World Bank, Development Research Center. Mimeo.

———; A. A. Powell; and R. A. Williams. 1977. *Patterns in household demand and saving*. New York: Oxford U. Pr.

Luxemberg, R. 1969. *Social reform or revolution*. Colombo, Ceylon: Tr. Integer.

Lysy, F. J., and L. Taylor. 1977. *A computable general equilibrium model for the functional income distribution*. Washington, D.C.: The World Bank, Development Research Center.

McDonald, J. F. 1981. Capital-land substitution in urban housing: a survey of empirical estimates. *Journal of Urban Economics* 9(2):190–211.

McKinnon, R. 1973. *Money and capital in economic development*. Washington, D.C.: The Brookings Institution.

Massel, B. F. 1961. A disaggregated view of technical change. *Journal of Political Economy* 69:547–557.

Mazumdar, D. 1975. The urban informal sector. Bank Staff Working Paper No. 211. Washington, D.C.: The World Bank.

———. 1976. The urban informal sector. *World Development* 4(8):655–679.

———. 1979. Paradigms in the study of urban labor markets in LDCs. Staff Working Paper No. 366. Washington, D.C.: The World Bank.

Meadows, Donella et al. 1974. *Limits to growth*. New York: Universe Books.

Meesook, Oey A. 1974. Regional consumer price indices for Thailand. Working paper. Faculty of Economics, Thammaset University, Bangkok.

Merrick, Thomas, W. 1963. The informal sector in Belo Horizonte: a case study. Working paper. CEDEPLAR, Federal University of Minas Gerais, Brazil.

————, 1978. Employment and earnings in the informal sector in Brazil. *The Journal of Developing Areas* 10(3):337–354.

Mikesell, R. F., and J. E. Zinser. 1973. The nature of the savings function in developing countries: a survey of the theoretical and empirical literature. *Journal of Economic Literature* 11(1): 1–26.

Mills, Edwin S. 1967. An aggregative model of resource allocation in metropolitan areas. *American Economic Review* 57(2):197–210.

————. 1972. *Urban economics*. Glenview, Ill. Scott, Foresman, and Co.

————, and K. Ohta. 1976. Urbanization and urban problems. In *Asia's new giant*, ed. Hugh Patrick and Henry Rosovsky. Washington, D.C.: The Brookings Institution.

————, and B. N. Song. 1977. Korea's urbanization and urban problems, 1945–1975. Working Paper No. 7701. Seoul, Korea: Korea Development Institute.

Mirrlees, J. 1975. A pure theory of underdeveloped economies. In *Agriculture in Development Theory*, ed. L. Reynolds. New Haven: Yale U. Pr.

Mohan, R. 1977. Development, structural change and urbanization: explorations with a dynamic three sector general equilibrium model applied to India, 1951–1984. Ph.D. diss., Princeton University.

————. 1979. *Urban economic and planning models*. Baltimore: Johns Hopkins U. Pr.

————. 1980. The people of Bogota: who they are, what they earn, where they live. Staff Working Paper No. 390. Washington, D.C.: The World Bank.

Morawetz, D. 1974. Employment implications of industrialization in developing countries. *The Economic Journal* 84(335):491–542.

Morley, S., and J. G. Williamson. 1977. Class pay differentials, wage stretching and early capitalist development. In *Essays on economic development and cultural change*, ed. M. Nash. Chicago: U. of Chicago Pr.

Musgrove, Philip. 1978. *Consumer behavior in Latin America*. Washington, D.C.: The Brookings Institution.

Muth, Richard F. 1969. *Cities and housing*. Chicago: U. of Chicago Pr.

———. 1971. The derived demand for urban land. *Urban Studies* 8: 243–254.

National Economic Council. 1973. *The 1961 interindustry accounts of the Philippines*. Manila.

Nelson, Joan. 1970. The urban poor: disruption or political integration in Third World cities. *World Politics* 22(3):393–414.

Nichols, D. 1970. Land and economic growth. *American Economic Review* 60(3):332–341.

Nishimizu, M., and J. M. Page. 1981. Total factor productivity growth, technological progress and technical efficiency change. Development Economics Department, The World Bank. Mimeo.

———, and S. Robinson. 1982 ongoing. Sectoral productivity change: a comparative analysis of four countries. In *Sources of growth in developing countries*, ed. H. B. Chenery et al.

Nordhaus, W. and J. Tobin. 1972. Is growth obsolete? In *Economic growth: fiftieth anniversary colloquim V*, National Bureau of Economic Research. New York: Columbia U. Pr.

Ortmeyer, D. 1979. An analysis of the effects of growth policies on domestic savings behavior in the Republic of Korea. Ph.D. diss. University of Wisconsin, Madison.

Palanca, E. H. 1974. Structure of the Philippine economy: a comparative study of the 1961 and 1965 input-output tables. *Philippine Economic Journal* 8(1):41–56.

Papanek, G. F. 1973. Foreign aid, private investment, savings, and growth in LDC's. Journal of Political Economy 81(1). 120–130.

Patrick, H. 1966. Financial development and economic growth in underdeveloped countries. *Economic Development and Cultural Change* 14:174–189.

Perera, D. 1967. A preliminary input-output table for Ceylon. *Central Bank of Ceylon Bulletin* (July):17–34.

Perlman, Janice E. 1976. *The myth of marginality: urban poverty and politics in Rio de Janeiro*. Berkeley: U. of California Pr.

Phelps-Brown, H. 1977. *The inequality of pay*. Oxford: Oxford U. Pr.

Prebisch, Raul. 1950. *The economic development of Latin America and its principal problems*. New York: UN, Economic Commission for Latin America.

Preston, S. 1979. *Patterns of urban and rural population growth*. New York: United Nations, Population Division.

Renaud, B. 1979. National urbanization policies in developing countries. Staff Working Paper No. 347. Washington, D.C.: The World Bank.

Republic of the Philippines. 1963. The 1961 interindustry accounts of the Philippines. Manila: Office of Statistical Coordination and Standards.

Reynolds, Clark W. 1979. A shift-share analysis of regional and sectoral productivity growth in contemporary Mexico. Working paper. Laxenburg, Austria: International Institute for Applied Systems Analysis.

Reynolds, L. G. 1965. Wages and employment in a labor surplus economy. *American Economic Review* 55:19–39.

Rodgers, G.; M. Hopkins; and R. Wéry. 1978. *Population, employment, and inequality*. West Mead, England: Saxon House.

Rogers, A. 1977. *Migration, urbanization, resources, and development*. Laxenburg, Austria: International Institute for Applied Systems Analysis (RR-77-14).

———. 1982. Sources of urban population growth and urbanization, 1950–2000: a demographic accounting. *Economic Development and Cultural Change* 30(3):483–506.

Rosen, Sherwin. 1979. Wage-based indexes of urban quality of life. In *Current issues in urban economics*, ed. P. Miewzkowski and M. Straszheim. Baltimore: Johns Hopkins U. Pr.

Sabot, R. 1975. The meaning and measurement of urban surplus labour. Washington, D.C.: The World Bank. Mimeo.

Sahota, G. S. 1968. An economic analysis of internal migration in Brazil. *Journal of Political Economy* 76:218–245.

Sakong, I., and G. Narasimham. 1974. Interindustry resource allocation and technological change: the situation in Indian manufacturing. *The Developing Economies* 12(2):123–132.

Sanderson, Warren C. 1980. *Economic-demographic simulation models: a review of their usefulness for policy analysis*. Laxenburg, Austria: International Institute for Applied Systems Analysis (RM-80-14).

Sato, K. 1967. A two-level constant elasticity of substitution production function. *Review of Economic Studies* 34(2):201–218.

———. 1972. Additive utility functions with double-log consumer demand functions. *Journal of Political Economy* 80:102–124.

Schmidt, R. M. 1981. The demographic dimensions of economic-population modeling. Ph.D. diss., Duke University, Durham, N.C.

———. 1983. Incorporating demography into general equilibrium modeling. In *Modeling growing economies in equilibrium and disequilibrium*, ed. A. C. Kelley, W. C. Sanderson, and J. G. Williamson. Durham, N.C.: Duke Pr. Policy Studies.

Schultz, T. Paul. 1979. Effective protection and the distribution of personal income by sector in Colombia. Discussion Paper No. 316. Economic Growth Center, Yale University.

―――. 1982. Lifetime migration within educational strata in Venezuela. *Economic Development and Cultural Change* 30(3): 559–593.

Schultz, T. W. 1961. Investment in human capital. *American Economic Review* 51:1–17.

―――. 1972. Investment in human capital in poor countries. In *Macroeconomics: selected readings*, ed. W. L. Johnson and D. R. Kammerschen. Boston: Houghton Mifflin Co.

―――. 1978. *Distortions of agricultural incentives*. Bloomington: Indiana U. Pr.

Shaw, E. 1973. *Financial deepening in economic development*. New York: Oxford U. Pr.

Shaw, Paul R. 1978. On modifying metropolitan migration. *Economic Development and Cultural Change* 26(4):677–692.

Sheira, A. Z. 1968. Inter-industry relations in North Africa. *Agricultural Bulletin for Africa* 10:27–48.

Simmons, Alan B. 1979. Slowing metropolitan city growth in Asia: policies, programs and results. *Population and Development Review* 5(1):87–104.

Simon, J. L. 1976. Population growth may be good for LDC's in the long run: a richer simulation model. *Economic Development and Cultural Change* 24:309–337.

―――. 1980. Resources, population, environment: an oversupply of bad news. *Science* 208:1431–1437.

Sjaastad, L. A. 1962. The costs and returns of human migration. *Journal of Political Economy* 70:80–93.

Solow, R. M. 1957. Technical change and the aggregate production function. *Review of Economics and Statistics* 39:312–320.

Song, Byung Nak. 1975. The production structure of the Korean economy: international and historical comparisons. Working Paper No. 7508. Seoul: Korea Development Institute.

―――, and R. J. Struyk. 1976. Korean housing: economic appraisal and policy alternatives. Working Paper 7603. Seoul: Korea Development Institute.

Sovani, N. V. 1962. The analysis of overurbanization. *Economic Development and Cultural Change* 12:216–222.

Srinivasan, T. N. 1977. Development, poverty, and basic human needs: some issues. *Food Research Institute Studies* 16(2).

Stark, Oded. 1980. On slowing metropolitan city growth. *Population and Development Review* 6(1):95–102.

Stern, J. L., and J. D. Lewis. 1980. Employment patterns and income growth. Staff Working Paper No. 419. Washington, D.C.: The World Bank.

Stiglitz, J. 1974. Wage determination and unemployment in LDC's. *Quarterly Journal of Economics* 88(2):194–227.

Streeten, P., and S. J. Burki. 1978. Basic needs: some issues. *World Development* 6(3):411–421.

Suh, S. M. 1979. The patterns of poverty in Korea. Working Paper No. 7903. Seoul: Korea Development Institute.

Taylor, L. 1979. *Macro models for developing countries.* New York: McGraw-Hill.

Thomas, Vinod. 1978. The measurement of spatial differences in poverty: the case of Peru. Staff Working Paper No. 273. Washington, D.C.: The World Bank.

———. 1980. Spatial differences in the cost of living. *Journal of Urban Economics* 8:108–122.

Thorn, R. S. 1967. The evolution of public finances during economic development. *The Manchester School of Economics and Social Studies* 35:19–53.

Todaro, M. 1969. A model of labor, migration, and urban unemployment in less developed countries. *American Economic Review* 59(1):138–148.

Tsao, Y. 1982. Productivity growth in Singapore. Ph.D. diss., Harvard University.

Tybout, J. 1981. Credit rationing and firm financial behavior in developing countries. Department of Economics, Georgetown University (June). Mimeo.

Uneo, H., and S. Kinoshita. 1968. A simulation experiment for growth and a long-term model of Japan. *International Economic Review* 9:114–148.

United Nations. *Demographic Yearbook.* Various years. New York: United Nations.

———. 1965. *Economic bulletin for Asia and the Far East.* Volume 15, no. 4. Bangkok.

———. 1976. *Global review of human settlements: a support for habitat.* 2 vols. Oxford: Pergamon Pr.

———. 1981. *Monthly Bulletin of Statistics.* Vol. 35, no. 7 (July)

———. 1982. *Yearbook of National Accounts Statistics 1980.*

United Nations. Department of International Economic and Social Affairs. *Yearbook of international trade statistics.* Various issues.

————. 1980. *Patterns of urban and rural population growth.* Population Studies No. 68.

United States. Bureau of the Census. 1975. *Historical statistics of the United States, colonial times to 1970.* Part I. Washington, D.C.: GPO.

Uzawa, H. 1961. On a two-sector model of economic growth: I. *Review of Economic Studies* 29:40–47.

————. 1963. On a two-sector model of economic growth: II. *Review of Economic Studies* 30:105–118.

Walters, Dorothy. 1970. *Canadian growth revisited, 1950–1967.* Staff Study No. 28. Economic Council of Canada.

Watanabe, T. 1968. Industrialization, technological progress, and dual structure. In *Economic growth: the Japanese experience since the Meiji era,* ed. L. Klein and K. Ohkawa. Homewood, Ill. Richard D. Irwin.

Weisskopf, T. 1972. The impact of foreign capital inflow on domestic savings in underdeveloped countries. *Journal of International Economics* 2(1):25–38.

Williamson, J. G. 1971. Capital accumulation, labor saving and labor absorption once more. *Quarterly Journal of Economics* 85(1):40–65.

————. 1974. *Late 19th century American development: a general equilibrium history.* Cambridge: Cambridge U. Pr.

————. 1979. Why do Koreans save 'so little?' *Journal of Development Economics* 6(1):343–362.

————. 1981. Urban disamenities, dark satanic mills and the British standard of living debate. *Journal of Economic History* 41:75–84.

————, and L. de Bever. 1977. Saving, accumulation, and modern economic growth: the contemporary relevance of Japanese history. *The Journal of Japanese Studies* 4:125–167.

————, and P. H. Lindert. 1980. *American inequality: a macroeconomic history.* New York: Academic Pr.

Willis, R. 1979. Comment on internal migration in developing countries: a survey. In *Population and economic change in less developed countries,* ed. R. Easterlin. Chicago: University of Chicago Pr.

Wingo, Lowden. 1961. *Transportation and urban land.* Washington, D.C.: Resources for the Future.

Woodruff, A. M., and J. R. Brown. 1971. *Land for the cities of Asia.* Hartford, Conn.: Lincoln Institute.

Yap, L. 1972. Internal migration and economic development. Ph.D. diss., Harvard University.

————. 1976a. Internal migration and economic development in Brazil. *Quarterly Journal of Economics* 90(1):119–137.

————. 1976b. Rural-urban migration and urban underemployment in Brazil. *Journal of Development Economics* 3(3):227–243.

————. 1977. The attraction of cities: a review of the migration literature. *Journal of Development Economics* 4:239–264.

Yotopoulos, P. A. 1977. The population problem and the development solution. *Food Research Institute Studies* 16(1) [Stanford, Cal.].

————, and J. Nugent. 1976. *Economics of development: empirical investigations*. New York: Harper & Row.

Zarembka, P. 1972. *Toward a theory of economic development*. San Francisco: Holden-Day, Inc.

Zelinsky, W. 1971. The hypothesis of the mobility transition. *Geographic Review* 61:219–249.

Index

accumulation: capital and impact multipliers and, 115, 116; city growth and, 107–108; growth trends and, 85, 146–48; housing stock, 129; human capital, 14; increased demand for skilled labor and capital, 10; land, 43; model dynamics and, 68–73; post-OPEC capital, 129; post-OPEC price trends and, 159; RDC and, 80–81; rising urban rates of, 8; savings and, 61; structural change and long-run, 146–48; treatment of, 67–68

agriculture, 8, 19, 148; capital stock and, 80; constraint on urbanization and land for, 9; decline in, 86; Green Revolution and, 70, 176, 183; growth in output of, 129; land scarcity and, 138, 180–81; land stock and, 43, 48, 50, 127; policy and, 25; production function, 24; underdeveloped economies and, 21

balance of payments, 50–52

BASELINE trend model: forecasts and, 148, 151–54, 156, 157–58, 159, 160, 166–67, 169–73; model forecasts and defining, 143-46

Bergman, L., 17

Bruno, Michael, 106

capital: city growth slowdown and, 138; growth rate of, 146; immobility of, 120; modeling and, 20–21; rapid rates of urban accumulation of, 10; skilled labor and, 21, 22. See also foreign capital

capital goods, 101, 115

capital markets, 101; model and, 15; model and "productive," 34–37; relative austerity of, 180; segmentation of, 96

capital stock: accumulation rate for, 85; net investment and, 68; RDC and, 79–80

Cheetham, R. J., 8, 29

Chenery, H. B., 23, 77, 97, 145

city growth, 82, 90; BASELINE trend model and, 143–46, 148, 151–54, 156, 157–58, 159, 160, 166–67, 169–73; capital accumulation and, 107–108; capital-intensive nature of, 4, 5; comparative assessment of, 111–15; demographic projections and, 154–58; foreign capital and, 169–71; fuel and imported raw material scarcity and, 105–106; labor and demographics and, 166–69; land and labor and, 108–110; long-run accumulation and structural change and, 146–48; long-run predictions and, 148–54; migration and, 104, 109–110, 148–49, 151, 152, 153, 154, 158–59; migration and urbanization and, 93; OPEC price shock and, 126–27; population pressure and, 125; prices and natural resources and, 159–66; productivity and, 171–76; RDC prototype and, 75; relative rents and, 47; short-run constraints on, 104–105; sources of slowdown in, 132, 134–38, 141, squatter policy and, 122–23; STABLE model and, 143, 149–51, 152, 153, 154; structural evolution and, 111–15; unbalanced productivity and, 102–104; urban wage policy and, 119–22. See also urbanization; individual entries, e.g., employment; imports; income; labor force; land, etc.

Coale, A. J., 10, 14, 56, 62, 108, 158

commodity-producing sectors, 19

constant elasticity of substitution (CES), 21–22

construction costs, 64

Corden, W., 30–31, 33, 119–22

cost-of-living differentials, 82; defined, 14; housing scarcity and, 153; importance of, 184; migration research and, 6–7; model and, 96–97; real earnings and, 110; rents and spatial, 16

cost-of-living indexes, 34; household types and, 61

country choice, RDC prototype and, 75

LIBRARY OF CONGRESS CATALOGING IN PUBLICATION DATA

Kelley, Allen C.
  What drives Third World city growth?

  Includes bibliographical references and index.
  1. Cities and towns—Growth—Mathematical models.
2. Cities and towns—Developing countries—Growth—
Mathematical models.   3. Equilibrium (Economics)
I. Williamson, Jeffrey G., 1935–   . II. Title.
HT371.K44   1984   307′.14′0724   84–2070
ISBN 0-691-04240-3
ISBN 0-691-10164-7 (pbk.)

ALLEN C. KELLEY is James B. Duke Professor of Economics at Duke
University, and JEFFREY G. WILLIAMSON is Laird Bell Professor of
Economics at Harvard University. They are coauthors of *Dualistic
Economic Development* and *Lessons from Japanese Development*
(Chicago, 1972 and 1974).

8792